T0271235

SETH: CONVERSATIONS

Conversations with Comic Artists   M. Thomas Inge, General Editor

Seth: Conversations

Edited by Eric Hoffman and Dominick Grace

University Press of Mississippi   Jackson

Works by Seth

Palookaville, 22 issues (1991–2015)
It's a Good Life, If You Don't Weaken (1996)
Vernacular Drawings (2001)
Clyde Fans, Book One (2004)
*Bannock, Beans and Black Tea: Memories of a Prince Edward Island Childhood in the
    Great Depression* (2004) (with John Gallant)
Wimbledon Green: The Greatest Comic Book Collector in the World (2005)
Forty Cartoon Books of Interest (2006)
George Sprott (1894–1975) (2009)
The Great Northern Brotherhood of Canadian Cartoonists (2011)

www.upress.state.ms.us

The University Press of Mississippi is a member of the Association of American University
    Presses.

First printing 2015
∞
Library of Congress Cataloging-in-Publication Data

Seth, 1962–
  [Interviews. Selections]
  Seth : conversations / edited by Eric Hoffman and Dominick Grace.
      pages cm. — (Conversations with comic artists series)
    Collection of interviews originally published in various sources.
  Includes index.
  ISBN 978-1-62846-130-5 (hardback) — ISBN 978-1-62846-131-2 (ebook) 1. Seth, 1962––
      Interviews. 2. Cartoonists—Canada—Interviews. I. Hoffman, Eric, 1976– editor. II. Grace,
      Dominick, 1963– editor. III. Title.
  PN6733.S48Z46 2015
  741.5'971—dc23   2014024115

British Library Cataloging-in-Publication Data available

CONTENTS

Introduction   vii

Chronology   xvii

Interview   3
   Michael Strafford / 1985

An Interview with Seth   7
   Dylan Williams / 1995

An Interview with Seth   68
   Bryan Miller / 2004

Seth Interview   77
   Dave Sim / 2005

Retro Man   89
   Gerald Hannon / 2006

On Cartooning   100
   Rebecca Bengal / 2006

Talking to Seth   111
   Thom Ernst / 2009

Comics Reporter Sunday Interview: Seth   121
   Tom Spurgeon /2009

Interview with Seth   145
    Eric Hoffman and Dominick Grace / 2013

Index   223

INTRODUCTION

Seth, born Gregory Gallant in Canada in 1962, is one of the most significant artists to emerge in the alternative comics boom of the 1980s, as a cartoonist, designer, and comics historian. As we have discussed elsewhere (see the introduction to *Chester Brown: Conversations* [2013]), the 1980s was a fascinating transitional period for the comics industry. Most "mainstream" (i.e. superhero-focused) publishers had died out, leaving Marvel and DC as the primary forces on the newsstands. Companies providing some sort of alternative to the hegemonic superhero world—e.g. Warren, or the underground publishers—were also shrinking or dying out. However, several factors conspired to create an environment receptive to new developments in comics. One of these was the development in the 1970s of the direct comics market, whereby comics stores could order books directly from distributors on a nonreturnable basis (in contrast to the longstanding returnable distribution system). This was a key factor in the proliferation of comics specialty stores, which could get books more cheaply and easily via the direct market than they could under the old newspaper and magazine distribution system. Coupled with this development was the growth of comic book conventions—again, a phenomenon that began in the early 1970s and flourished by the end of the decade.

These twin forces provided not only a venue for mainstream books to be more widely disseminated but also the development of a growing market of readers interested in comics as a legitimate cultural medium. Instead of finding their comic fixes haphazardly in convenience stores or on newsstands, comics fans could now, in many cities, find them in shops that specialized in comics. These shops provided a reliable source for new books as well as an increasing stock of back issues. Readers could now easily find the books they wanted—and many other books of which they had never heard before. The creation of this market benefited more than just the established publishers—though it came too late to save many stalwarts, such as Charlton, Gold Key, Dell, and others—and it remains a fascinating period in comics history, providing a pathway for new publishers to get their books distributed and noticed. The alternative/ground-level comics movement was born.

Charles Hatfield discusses the birth of the alternative comics movement in *Alternative Comics: An Emerging Literature*, noting that the term "ground-level" was applied to such books because such "they attempted to reconcile underground and mainstream attitudes" (26), for example by wedding the fantasy tropes of the mainstream with the look and sensibility of the underground—black and white art, more explicit sexual and violent content, and, most importantly, perhaps, a more idiosyncratic and personal perspective. The first wave of such books includes those with essentially mainstream narrative drives—the fantasy series *The First Kingdom* (1974–1977) by Jack Katz, for example—and in many cases the creative powers of mainstream talent seeking slightly more creative freedom. The second wave saw a more coherent and professional approach in the emergence of new companies (e.g. Pacific, which provided a home for Jack Kirby's later superhero work, or Eclipse, which published many more graphic but still essentially mainstream titles). The third wave of the early to mid-1980s saw a ground-level comics world in many respects still heavily invested in mainstream sensibilities (one of the key books of this period is Howard Chaykin's *American Flagg!* [1983–1988] for First Comics, a visually dense, relatively sophisticated satirical science fiction dystopian narrative that is nevertheless firmly rooted in mainstream genre tropes), yet which also saw the emergence of artists—and publishers—with more ideologically driven commitments to significant alternatives to the mainstream, and a far more diverse and eclectic approach to style and narrative. This period also saw the proliferation of artists interested in taking comics beyond the limits of mainstream tropes and of publishers interested not merely in providing somewhat more adult and sophisticated variations on superhero power fantasies but also in opening up comics as a medium capable of exploring any subject matter. If publishers such as Pacific, Eclipse, First, or Vortex closely approximate the mainstream aesthetic, ones like Raw (founded by Art Spiegelman and Françoise Mouly in 1980 in the wake of the demise of the underground comic *Arcade* as a new forum for avant-garde comics), Fantagraphics (founded in 1976 and initially the publisher of *The Comics Journal* [1977–present], this publisher put its aesthetic theories into practice when it began publishing comics in 1981) and Drawn & Quarterly (founded in 1990 by Chris Oliveros, on the model of Speigelman and Mouly's *Raw* magazine [1980–1991], to publish art comics) set out to redefine what comics could be.

Seth, along with several other major comics talents, emerged in the 1980s and benefited from this fertile environment. Like many of his contemporaries,

Seth was influenced by both mainstream comics and underground comix, as well as by the DIY aesthetic of the punk and new wave movements. Indeed, he traces his pseudonym, with some embarrassment, to his involvement with youth culture: "I was involved with the punk scene and the nightclub scene and I got heavily involved in creating a whole new persona for myself and eventually that also involved coming up with a new name," he tells Thom Ernst in one of the interviews collected here. He notes elsewhere, "I wanted a scary pseudonym and I made [a] list of names. I picked Seth. I shudder to imagine what else was on that list. Thank God that Seth is, at least, a real name. It could have been much worse" (Stukavsky n.p.).

However, Seth's early career hews closer to the mainstream than to the alternative or underground. His first significant work was on Dean Motter's *Mister X* (1983–1990, with numerous subsequent revivals), published by Vortex, on which Seth followed the Hernandez Brothers (who were themselves alternative mainstays with their Fantagraphics-published series *Love and Rockets* [1982–present]). Seth drew issues 6–13 (December 1985–June 1988) in a cartoony retro style incorporating elements of Bauhaus and Russian Constructivism; the book's Radiant City looked like the future as imagined in the 1930s. Stylistically, this retro sensibility is consistent with Seth's interests—his comic works often seem to fulfill his desire to evoke (and inhabit) what he calls in an interview with Bryan Miller collected here, a more "genuine" and less "vulgar" and increasingly rarefied past—yet *Mister X* was essentially a mainstream-style melodrama about the near-future dystopian city, built upon the principles of "psychotecture" (a melding of psychology and architecture, which means that the city's design influences the minds of its inhabitants) from the designs of the eponymous character, who is now an antiheroic outlaw architect loner attempting to wrest back control of the city. Narratively, this is far from typical territory for Seth who, though he was heavily influenced by mainstream comics in his teen years (even designing and creating stories set in his own Marvel-style universe—discussed in M. Todd Hignite's "Seth in the Studio"), is one of the least mainstream-inflected figures of the alternative comics movement, in contrast to many of his peers.

After *Mister X*, Seth focused on commercial illustration for a couple of years. Illustration remains a major component of his career. More than most of his peers, Seth has a foot set firmly in the commercial camp as well as in the fine art camp. He discusses this balancing act in several of the pieces here. He has done numerous book covers and internal illustrations and has designed several books and series, most notably perhaps the Fantagraphics-published *The Complete Peanuts* (2004–present), one of the earliest of the current crop of classic comic strip reprints and arguably influential on the design of many subsequent series. He has also done design work for releases of John Stanley's comics (another influence) and one of his favorite Canadian cartoonists, Doug Wright, among others. Consequently, his influence and importance spread well beyond the confines of comics, though his own clear distinction between commercial work and his comics makes apparent where he sees his more significant work to lie.

That significance to comics begins with *Palookaville* (1990–present, 22 issues as of 2014), published by Drawn & Quarterly. Seth's comic emerged relatively late compared to the seminal alternative comics of his contemporaries (e.g. the Hernandez's *Love and Rockets* began in 1982, Chester Brown's *Yummy Fur* [1983–1994] in 1983, Peter Bagge's *Neat Stuff* [1985–1989] in 1985, Dan Clowes's *Eightball* [1989–2004] in 1989), so by the time he reentered the comics world, the alternative revolution had opened up possibilities considerably from where they had been even a few years before. The diversity of work by these and other artists had established that alternative comics need not resemble mainstream comics even superficially but might be drawn in a variety of styles and encompass almost any sort of narrative. There was space in the market for a style as idiosyncratic and unique as Seth's.

In addition to the mainstream influence that informed some of his juvenile and early work, Seth was also heavily influenced by a wide array of other comics models, from the undergrounds to newspaper strips and classic cartooning. Many of the interviews here delve into Seth's influences, including the revelation that for Seth, Robert Crumb was perhaps the key influence, as he discusses in several interviews—also acknowledging that people are surprised to hear this. Looking at Seth's work, one might not see an obvious Crumb influence, yet Seth does share with Crumb a fascination with earlier historical periods and a desire to invoke them in his work. He also shares with Crumb a history in commercial illustration, though unlike Crumb, Seth has not left illustration behind. Their work may not look similar, but complementary aesthetic senses inform their art.

If Crumb is invisible, the influence of the cartoonists of the *New Yorker* and other magazines from the golden age of cartooning is overt in Seth's work. Indeed, his first graphic novel, *It's a Good Life, If You Don't Weaken* (1996, originally serialized in *Palookaville* 5–9), explicitly announces Seth's fascination with the past and with earlier cartooning styles. The story takes one of its cues from the then-popular movement towards autobiography in alternate comics (by the early 1990s, figures such as Joe Matt, Joe Sacco, Chester Brown, and others began something of an alternative comics movement by making themselves characters in their own work), traceable back to au-tobiographical comics by figures such as Crumb and Harvey Pekar, or more transformatively, Art Spiegelman in *Maus*. *It's a Good Life* seems to be part of this movement, as it follows "Seth" and his quest to track down work by the elusive cartoonist Kalo. What was not evident in the story, and indeed is never acknowledged within the work itself, is that Kalo never existed, and the Kalo cartoons Seth provides as evidence are his own pastiche work. By delib-erately blurring the line between fact and fiction, the book grapples with the fact that autobiography is always at some level fictional. As Katie Mullins has asserted, "Indeed, the fictional Seth is a kind of comics creation: a character whose actions and ideologies are influenced and formed by various—mostly mainstream—canonical comics' plots, characters, and philosophies" (n.p.).

To a degree, Seth's subsequent graphic novels continue to expand on the preoccupations and themes of *It's a Good Life*. *Clyde Fans*, which began its serialization in *Palookaville* in issue 10 (1998) and is (as of 2015) unfinished, focuses on two brothers and their electric fan company. A present-day narra-tive is balanced against narratives set in the 1950s, 1960s, and 1970s, track-ing the lives of Abe and Simon Matchcard. The visual style is highly polished and contemplative, the narrative deliberately paced (Seth has acknowledged that serialization over a decade and a half is "not a good way to read it," as he discusses in the final interview included here), the characters mundane and flawed. Seth allows himself to ramble, as he says, to let the narrative mean-der and be as long as it needs to be; plot is far less important than mood or characterization, as Seth deals with the inescapable grinding of time and its inevitable losses. Yet the charge of nostalgia that such a theme might sug-gest—that has often been directed at Seth's work, and that he addresses in several of these interviews—is an overly simplistic way of reading. The loss of the past may be melancholy, but Seth's work does not view the past wistfully or longingly. Certain aspects of the past—its objects and aesthetics—are cel-ebrated, perhaps, but not idealized.

If *Clyde Fans* is a deliberately paced, highly polished, meandering work, Seth's other graphic novels treat his interest in the past, history, place, and the complexities of fact and fiction in more economical and fluid ways. Seth's *Palookaville* style is complemented by a looser, cartoonier style derived from his sketchbook works. He has published one sketchbook collection, *Vernacu-lar Drawings* (2001), but has also in recent years released several books that had their genesis in other serialized venues or from sketchbook cartoons be-fore emerging as fully formed work. *Wimbledon Green* (2005), for instance, emerged from a figure he first drew in his sketchbooks. It might be seen as a sort of companion piece to *It's a Good Life*, with the titular character a more satirical treatment of the comics-obsessed fan and the at times isolating and alienating practice of collecting. Seth's characteristic interest in questions of persona and identity are of course also explored; questions about Wimbledon Green's agenda and even his reality are central to the book as it unfolds in a fragmented and subjective sequence of documentary-style linked strips, in which a variety of characters routinely break the fourth wall and address the reader directly. As such, this focus on the "reality" of the central character remains a concern in Seth's following major works.

George Sprott (1874–1975) (2009), for instance, was originally serialized in one-page installments in 2006/7 in the *New York Times*, a format the polar opposite of the long, contemplative chapters of *Clyde Fans*. Where that work allows for expansion and rambling, *Sprott* required a high degree of focus and self-containment. *Times* readers may not have seen or read each installment, so each strip had to be designed both to be self-contained and part of the larger whole. As a consequence, the work—similar to *Wimbledon Green* but at a larger size and with polished art in the *Palookaville* style—is structured as a series of vignettes, again across time, that detail the life of a small-town television personality, and again from various perspectives. Seth's fascination with persona and self-mythologizing, his interest in time and the past, and his desire to evoke a precise sense of space coalesce in this brief but dense narrative. It may be his most successful work to date, or at least the completed work with which he is happiest, as he suggests in his interview with Hoffman and Grace.

Seth's interest in place and the physical world led him to a project (never realized) for which he decided to craft a locale first, in which to set the story. This led first to an expanding history of the city, Dominion, Ontario, written in his notebooks, and then to Seth's construction of cardboard models of Dominion's buildings. To date, he has constructed over eighty of these, with more to come, and they have toured art galleries as their own separate display. *Clyde Fans* is the first work with segments explicitly set in Dominion, and photographs of these models have appeared in recent issues of *Palookaville*, as well as being interspersed throughout the collected *Sprott*, which is also set in Dominion. It has now become Seth's *place*, perhaps his version of Twain's Hannibal, Missouri, Hardy's Wessex, or, perhaps more appropriately for this Canadian artist, Stephen Leacock's Mariposa (Seth has in fact provided lush illustrations for a new edition of Leacock's *Sunshine Sketches of a Little Town* [2013]). If the past in Seth's work is nearly always romanticized—that is, forced to fit those distinct parameters of cultural artifacts with which Seth fashions his narratives—then Dominion can be seen as a necessary creation for the preservation of this idealization. Indeed, place has always been important in Seth's work—see his remarks on the importance of Radiant City to the story of *Mister X* in Michael Strafford's 1985 interview, included here—yet his creation of Dominion makes its physical rooting even more central.

Place emerges as the primary focus of his most recent graphic novel, *The Great Northern Brotherhood of Canadian Cartoonists* (2011), which is not properly speaking even a narrative but another sketchbook/Dominion project given expanded life in graphic novel form. Here Seth offers perhaps his most radical metafictive work, as the book imagines an alternate Canada in which cartooning and comics receive serious and sustained respect (though now waning, of course—time and loss remain central concerns), and the narrative (such as it is) merely explores the now largely abandoned meeting place of the GNB Double C, as this organization is affectionately known, largely in the form of a guided tour of the GNB Double C's Dominion, Ontario branch headquarters. "Seth" again narrates, providing mini biographies and samples of the work of many of the Brotherhood. Most of these are in fact imaginary creators and comics, but Seth weaves in a few real figures, such as Doug Wright, giving the work an oddly liminal status, locating it even more starkly on the border between fact and fiction than is the case with *It's a Good Life*.

Seth has produced many other comics and illustrations and designs, too numerous to discuss in detail here (a select number are included in this book's chronology), which reflect not only his productivity but also his ubiquity and importance in contemporary comics. His art graces the covers and interior pages of major magazines and books; he has provided innovative and influential designs for numerous books and series, comics-related and otherwise; and he continues to produce profound and thoughtful comics that go against the grain of most other artists. In his interview with Tom Spurgeon, he describes himself as "a contrarian." He might be better described as *sui generis*: a true original.

This book gathers together interviews from early in his career to a new one conducted specifically for this book, in which Seth's influences, ideologies of comics and art, major thematic preoccupations, and major (as well as some minor and even nonexistent) works are explored, from numerous perspectives—appropriately enough, given Seth's own complex and multifaceted artistic endeavors. The first, Michael Strafford's 1985 piece, is a brief interview with twenty-three-year-old Seth at the beginning of his career, shortly after he began providing artwork for Dean Motter's *Mister X*. Seth discusses his aesthetic choices in illustrating the series, in particular his utilizing the work

Seth channels Doug Wright. From *The Great Northern Brotherhood of Canadian Cartoonists* © Seth. Used with permission from Drawn & Quarterly.

of Bauhaus and Russian Constructivism architecture which foreshadows his later concern with architecture in his creation of Dominion City.

Dylan Williams's expansive 1994 interview with Seth near the beginning of his professional career, following the positive critical reception of his comic *Palookaville*, finds Seth in the midst of his creation of *It's a Good Life, If You Don't Weaken*. Seth discusses the pros and cons of serialization as opposed to producing graphic novels, arguing in favor of serialization, at least from an economic standpoint. Seth discusses the changing economics of the medium on the eve of the collapse of the speculator bubble. Also addressed here is Seth's early magazine work, his collaborations with Dean Motter on *Mister X* and his key associations with fellow Toronto-based artists Chester Brown and Joe Matt, and his technical methods, along with a candid discussion of various comics artists whom he admires or who have influenced his work.

Bryan Miller's 2004 interview explores collecting and nostalgia—key Seth themes—before the discussion turns to *Clyde Fans* and then to Seth's work as a designer. Seth also comments on autobiographical comics and the differences between mainstream, alternative, and underground work, as well as the relationship between comics and other media.

Dave Sim's interview from 2005 is part of a series entitled "Advise and Consent," interviews discussing creators' use (or non-use) of editors. Seth discusses his views on editors and creative input, specifically his preferences against using either prior to publication. The interview expands to a more general discussion of authenticity among so-called "independent" comics artists and the difficulty of remaining entirely free from influence, either from other artists or from critics and the so-called artistic "establishment."

Gerald Hannon's fascinating and revealing 2006 profile for the magazine *Toronto Life* provides an excellent brief biography of Seth, rich in detail, as well as an insightful discussion of his singular oeuvre, offering a descriptive and insightful window into Seth's daily life and the challenges and rewards of being an "alternative" comics artist. Rebecca Bengal's 2006 piece is a short yet rewarding interview from the PBS series "On Cartooning," focusing primarily on Seth's technique and aesthetics, his influences, his illustrative strategies, and narrative devices. Also under discussion is Seth's relationship to his characters, his working process, and what separates his comics work from his commercial work and the cultural legitimacy of the comics artist in the twenty-first century.

Thom Ernst's 2009 interview explores the history of Seth's adoption of his *nom de plume* and then continues its interest in names as Seth and Ernst discuss the problematics of terms such as graphic novel, comics, and others used in attempts to define Seth's medium. This piece offers Seth's most extended theorizing on the nature of comics as a medium, which leads into a discussion of genre more generally and of filmic adaptations of comics. Tom Spurgeon's extensive 2009 interview goes into revealing detail about the genesis of *George Sprott* as a serial publication in the *New York Times*, as well as into Seth's inspiration and influences for the book. The complex nature of serial production and the artist's ongoing relationship with the work in that context, and the challenges of converting it to a book, are discussed, as are the technical aspects of the strip, which provide insight into Seth's aesthetic choices. Seth also comments in detail on characterization and narrative strategies in the work. Seth's interest in persona and some of his influences, notably Doug Wright, are addressed illuminatingly, and Seth's design work gets comprehensive treatment as well.

Finally, our new major interview with Seth ranges widely and comprehensively across his career, revisiting much of his earlier work as he looks back on it now, exploring his expansion into installation art and film, and looking forward.

ACKNOWLEDGMENTS

We gratefully acknowledge the original interviewers and publishers for their permission to reuse their work in this collection. The selection process during this project was challenging; though we believe the interviews collected here offer a satisfying and illuminating range of insights into Seth's work, space limitations have necessitated some hard choices and the exclusion of several worthy pieces. We wish also to thank Walter Biggins and Vijay Shah, at the University Press of Mississippi, for their work shepherding this book through the publication process, and Anne Stascavage for her always meticulous editing. Thanks also to Drawn & Quarterly for permission to use Seth's art and for providing scans. Finally, our sincere thanks go to Seth, who graciously and generously supported this project.

EH
DG

Works Cited

Hatfield, Charles. *Alternative Comics: An Emerging Literature*. Jackson: University Press of Mississippi, 2005.

Hignite, M. Todd. "Seth in the Studio." *Comic Art* 6 (2004): 28–49.

Mullins, Katie. "Questioning Comics: Women and Autocritique in Seth's *It's a Good Life, If You Don't Weaken*." *Canadian Literature* 203 (2009): 11–27, 201. Online

Stukavsky, Ann (January 1, 2010). "Drawn Together: Seth and the Newspaper." *the newspaper: The University of Toronto's Independent Weekly*. Online. Retrieved May 25, 2013.

SELECTED CHRONOLOGY

1962	Born Gregory Gallant, September 16, in Clinton, Ontario, to John Henry Gallant and Violet Daisy Gallant (née Wilkinson), one of five children. Raised in a series of small Ontario towns.
1980	Moves to Toronto to study at the Ontario College of Art in Toronto, Ontario, which he attends until 1983.
1982	Adopts *nom de plume* "Seth."
1985	Begins work on Dean Motter's *Mister X* comic for the Toronto-based Vortex Comics, beginning with issue 6 (cover dated December 1985) and ending with issue 13 (cover dated June 1988).
1986	Meets cartoonist Chester Brown.
1988	Various commercial artworks published in Canadian magazines. Two very early and important jobs from that first year that launched Seth's commercial art career were a cover for *Saturday Night Magazine* and a full-page feature in *Toronto Life Fashion* ("Jacque the Happy Lumberjack"). Subsequent commercial artwork has appeared in the *Atlantic, Forbes, Globe and Mail, Mother Jones,* the *National Post, New York Magazine, New York Times,* the *New Yorker, Saturday Night,* the *Washington Post, CNQ (Canadian Notes and Queries),* the *Walrus,* and many other publications too numerous to list.
1991	First two issues of *Palookaville* published by Montreal, Quebec-based Drawn & Quarterly. Meets cartoonist Joe Matt.
1993	Third and fourth issues of *Palookaville* published. Begins first serial, *It's a Good Life, If You Don't Weaken,* in the fourth issue.
1994	Fifth and sixth issues of *Palookaville* published.
1995	Seventh and eighth issues of *Palookaville* published.
1996	Ninth issue of *Palookaville* published. *It's a Good Life, If You Don't Weaken* subsequently published in collected format.
1997	Next major storyline, *Clyde Fans,* begins in the tenth and eleventh issues of *Palookaville.* Wins Ignatz Award for Outstanding

	Artist for *Palookaville* and Outstanding Graphic Novel or Collection for *It's a Good Life, If You Don't Weaken*.
1998	Twelfth issue of *Palookaville* published.
1999	Thirteenth issue of *Palookaville* published. Moves to Guelph, Ontario.
2000	Fourteenth issue of *Palookaville* published. *Clyde Fans Part One* collection published in comic book format.
2001	Selected drawings from sketchbooks published in *Vernacular Drawings*. Fifteenth issue of *Palookaville* published. Participates in group exhibit *Substitute City: Artists Infiltrate Toronto* held at the Power Plant in Toronto. Essay "John Stanley's Teenage Trilogy" published in *The Comics Journal*.
2002	Marries Tania Van Spyk. Solo Exhibit at the Napoli Comicon in Naples, Italy. Provides cover and interior art for Aimee Mann compact disc *Lost in Space*.
2003	Sixteenth issue of *Palookaville* published.
2004	Designs the first two volumes of the *New York Times* bestselling *The Complete Peanuts*; twenty-five volumes are projected to be completed by 2016. *Clyde Fans, Book One* (collecting *Clyde Fans* parts one and two) published in hardcover. Seventeenth issue of *Palookaville* published. Collaboration with father, John Gallant, *Bannock, Beans and Black Tea: Memories of a Prince Edward Island Childhood in the Great Depression*. Provides cover for August 23, 2004, cover of the *New Yorker*, the first of several. Interview and feature in *Comic Art* no. 6. Included in significant *New York Times* graphic novel feature, "Not Funnies" and in *McSweeney's Quarterly Concern* number 13 (edited by Chris Ware). Pens essay, "Chris Reynolds: An Appreciation" for *The Comics Journal*.
2005	Sketchbook work *Wimbledon Green: The Greatest Comic Book Collector in the World* published. Eighteenth issue of *Palookaville* published. Exhibit Present Tense: Seth held at the Art Gallery of Ontario; single-page story "Hush" purchased by the Art Gallery of Ontario for its permanent collection. Cofounds Doug Wright Awards with Brad MacKay. Wins Doug Wright Award for *Clyde Fans, Book One*. Awarded the PEI Museum Heritage Award for *Bannock, Beans and Black Tea*, and the Eisner Award for Best Publication Design and a special Harvey Kurtzman Award for Excellence in Production/Presentation for *The Complete Peanuts*. Excerpt from *Wimbledon Green* ("Jonah") published in the *New Yorker*.

2006   Begins serialization of *George Sprott* in the September issue of the *New York Times Magazine*; twenty-five installments are published, running to February 2007. Exhibit Seth shown at the Macdonald Stewart Gallery in Guelph, Ontario. A small book, *Forty Cartoon Books of Interest*, designed and written by Seth, published (a supplement to *Comic Art* no. 8). Designs *The Portable Dorothy Parker* for Penguin books. Profile in *Toronto Life*. Designs (and is included in) Ivan Brunetti's *Anthology of Graphic Fiction, Cartoons, and True Stories*.

2007   *George Sprott* continues in the *New York Times Magazine*. Designs inaugural pamphlet for the Center for Cartoon Studies in White River Junction, Vermont, which is used to establish the school's identity. Selection from *Wimbledon Green* included in *The Best American Comics 2007*, edited by Chris Ware. Exhibit Uninked shown at the Phoenix Art Gallery in Phoenix, Arizona.

2008   Nineteenth issue of *Palookaville* published. Dominion City and Beaver City models exhibited as part of the RENDER Project at the University of Waterloo Art Gallery in Kitchener-Waterloo. Designs accompanying installation piece *The North Star Talking Picture House*, a full-scale cardboard theater showing silent films chosen by Seth. Selection from *George Sprott* reprinted in *The Best American Comics 2008*, edited by Lynda Barry. Awarded the Communications Arts Gold Award for Excellence for one of his *New Yorker* covers. Article "Seth on Thoreau MacDonald" published in *The Devil's Advocate* magazine.

2009   Designs Drawn & Quarterly's John Stanley Library; nine volumes published to date. Provides design for and coedits *The Collected Doug Wright: Canada's Master Cartoonist*. *George Sprott (1894–1975)* (collecting the *New York Times* series) published. Wins Inkpot Award. Dominion exhibit shown at the Dundas Historical Museum in Dundas, Ontario and Dominion and The Wine King at the Niagara Arts Centre in St. Catharines, Ontario.

2010   Exhibit An Exhibition of Drawings shown at the Adam Baumgold Gallery in New York City. Dominion exhibited at the Museum London in London, Ontario. *Palookaville* 20 published, for the first time as a hardback "annual." Redesigns the entire magazine *CNQ* beginning with issue 79; provides covers for every issue since (now up to issue 88). *George Sprott* awarded the Doug Wright Award. First volume of Seth-designed reprints of *Doug*

Wright's Family published as *Nipper*; three volumes have been published to date.

2011   A sketchbook work, *The Great Northern Brotherhood of Canadian Cartoonists* (a.k.a. *The G.N.B. Double C*) published. Exhibition of G.N.B. Double C drawings held at the Adam Baumgold Gallery. Awarded the Toronto Harbourfront Festival Prize. Essay "Creating a Personal Vernacular Canadian Design Style" published in *The Devil's Advocate.*

2012   Designs *About Love: Three Stories by Anton Chekhov f*or Biblioasis. Begins collaboration with Lemony Snicket on All the Wrong Questions series of books for Little, Brown.

2013   *Palookaville 21* published. Exhibit It's a Good Life, If You Don't Weaken (And selected Early Works) shown at the Adam Baumgold Gallery. Designs deluxe edition of *Sunshine Sketches of a Little Town* by Stephen Leacock for McClelland & Stewart. Second volume of All the Wrong Questions, *"When Did You See Her Last?"* published.

2014   *File Under 13: Suspicious Incidents*, companion to All the Wrong Questions volume published. Documentary on Seth, *Seth's Dominion*, directed by Luc Chamberland premieres at Ottowa International Festival; includes never-before-seen puppet show "The Apology of Albert Batch" and significant animation based on Seth's work. "Shouldn't You Be in School?," third of All the Wrong Questions published.

2015   *Palookaville 22* published. "Why is This Night Different From All Other Nights?," fourth and final All the Wrong Questions volume published.

SETH: CONVERSATIONS

Interview

MICHAEL STRAFFORD / 1985

Arken Sword (1986) 28–29. Reprinted by permission.

Seth's interview was conducted [at the UK Comic Art Convention in 1985] by Michael Strafford and comes from the second issue of his cassette magazine *Comicast*.

Seth: I came to Toronto, Canada, about five years ago. Before that I'd always wanted to be a comic book illustrator with fairly typical ideas of what I wanted to do. I had piles of horror strips, and superheroes et cetera. Then I went to art school and over two years I got disenchanted with comics and I gave them up. I was in the commercial design department, but after the third year of that I became disenchanted with that too because I didn't want to be drawing brillo pads for the rest of my life. So I dropped out of school and spent a year bumming around. At the end of that year, in which I really didn't do anything, I got my portfolio back together and started working on my comics again. By this time I felt that I had matured as an artist and had learned new influences. I found that I had a direction of my own for a change. It was co-incidentally around this time that I came across Bill [Marks] and Vortex who were looking for a new artist on *Mister X*. I was also involved with a group of artists called The Circle, who were a sort of minimalist comic art movement who were working towards simplicity [in] style and content.

Michael: How do you think you've followed the Hernandez Brothers?
S: They're a hard act to follow, because they're very good. I'm a big fan of theirs. I felt their problem on *Mister X* was that Jaime is an amazing artist for figure drawing but he doesn't seem to have a great love of architecture, and to me the protagonist of *Mister X* is the city. Radiant City is the main character. If Mister X is the main character, then you have to explore him too much,

and since he's an enigma, it becomes very hard in that direction. So I feel that in certain areas I probably enjoy working on the series more than they did, because I have a great love for the Bauhaus, the Russian Constructivists, and the international style of architecture, which are a lot of the influences the book comes from. It's really hard to follow Jaime because he's such an excellent figure drawer and I don't feel as confident about my figure drawing as I do about my architecture.

M: *Mister X* is designed as a whole package rather than a strip with a cover stuck around it. Do you prefer this?
S: Yes, I do. I really think that it's important to work as an entire package. Dean created *Mister X* to be the very pinnacle of comic art, to be a venue for all the very best elements of design. That follows exactly what I feel too. I'm striving to create a really slick, concise package. I like the way that the cover integrates with the interior graphics, which integrates with the rest of the book. I design everything as a spread, which sometimes confuses the colorist. I like every spread to work perfectly, so I make sure I know where the text and ad pages go. I like the book to work as a complete design element and not to be chopped up. I remember in the late sixties that Marvel would take Jack Kirby's pages, cut them in half, and put ads in the bottom. That's just abominable. That shows the lack of concern they have for comics as an art medium.

M: How is the more avant-garde art taken across in America / Canada?
S: It's really a shame because it's pretty much the same all over the world, I think. There's a very small hardcore crowd that will look at alternative work, and the rest of the comics market doesn't seem very interested. They're too busy with the mainstreams. Even *Love and Rockets*, which I believe is a very successful small press book, sells about 8,000–10,000 copies. Things like *Raw*, *Weirdo*, all the small presses, reach an audience that isn't really that connected with the regular comic book world. I used to have a pet theory that there was a comics wall, with Marvel and DC on one side, and *Raw* and the like on the other. I thought that *Mister X* and *Love and Rockets*, for example, could stand in between. I don't really go with that theory anymore. I tend to regard comics as a whole now. I try to hope that you can reach both markets at the same time. I tend to hope that there are people at Marvel who read *Raw*.

M: Would you like to work on an anthology like *Love and Rockets*, where you have short stories that are vaguely interconnected?
S: Yes and no. I'd like to work in a short-story format, but I don't think I'd

Radiant City. From *Mister X*. Courtesy of Vortex Comics Inc. © 2013.

like to interconnect them. Ideally, I'd like to do concise packages that had, say, six-page installments over ten issues, that finished off, leaving those characters for good. Then I could start on something new. I like the idea of having a beginning and an end. Sometimes I feel that one of the biggest problems with the comics market is that there is no end to comics characters. They go on for eternity. A lot of the time there's a lot of wasted space, a lot of self-indulgence.

M: Are you ever self-indulgent?
S: Oh, for sure. I always try to keep the storytelling as the main point, but occasionally there'll be something I really want to draw. Like, I may want to throw in a cityscape, and I'll contrive it, as long as it tells a story.

M: You said earlier that the book is based around the city. Are you trying to put emotional content into the structures of the city itself?
S: Yes, I am. Just lately I've been giving some thought to reworking the way I draw the city. I'm going to be using more oblique angles. I'm not going to be as dramatic as, say, *The Cabinet of Dr. Caligari*, but I'm going to give a bit more of a demented feeling to the city, as though the psychotecture was working.

M: Do you have any input on the writing side?
S: We sit down and toss ideas back and forth, but it is Dean's creation, so I leave the direction to him. We discuss new ideas and new characters, and Dean is pretty open to that. He allows me free rein when I'm working on back-up strips. He doesn't force break-downs on me, or how a character should look. He lets me do what I think is right.

M: Does the book have an end?
S: Dean claims there is an ending. I don't know it. I don't know when it will end or if it will end. It's a commercial property, so I don't think Bill Marks would want to end it in four years' time if it was selling well, and it was still a quality comic.

M: Will you be working on anything else?
S: Not at the moment. I'm concentrating on working on my skills as an artist, and later as a writer, too. I feel I'm ready to publish a book of my own, but I don't think I'm fast enough to do *Mister X* and my own book every two months. I'm enjoying working on *Mister X* anyway.

An Interview with Seth

DYLAN WILLIAMS / 1995

Destroy All Comics 2.2 (February 1995) pp. 1–27. Reprinted with permission.

Seth: My very first influences in comics or cartooning, the first things that interested me in it, would be a combination of a few newspaper strips. The first would be *Peanuts*, of course. *Peanuts* has been a lifelong interest, and I don't think a point will ever come where I don't love it as much as I do now. Around that same time, there was a Canadian editorial cartoonist [for the *London Free Press*, in London, Ontario] who signed his work Ting, although his real name was Merle Tingley, who came to my school when I was in grade one or two and gave a little lecture, and after that . . . I think I was always following his work anyways, because like a lot of editorial cartoonists he had a little mascot creature in his drawings that was a worm! You had to look for it in the cartoon, so that was enough to make me interested in it when I was that young, 'cause obviously I wasn't interested in the subject matter. He really inspired me and made me see that people were cartoonists, that there were actually people doing this. That, and my parents used to have certain strips they really liked, which I mentioned in *Palookaville*. *Nancy* and *Andy Capp*, that my mother really liked, were real big favorites of mine, and still are, and this strip called *Little Nipper* by Canadian cartoonist Doug Wright was another thing that I still think is a great strip. These things were probably the first things that got me interested. Like any kid, I was reading a few comics at that time, I was reading *Heckle and Jeckle* and *Richie Rich* and *Archies* and stuff.

Dylan Williams: Did your parents have any anthologies of the cartoonist's work, or did they just get it in the paper?

Seth: Just from the paper. There were a few paperbacks around the house, but the truth is, there weren't ever many books around my family's house.

The formative influence of comic strips on Seth. From *It's a Good Life, If You Don't Weaken* © Seth. Used with permission from Drawn & Quarterly.

I think my interest in reading and cartooning is something that really just sprang . . . I don't even know how it came about, except that I liked the stuff. Because there was no tradition in our family towards the arts in any way, like nobody in my family even was much of a reader.

Williams: Did you get the *New Yorker*?
Seth: No, my family was definitely lower middle class. At one point or another, we were even living in a trailer park. So, definitely as a young man I wasn't flipping through the *New Yorker* or the *New York Times* or anything. My dad was a mechanic when I was really young, and later he was a shop teacher.

I've got to give him credit though. He had a grade three education, and he managed to up it, and go back to school and go through teachers college and everything, so in retrospect, it's kind of impressive.

I remember sometime in grade school, actually it was at summer camp, I read some Marvel comics. They were Kirby *X-Men*. They were in a big box, so they hadn't just come out or anything, and this fired me up. This really got me interested in comic books in a way I'd never been before.

Williams: It's funny, when I think about Kirby stuff, those are the ones that I think are the least great, but even then they are so great.

Seth: When I look at those, I still have all of them around here somewhere, that stuff just looks great to me. There's a real nostalgic charm to it that's unmistakable. It's really appealing to me. For some reason that got me fired up, and when I got back home, I remember I started watching the *Spider-Man* cartoon on TV and stuff, and then I remember, it kind of clicked together one day, "Hey, Spider-Man's in a comic book," so I started buying comic books, and within a few years I was a total Marvel addict. I went through this period, through most of my teen years, of buying and reading every single Marvel comic that ever came out. That's where I developed my drawing ability. If I hadn't loved comic books, I wouldn't have spent that much time drawing. I think it's probably true of an awful lot of people who do comics, since the fact that they were kind of an outsider to the scene. I was definitely a loser in high school. If they had a drawing ability, they would produce their own comic books. I must have drawn hundreds of comic books when I was in high school, all superhero crap, and some horror stuff.

Williams: There should be some therapy group for kids like that.

Seth: To keep them from ending up at Marvel. I see some groups for those kids, but they don't look too good. They're role playing groups in the back of a comic shop or something. I was fortunate that I didn't know a single other person who read comic books until I was in my twenties. I was horribly ashamed of it, in fact, so there was no way I was going to tell anyone in high school that I was reading comic books. I figured, "I'm enough of a loser, I don't need to add this to the group. They have plenty of reasons to hate me as it is." But that's where I think I really developed my drawing abilities. If it hadn't been for that I probably wouldn't be able to produce a comic book now.

I guess it was around when I went to art school that I lost interest in those Marvel comics, but I still had interest in the medium.

Williams: And you were just doing painting?

Seth: Sure, yeah, I was in a more commercially oriented department.

Williams: Were you in illustration?

Seth: I was in what they called communication and design, which incorporated any kind of artwork that was for commercial purposes. I took illustration courses, and I took graphic design courses, and production art, and technique. All those things. But halfway through art school, I really realized, "This doesn't do me any good. At the end of this I'm going to end up working on the Jell-O account or something, this isn't going to make me a cartoonist," so I kind of got disenchanted with the whole thing, and that's when I . . .

Williams: So you still wanted to be a cartoonist?

Seth: Yeah, even during all this I still wanted to be a cartoonist, I just didn't know what the hell I was going to do with it. I was really kind of mixed up. There's only been one point in my whole life, since I was a kid, where I didn't think I was going to be a cartoonist, and that was in my third year of art school, and I was really fucked up, and I thought, "This ain't going to happen. This is a dream." I guess this actually would have been right after I dropped out of art school, because I hadn't even drawn anything for about eight months, and I thought, "I'm not going to be a cartoonist. I'm not going anywhere. I'm working at a shitty job, and I'm not doing any art, and what was I thinking anyway, I don't even know what I'm going to do."

Williams: What kind of job was it?

Seth: I was working in a jewelry factory, assembling costume jewelry. And I was also really fucked up on drugs at that point too, so life really didn't seem like it was heading anywhere.

Williams: So, how much art school did you have?

Seth: I was there for about two and a half years.

Williams: Did you learn all the basics of drawing?

Seth: I guess so. I start to wonder what you really learn in art school. It's a good place to kill time.

Williams: It depends on the teacher. If the teacher is really teaching you stuff, then it's important, but if it's one of those, "draw how you feel," kind of things . . .

Seth: Yeah. First of all, I think I was too young when I was there. I just wasn't prepared to learn. The truth is, I didn't really have a clue. I remember being in graphic design class, and I didn't even know what graphic design was when I was nineteen years old! I would look at the stuff, and it would seem like some sort of a magic thing to be able to get a graphic design that you would get an A on. I didn't know how it worked. Now, it's like an instinctual thing. You look at something and you can tell what's good graphic design and what isn't, but at that point I was completely lost. I was an idiot, and I didn't learn anything really useful when I was in art school. I feel like most of my learning has come through self-teaching, because you have to learn when you're ready.

Williams: I really think that most art school is a fraud because nobody is really ready to sit down and learn that stuff when they're nineteen.
Seth: Exactly.

Williams: You have to be like twenty-five, or you have to be mature enough to actually digest the stuff.
Seth: I mean, what the hell do you know about anything when you're nineteen, and how can you translate that experience into any sort of an artistic statement? It's pointless. I think the best thing you might get out of art school is a lot of life-drawing classes. That was always fun. I don't know if it helped my drawing, but I sure enjoyed it. It's always a pleasure to draw from the figure.

Williams: Yeah, I agree. If you sit down and actually look at things . . .
Seth: It's definitely something every cartoonist should do.

Williams: I spent three years straight, all the way through the summer and everything, just going to figure drawing classes.
Seth: It's definitely important, because you really can't learn to draw from other cartoonists.

You can learn to emulate their stylistic tics, but it's not going to help you draw any. When it really comes down to the basics of drawing and composition, you can't learn that from anybody else. You've got to learn that yourself.

Williams: What renewed your interest in cartooning?
Seth: I guess when I was about twenty, when I was in art school, I pretty much lost interest in cartooning, for a while. That's because I stopped reading

the Marvel comics. I was still interested in comics, but I just didn't realize there was such potential to the medium. So for a couple of years there I just stopped doing any kind of cartooning. I was just goofing around. I dropped out of art school. I started doing a lot of drugs and stuff, and then I read an ad that Vortex Comics was looking for an artist or something. I went up there and showed them some stuff that I had and they didn't care for it, but this guy Ken Steacy . . . I don't know if you've ever heard of him . . .

Williams: The airbrush guy.

Seth: Yeah. He took me out to the comic shop, because I told him I wasn't reading any comics and he said, "You gotta buy this *Love and Rockets*." So this would probably be '82 or '83, and so I picked up issue number three and I started reading *Love and Rockets*. For a while that's all I read, then I started branching out and reading some other stuff. I was picking up Chester [Brown]'s minicomic *Yummy Fur*, and . . .

Williams: Did you know Chester then?

Seth: No, I didn't. I wrote him a letter sometime around then, and that's when we made our first contact. We didn't really meet until we both worked at Vortex a couple of years later.

Then I started to get interested in comics again, and started to read some of the undergrounds I'd read as a teenager, but didn't really understand. I started to pick up on Crumb, and started to dig more deeply into the alternative comics scene. I started reading *Weirdo* and *Raw*, and stuff like that.

Williams: Was that stuff available at any store around there?

Seth: Yeah, it was actually pretty easy to find here in Toronto. Toronto is not bad for . . . The Beguiling wasn't open yet, which, in my mind, is probably the best comic shop I've ever seen.

Williams: That's what everybody says. Except Quimby's, which sounds like it's pretty close.

Seth: I haven't heard much about that, but there were a couple of comic shops here that were pretty good. There's a place called the Dragon Lady that had a lot of old stuff, and there was a place called the Silver Snail that carried a fair amount of alternative stuff at that time, although it's pretty much a mainstream store now. But, it was easy enough to find this stuff . . . *American Splendor* and things like that, so I got my interest in cartooning revitalized around that time, and that's when I ended up drawing *Mister X*.

Williams: There was some other comic that somebody told me you drew for Vortex.

Seth: I did a bit of stuff in their *Vortex Magazine*. They had an anthology title, but besides that I didn't do anything for them but *Mister X*.

Williams: What did you feel about doing the *Mister X* stuff?

Seth: In retrospect, I didn't have any moral qualms about it. Looking back on it, I probably should have had some moral qualms about coming on after the Hernandez Brothers, after Bill had supposedly screwed them around, but the truth is, I didn't really know anything about that at that time. I'd just started reading *The Comics Journal*, and by the time I was working on *Mister X* it wasn't common knowledge that Bill had screwed them around. I suppose I should have made some sort of a moral choice after that, but I just stuck with it. As an esthetic choice, at that point, I didn't really have any esthetic problem with *Mister X*. Not until I'd been working on it for a while. I really liked what the Hernandez Brothers had done on it. Looking back on it now, I can really see that the stuff they did on it was really second rate compared to their *Love and Rockets* work, but at the time it seemed great to me. So, I was happy to get the job at first.

Williams: Great by regular standards too.

Seth: Yeah, exactly.

Williams: The best of the schlock.

Seth: Yeah. So, by the time I left the book it felt like I'd made a major mistake working on it. The only thing that I can say really good about it is that it forced me to draw a lot, and develop my style a bit. Whenever I look at those *Mister X*'s, which is almost never, I can really see that I was learning to draw better through them. From the beginning to the end it's a real inconsistent bunch of comic books. At least it prepared me for what came later. But if it was now, I certainly wouldn't be taking on a project like *Mister X*.

Williams: Have you ever talked to David Mazzucchelli, because what you're saying there sounds like what happened with him too.

Seth: Yeah, I guess so. I've only met David Mazzucchelli once and it was for about two minutes, so we didn't really have any time to talk. It seems like sort of a miracle to me that he got out of that world. He's the only one. I don't know anybody else who has gone into mainstream comics, real Marvel/DC, and ever come out to produce anything worthwhile.

Williams: Really it's the opposite. There are all these underground guys who are now ending up working for Marvel and . . .
Seth: Yeah, that's sad.

Williams: It's horrible.
Seth: I just think those places are soul destroying. You can't go in there when you're twenty years old, and then five years later, after doing that, come out, and still have an artistic vision. It just warps you. You're surrounded by all these people who think the same way and have the same interests, and I think you probably get sucked in, like any kind of a corporate structure. I'm sure that if I'd gone to Marvel Comics at nineteen, and they'd said, "You can draw our books," I'd just be a hack now, 'cause there's no way you can survive it.

Williams: I think if you have a strong enough vision, like with Mazzucchelli, I think that's what it is. His vision is so intense.
Seth: His old friends there must think he's nuts.

Williams: Actually, he has this great story about Rob Liefeld looking at his stuff and going, "What happened to him? Oh my God! This doesn't make any sense."
Seth: I believe it. They must just think he's a kook.

Williams: Which is great!
Seth: Yeah. Well, considering none of those guys can draw, they're certainly nobody to be judging anything.

Williams: Did you have a lot of freedom on *Mister X* to do stuff, or did he just, I don't know . . . I haven't even read those actually.
Seth: Well, don't bother. Yeah, I had a lot of freedom. The guy I worked with, Dean Motter, who was the writer, he would basically just give me the dialogue for the book, and I would just break it down, and design the characters and whatever. But even so, it's not a satisfying experience even when you have that much control. You're not writing it and you're not coloring it, and they won't even let you do the cover. It's kind of soul destroying too, when you're drawing the book and they say to you that you're not good enough to do the cover. It makes you wonder, "Why am I good enough to draw the insides of the book, then?" Ultimately, I just don't believe in working with writers anyway. I think it's a pretty rare exception when that works out.

Williams: If there's a collaboration, isn't . . .

Seth: I guess that's why I have this opinion. I can't collaborate, so I judge everything from that. I find it hard to imagine . . . I suppose I could collaborate with Chester, but then I often think, "but, what's the point?" Both of us can just do our own work. We don't need to get together on anything. It's rare for me to find anybody that I can enjoy working with that much that I'd ever want to collaborate with them.

Williams: I'd like to see you and Chris Ware do something.

Seth: That would be interesting. I just can't imagine it.

Williams: How did you get into illustration?

Seth: That was a plan on how to get out of comics, so I could do my own comic. When I left *Mister X* . . . I had a friend Maurice Vellekoop . . . you've probably seen his work in *Drawn & Quarterly* [comics anthology published from 1990–92 by Drawn & Quarterly], well, he's a big illustrator, and I could see he was making a lot of money. I thought to myself, there's no way I could work on *Mister X*, for example, and do a comic book of my own on the side. It's just too much work. But I thought if I did illustration, I could make more money for less work, and still manage to get my comic book out on the side. But that really didn't work out too well, because for the first couple of years of illustration I had to work so hard to build up any sort of a career that I was working seven days a week on illustration.

Williams: Was this before *Palookaville* came out?

Seth: Yeah, this was the couple of years in-between those two books. So, finally it was so busy I just had to say, I'll have to schedule my time better and do less illustration, and get the comic done. So basically that's what I've done now. I just take as much illustration as I need, and just use the other time on the book. Ultimately it worked out, but for the first couple of years . . .

Williams: Do you have people coming to you for jobs?

Seth: It depends, it's really hot and cold. It's scary being a freelancer, but I've had steady work for the last five years. There's been some points where I've been down to my last buck, and I'll get scared and start thinking, "I better find a representative, or something," because the work's drying up, but then some more always comes. The recession was kinda tough, because illustration really dropped, but the last six months, or whatever, it's been really good. I've been getting lots of work and I've been able to have enough money to take a month off to work on the comic, and stuff like that. So, it's been pretty good lately, but I'd like to get out of illustration.

Williams: Where have your illustrations appeared?
Seth: Well, they appear mostly in Canadian magazines.

Williams: Like travel magazines, or stuff like that?
Seth: Lifestyle magazines, newspapers. I do a lot of work for one of the newspapers here in town. In lifestyle magazines I do a lot of restaurant illustrations. I've done work for *New York Magazine* and the *Washington Post*. I almost did some work for the *New Yorker* this year, but that didn't work out. I did a cover for them, but it ended up getting killed.

Williams: Wow.
Seth: It didn't see print. It was pretty disappointing for me because I was really looking forward to seeing it on the cover, but it didn't come through.

Williams: I'd think they'd see your style and go, "This guy is for us."
Seth: I'd like it, but . . . they sent me a thing telling me all the new holidays coming up, if I want to submit some ideas, so . . . we'll see. I was pretty bummed out when the cover didn't see print, so I've got to build up my enthusiasm again, to try to work up some ideas.

I don't really like their system. They send out these newsletters to everybody. So you've probably got like fifty people competing for that Valentine's Day cover, and they probably just pick the best one. I prefer the old commission idea, when they call you up and commission you specifically.

Williams: That's treating it like art. They don't want to do that anymore.
Seth: Yeah, well, I just wanted that big fee too. They pay very well.

Williams: That's what I hear.
Seth: But once you get in, it seems like it's pretty good. People like . . . who has been doing covers lately a lot . . . well, certainly Art Spiegelman has.

Williams: David Mazzucchelli's done a couple.
Seth: Yeah, Mazzucchelli really seems to have his foot in the door now. I must have seen like three or four covers by him so far.

Williams: There's a [Lorenzo] Mattotti cover on the new one.
Seth: I think he's already done a cover for them, so that would make sense. And I've seen [Mark] Zingarelli . . . quite a few cartoonists are doing stuff for them now, which is good, 'cause that's like the old tradition. I prefer that than getting illustrators to do the covers.

Williams: Yeah, Evan Dorkin has a theory that with comic artists getting more illustration jobs, that it's maybe gonna open people's minds up to comic books.
Seth: I think he's kidding himself . . .

Williams: Nothing will do it.
Seth: Yeah, I'm pretty cynical about that.

Williams: What makes you choose the specific events you write about? Is it that they just stick in your mind and they keep on coming up?
Seth: You mean like the specific events within the story, or the different storylines in general?

Williams: The different stories in particular. Are they things you want to deal with, or are they just unresolved issues?
Seth: For the first three issues [of *Palookaville*], I look at them really differently than from issue number four on. Especially with the first issue, I feel like, this was my first comic story, and I think I made a fatal mistake. I picked something which is like a good anecdote, which is the kind of thing you might tell to some friends, to get some laughs or whatever, but a good anecdote very rarely makes a good story. I don't really feel like I knew what I was doing with the first issue.

With the storyline that started in the second issue, that ran in two and three, I felt like I had a better grasp of what I wanted to do, but I still didn't really know how to pull it off. When I look at that story now, I see that it should have been at least six issues long, and I should have paced it really differently. But, I had to do those to learn, first. Starting with issue number four I really felt like, "Now I know what I want to do and how to approach it." The way I look at it now, I would pick a story that has some potency, beyond being just something interesting that happened to me. This is kind of my complaint with a lot of autobiography, like what Dennis Eichhorn does, for example. It's too much of, "Here's some weird shit that happened to me," and there's not

Seth and Chet discuss Kalo. From *It's a Good Life, If You Don't Weaken* © Seth. Used with permission from Drawn & Quarterly.

any real introspection attached to it. I feel like there has got to be a point in telling a story. Obviously, or then there's no point in telling it. So now, I would pick a story more for what I want to say with the story, rather than with the specific events of it. In my mind, the events are secondary.

In *It's a Good Life, If You Don't Weaken* the search for Kalo is more of a catalyst for the story. It's just the motor that makes it run. To me, it's not the most interesting thing about it.

Williams: What's the most interesting thing about it?
Seth: The most interesting thing would be my underlying points of what I'm

trying to say about life, which will involve why Kalo is in the story, but it has a lot more to do with basically trying to explain how I feel about the world, and that's just the plot to build it around.

Williams: That's a big point for a lot of cartoonists, when they start realizing there should be a purpose.

Seth: Yeah, exactly. So much of cartooning has had to do with entertaining, and because of that I don't think most people come to the medium thinking they have to have something to say. They just think they have to manage to entertain people. So you get into this whole thing where you do one- or two-page stories, and if you get somebody to laugh, that's good. They never really reach that point where you really have to say something, which of course, is the most important thing if you're going to be a writer of any sort.

Williams: Yeah, most people don't approach it like it's writing.

Seth: Exactly. You've got too many people who've definitely spent too many years working on their drawing. They didn't realize they had to work on their writing too. It certainly happened to me. I mean, I'm thirty-two years old, and I'm just figuring what to do with the writing now, I'm just starting to figure it out.

Williams: When was the stuff in *Drawn & Quarterly*, in relation to *Palookaville*?

Seth: I think the first thing I had that appeared in *Drawn & Quarterly* came out before *Palookaville*, and then the next stuff probably came concurrent to the first couple of issues.

Williams: So that's probably the first thing you'd ever written?

Seth: I guess I wrote a couple of really crappy things in that *Vortex Magazine*, and I guess I did a couple of one-page strips here and there, before. But, I would probably put that as the first stuff I'd be willing to admit to.

Williams: It's interesting to see a progression in artists.

Seth: It's always more interesting to see from the other side, but it's pretty painful to look at your own early stuff.

Williams: Oh yeah.

Seth: But, it never bothers me to look at early stuff by other cartoonists that's really bad. I think it's interesting.

Williams: Personally, I'd kill to get any of the stuff Charles Schulz did before *Peanuts*.
Seth: *L'il Folks*. I've got the teenage stuff.

Williams: You've got the *L'il Folks* book?
Seth: No. No. Actually, I was thinking, in my next issue of *Palookaville*, I was going to put a request, if I have anybody who lives in Minneapolis-St. Paul to Xerox that stuff off the microfilm for me, and I'd gladly trade them some original art for it, because I'd really like to get my hands on that. There's two years' worth of it. I love that first couple of years.

Williams: I know, it's totally . . . That's a perfect example, like Schulz isn't proud of it at all. He thinks it's bad, so he's not going to reprint it at all.
Seth: Yeah, I was reading an interview with Schulz about a year ago where somebody was suggesting that he turn *Lil' Folks* into a book, and he was like, "Nope. Nope. I don't want that to see print." And it's too bad, 'cause I'd like to get my hands on it. I think the drawing was really beautiful too. It's definitely a different animal, that early *Peanuts* stuff and the *Lil' Folks*, than the later *Peanuts* stuff, but it's still nice. I like it.

Williams: That's why you should reprint your early stuff in one book.
Seth: Well . . .

Williams: Do you think about people not relating to your work at all? It's an issue to me. I do this stuff, I'm really interested in the fifties, and people don't relate to it at all, because it's not autobio, and it's not this, or whatever.
Seth: I don't think about it, because I don't think I really have that much connection with my audience, that I'm ever talking to them personally or anything. I get letters from people, and usually, you just get letters from people who like what you're doing. I don't know. Joe [Matt] and I have talked about this kind of thing, 'cause I think Joe is very conscious of his audience. He's aware of them. I don't think about it that way. When I'm writing the comic I just think, I pretty strongly just think, write what you want to read. I assume that my audience is smart enough, I could be overestimating them, but, to overlook these lifestyle differences. Sometimes I'm aware of it. I think, "Here, I'm insulting these trendies, they might be part of my audience and they might be pissed off," but I think, "You know, that's life."

Williams: Yours is the first comic I've read where I actually felt some kind of identification. Normally, like I read Joe [Matt]'s stuff, and I think he's a jerk, but his stories are always great, so I'm really interested in it, but I don't identify with his lifestyle, but with you, both Jeff LeVine [comics artist and editor of *Destroy All Comics*] and I, we can relate to the idea of going to a book store and poring through these racks of stuff, just to find this one thing that nobody else would care about.

Seth: I appreciate that, and I'm surprised to find out that most of the letters I get are from people who say they relate to that.

Williams: Wow.

Seth: So maybe there are more likeminded people out there than we think. Who knows? But yeah, I usually don't assume that the audience is going to relate, 'cause I feel kind of like an oddball sometimes.

Williams: But, it's just that you feel like you have to do it.

Seth: Yeah, exactly.

Williams: Crumb talks about that too.

Seth: I really related to Crumb when I was younger, especially, I remember that story, "That's Life," where he's looking for old records. That really struck a chord in me when I was about twenty-two. I don't feel that Crumb influenced me, but I feel that when I first read Crumb, there was that feeling that he confirms your own thoughts.

Williams: You don't feel so crazy.

Seth: Yeah, and I really did feel that his interest in old time things made me feel a certain confirmation that this wasn't a weird interest.

Williams: Are you aiming your story, *It's a Good Life*, at other cartoonists?

Seth: I guess that's in the back of my mind, but part of me . . . I'm thinking, I've seen plenty of movies about film directors, and hundreds of novels about authors, and I feel like I can relate to that. That's why I put the glossary in there though, because I figure, I don't assume the audience knows who I'm talking about, but it doesn't really matter. It's almost incidental if I'm talking about a cartoonist; what's more important is whatever point I'm trying to bring up about life. I'm just connecting it to cartooning because that's the way I am. I figure it's a good enough metaphor, 'cause [J.D.] Salinger can bring in haiku if he wants, so I figure I can bring in . . .

Williams: Hergé.
Seth: Exactly. I assume that an audience reading comics has some interest in cartooning, so they should be able to relate.

Williams: It's worked on a lot of people. I work in a comic book store, and they're interested in these other people 'cause you mention them.
Seth: That's good. I'd really like to think I'm turning on somebody to some artist or another.

Williams: That's my goal as an artist too . . . to make people aware of these older people who were so great.
Seth: Sure. There really is a ton of great cartooning out there, and it's a real shame that most cartoonists don't have much of an interest in it.

Williams: In the story where you're showing Chester [the Kalo cartoon], I totally identified with that. I have so many friends, I'll show them this great comic and they'll be looking at the ad pages or something like that.
Seth: You know, like I said, I think people have been trained to look at the past through the eyes of kitsch and it's hard for them to see the quality of things that aren't new and hip, unless it has some sort of a trendiness attached to it. Like suddenly the seventies are hip, but if it wasn't hip, I don't think anybody would be looking back at the seventies looking for any real quality or anything. And they're not bringing back anything from the seventies that was quality, they're just bringing back kitsch stuff, and I think that's the way pop culture operates. You can only appreciate things through a sort of ironic looking backwards, and that's bullshit.

Williams: "Wasn't it stupid that they did this, and funny, ha ha."
Seth: Exactly. Instead of seeing that some things in the past might have actually been superior. Certainly, looking at cartooning, you see an awful lot of evidence that things were better in the past. Like the newspaper strips for example. Such great strips. When you sit down and read a huge run of *Little Orphan Annie* . . .

Williams: Actually, that's the next thing on my list after this huge pile.
Seth: Once you get into it, it's so engaging. Harold Gray might be kind of right wing, but his actual storytelling is terrific. It's really fascinating stuff.

Williams: I think it's neat. Even if I disagree with the politics, or all that, of

the artist, it's really interesting to me when people are really opinionated. Because otherwise it's just bland and boring and lifeless. Like Steve Ditko, I don't know if you like him . . .
Seth: Sure, I love Ditko.

Williams: He's completely insane.
Seth: Totally.

Williams: And yet, he's doing these things that are really passionate. You can sense that he really believes in what he's doing.
Seth: Oh, yeah.

Williams: Even [if] it's . . .
Seth: It's crazy, but yeah, I think he's another example of someone interesting who actually got out of the mainstream in a way. It may be crazy stuff, but what other mainstream artist is out there, that passionate at that age? It's surprising actually.

Williams: A lot of them are, but they've been pushed down so far, that they can't put it into their work, that they feel nobody wants to hear about it, 'cause I've talked to a bunch of people and they all have the same kind of opinions on life and stuff, but they just don't want to put it into their work.
Seth: I can imagine that probably at this point it's hard for them to view cartooning as personal expression.

Williams: Yeah.
Seth: It's just been a job all these years.

Williams: Exactly.
Seth: I don't bother putting much personal expression into illustration. That's just, get it done and get the money.

Williams: Yeah, that's what they thought cartooning was, and yet they were so great.
Seth: I know, it's true.

I remember when I started *Palookaville*. It was right around the time I met Joe, and Chester had just started doing autobiography, and suddenly everybody seemed to be doing autobiography. It occurred to me, "Gee, I don't want it to look like I'm jumping on a bandwagon." The thing was, I'd come to the conclusion that what seemed to be the most interesting work at the time was [Harvey] Pekar [author of *American Splendor*], Lynda Barry, and stuff like that, that seemed to be autobiographical, and it inspired me to try it myself. Then, like a year later, there were like ten people doing it, and it seemed sad. I thought, "Jesus Christ!" This autobiographical thing . . . which actually, I'm getting out of soon.

Williams: Oh, really?

Seth: At the end of this storyline, the next piece I'm going to do will be fiction.

Williams: It seems like this story is not so much autobiographical as philosophical. It's your thoughts on things.

Seth: Yeah, It's certainly more constructed than a straight autobiographical piece. When I'm writing this, I'm not the least bit concerned with factual accuracy, whether I was in this spot, or that spot, or anything like that. I think that's a weakness of autobiography anyway, sticking to the facts too closely . . . unless you're writing your autobiography, but I don't really think of autobiographical comics that way.

Williams: Yeah, your stuff seems to transcend it. Even Joe Matt's stuff, that's its genre, but it's not, I don't know, I would read it if he was doing it as *Uncle Scrooge*. I would put him on the same level as Carl Barks. I think he has a real knack for storytelling.

Seth: Yeah, Joe is what I would call a real natural talent. I don't think I've ever met anyone with so much natural talent, that's not like an intellectual talent. He just does what he does. I don't think of him the same way I do of Chester. I really think Chester is a genius, and I don't know too many people I would class as a genius. He's a really individualistic thinker. I really feel his work comes out of the intellect, where with Joe I feel like it comes out of some reserve of natural talent. They're two different approaches entirely. They're both really different.

Williams: I think he's in this lineage of storytellers in comics, there's only been a few of, like Shelly Mayer [Sheldon Mayer, comic artist best known for his comic *Sugar and Spike* (1956–1971)], people who just had this story in them to tell. When I get *Peepshow* and take it home it's the first thing I read out of the whole stack because his stories are so gripping. I'm like that with *Uncle Scrooge* too.

Seth: You're right. It does have a real natural storytelling slant. It's not tricky. It's just very direct, and it really does work. I know Joe so well now it's getting hard to separate Joe and his work. I can't look at it as a casual reader anymore, because it's so connected to the creator in my mind. I'm judging it against what I know to be true or not, like how he's portraying himself and things like that . . . it's getting kinda close to home.

Williams: Does it get in the way of you criticizing his work?
Seth: No, I don't think so. I'm pretty brutal with Joe. We have that kind of relationship for some reason. I'm the bully and he takes it, and because of that I can be pretty harsh with him about him. We regularly, both Chester and I, both make fun of his *Peepshow* collection, the one from Kitchen Sink, especially those first fifteen pages. We're always picking on him for that.

That does seem really funny to me now, when I see him in a panel saying he fancies himself a bluesman; that cracks me up. That's like a total fantasy. We always pick on him about that one. We always pick on how wrong he is about himself in those interpretations of himself in those *Peepshow* pages. He's pretty easy-going though. He likes constructive criticism.

Williams: Do Chester and him do it back to you?
Seth: Sure.

Williams: Do they offer you a lot of criticism?
Seth: Yes and no. It's a funny thing. With each of us, when we finish an issue, and now that Chester is back in town this is definitely true, we'll get together and let the other two read it and take criticism. But I make it a point to only show them the issue when it's completely done. I'll take the criticism, but I'll never change anything, unless it's like a technical point. Like they say to me, "This really doesn't read, it looks like he's coming from the wrong direction," or something. I might take that and change something, same with Chester. He rarely will change anything if you don't like it, but we certainly might criticize each other back and forth.

Williams: Does it have any effect on your future work?
Seth: It might. I certainly respect their opinions, and things Chester has told me have certainly stuck in my mind and made me think about things I'm doing, especially from a technical standpoint. I have so much respect for Chester that I really will take his opinion to heart.

Williams: Are there any other artists that you correspond with?

Seth: I have casual correspondence with other cartoonists, but really not much in the way of criticism. I correspond lightly with David Collier [Canadian alternative cartoonist], but we don't really criticize each other's work or anything. We usually just say things like, enjoyed your last issue. But yeah, it's pretty tight here in Toronto, we're very close in discussing our work with each other.

Williams: It totally helps developing as an artist to have feedback.

Seth: Yeah. Chester has been a huge inspiration to both Joe and me. He's just light years ahead. I can't overestimate how much reading Chester's work has made me reevaluate how I think storytelling should be. I think Chester's greatest talent is how he tells a story. It's really his own approach.

Williams: I haven't read *Underwater* [Chester Brown's follow-up to *Yummy Fur* published by Drawn & Quarterly from 1994 to 1997] yet, but my girlfriend has read it and she was telling me about it, and I couldn't help but think of *Sugar and Spike*. I hate it when people try comparisons, but do you think that had any . . .

Seth: Influence on him? He's never read any *Sugar and Spike*. I was talking to him about *Sugar and Spike*, just in the last few weeks, 'cause I've been reading a lot of it lately, and I had to explain the premise of the strip to him because he didn't know anything about it.

Williams: Wow.

Seth: It's such a great strip.

Williams: It seems like, what he's getting at so far, from what I've heard secondhand, is the idea of children's interpretation of the world.

Seth: I think you're right, but I don't know, because the truth is, Chester doesn't really tell me what he's doing, and I don't ask either, because I know he doesn't want to talk about it. He wants you to just find out as you're reading it too, but from my impression that's what he's doing. It seems to me like he's showing how a child perceives the world and how he's gradually coming to understand language and things like that. At least that's my guess. I could be completely wrong.

Williams: And that's kind of what *Sugar and Spike* is about too.

Seth: Sure, although certainly from a lot more entertaining point of view.

Williams: Yeah. It's kind of like a weird combination of Joe and Chester. Yeah, Shelly Mayer is a genius. Have you ever read any of his *Scribblys* [*Scribbly* ran from 1948 to 1952]?

Seth: I've only read a little bit of it 'cause I can't get my hands on the original comics.

Williams: I have one that's worth a bunch of dollars that I bought for ten bucks.

Seth: Well, I'm putting feelers out now, and I'm telling myself I'm willing to pay the money, 'cause I want to get my hands on them pretty badly. They're right at the top of my list of old comics to get my hands on.

Williams: Have you seen the Smithsonian comic book [*The Smithsonian Book of Comic Book Comics* (1982) edited by Michael Barrier and Martin Williams, includes five *Scribbly* four-page stories]?

Seth: Oh yeah, there's a bit in there. There's also a bit in *The Greatest Golden Age Comics Ever Told,* from DC Comics, but just a bit, like four pages or something.

Williams: Do you like [EC artist Bernie] Krigstein at all?

Seth: I wouldn't say I'm a big fan. I like him. He's not on my big list of favorites. I like Johnny Craig better, if I had to pick between the two.

Williams: Man, that's a strange choice. I mean, I haven't heard other people say that. I like Craig too.

Seth: I think Craig has such a clean approach, and he tends to tell his stories less copy heavy, 'cause he was writing most of them, whereas Krigstein was working with [Al] Feldstein or whoever. I've always found EC Comics way too copy heavy. So, of the EC artists, I'm definitely drawn to Kurtzman and Johnny Craig. Especially Kurtzman.

Williams: I'm doing a big thing on EC Comics for the next *Destroy All Comics.* I know it's a dead horse, but . . .

Seth: It's still great stuff though. It's like a miracle that it's all in print in hardback.

Williams: And now they're coming out with some in a cheap format so the regular comic reader can buy it.

Seth: Yeah. I wish they'd do that with the *Lulu* stuff. I've got all the hardbacks, but wouldn't it be great if kids could buy those *Little Lulu* comics issue by issue again. They're some of the greatest cartooning ever done, in my mind.

Williams: That's why I think it's really important to do stuff like that glossary, because I think if you bring it up enough maybe people will start to be interested in it, so that there will be a readership. For all those *Popeye* reprints and stuff, there was no readership, so that just failed. They all lost money and nobody ever wanted to do them again. But if as an artist, you bring up an interest, then people might . . .

Seth: I hope so. When I was young it worked for me. When I was reading Salinger when I was nineteen, I started to develop an interest in Japanese poetry because of it. If there was anybody whose work I liked and they talked about another artist in it, I would check it out, because I respected their opinion.

Williams: I'm making a big point in everything I do to mention something.
Seth: I'm always bringing people to the apartment and showing them stuff.

Williams: Is that a picture of your apartment on the back of the *Peepshow* collection [Joe Matt's *Peepshow: The Cartoon Diary of Joe Matt* was published by Kitchen Sink in 1992]?
Seth: Yeah, it is.

Williams: I was rereading the issues of *Palookaville*, and then I went to the store and I looked at that graphic novel, 'cause you did that piece in the back and I noticed the *Little Lulus* and the *Tubbys* [*Marge's Tubby* published by Dell and Gold Key comics from 1953 to 1961] all on that little rack.
Seth: Yeah, it's my place. It's Joe pretending it's his place.

Williams: He really wants to own those comics.
Seth: I know. Well, Joe's too cheap to buy stuff. That's the problem.

Williams: Are people sending him stuff?
Seth: They send him View-Master reels. I've got a few of those too. I've actually been lucky enough that a few people have sent me great cartooning stuff. I've been amazed. I got a terrific collection of this cartoonist Roland Coe [*New York Post* cartoonist and influence on Seth; *Coe's Crosstown Carnival* was published in 1935] in the mail from one guy, and I was so happy. It's from 1936 or something, and it's just gorgeous stuff. And I got a couple of

other old gag collections from people through the mail who just sent them to me, and I was thinking, "This story is working out well. I didn't plan on this." But keep sending it. That's always nice. And of course, you get a million mini-comics.

Williams: Which is great too. Actually, I wish I got more. I don't really get anything.

Seth: One thing that's kind of depressing about it is sometimes you get more mini-comics than you do letters about your comic. You go to the mailbox and you see four envelopes . . . and you're like, oh no, because you're kind of hoping somebody had some comments on the last issue. Even so, actually it's been going pretty good. I've been getting a fair amount of mail lately.

Williams: Your stuff is really inspiring, to me at least.

Seth: I appreciate that.

Williams: I can't criticize it, because I think it's so good. It stands on its own.

Can you describe the techniques you use, like duo-shade, and brush and painting and stuff? How do you draw your strip?

Seth: Okay. First of all I work with a light table. What I do is I use Xerox paper . . . I always draw a grid out for each page, and then I do my panels one by one on separate sheets of paper, so that I can work them up at the light table, 'cause I like to do a lot of drawing on each panel until I get the compositions exactly the way I want. Then I tape that onto the page grid. After I have the issue penciled out, I use watercolor paper to draw on it, so I take this penciled page and I tape it on the back of the watercolor paper, and then I just slap that on the light table, and then I just go in with a brush and ink the whole thing. After that I do an overlay for where the grays will go and that's dropped in by the printer.

Williams: Oh. Everybody was theorizing that you use duo-shade.

Seth: No. I thought about playing around with that Craft-tint paper.

Williams: That's it.

Seth: I thought about trying it around, because Roy Crane [influential American cartoonist, creator of long-running strip *Wash Tubbs* (1924–1988)], his stuff is so great looking on it. Do you want me to talk about my color techniques?

Williams: Sure.

Seth: Basically, it's pretty straightforward. Most of the time I work with Dr. Martin's dyes for coloring. That's my basic method that I use most of the time, like the covers for numbers three and four. I just do a basic black and white drawing and then color it with Dr. Martin's dyes.

Williams: On overlay?

Seth: Nope, I dye it. Like an original watercolor painting, basically. I do a few other things, but mostly I use dyes.

Williams: The one thing I have no clue about is color.

Seth: Well, it's really something I think a lot of cartoonists have trouble with because you don't work with it that much. The first couple of years of illustration, I really had to struggle with learning color.

Williams: Did you learn it from school or . . .

Seth: No, I just . . .

Williams: Did Chester, Joe or anybody else help you?

Seth: I didn't know Joe then, and Chester just cut Rubyliths for his covers up until then. I knew in illustration I wouldn't be doing that, so I just basically decided to use Dr. Martin dyes and I spent a few months teaching myself how to use them. And for the first year of illustration I must have done every illustration over two or three times to get it right, because I just didn't have the technique figured out yet. Now it's pretty straightforward to me. I'm still learning to do better effects with it, but it's pretty easy once you get it down. I think the real talent is finally getting to a point where you have your color choices working out, 'cause there's always a tendency to be garish at first.

Williams: The cover for the new *Drawn & Quarterly* is really good, and moody.

Seth: I wasn't completely satisfied with the printing. A couple of undercolors showed up on the whites, so that kind of disappointed me, but besides that, it's okay.

Williams: It has some kind of feeling.

Seth: Well. I like a lot of folk art, so that inspired me to start painting with house paint a few years ago. It's a great medium actually. It really lays down great.

Williams: Yeah.

Seth: And you can mix colors really well too, and you get a ton of paint of course, so it's really great.

Williams: I'm doing a piece in acrylics actually. It's going to be my first painted thing.

Seth: Acrylics are a good medium for easy control. I'm going to try to figure out gouache soon, actually. I know Julie Doucet does some great stuff in gouache. She's really skilled with it.

Williams: Like what kind of stuff?

Seth: Like her covers for *Dirty Plotte*. They were all done in gouache and a really nice job too. Fiona Smyth [Canadian painter] is really good at it too.

Williams: She's one of my favorite cartoonists nowadays.

Seth: I've known Fiona for years. She went to art school with me, actually.

Williams: She's doing the future too, for me. She's taking the past, but she's also building something new out of it.

Seth: It's interesting that she's suddenly come into comics, because she's primarily a painter. Her and Maurice Vellekoop, we all went to art school at the same time and they both entered into comics just from playing around with them for a few years. Now they seem to be doing quite a lot of them.

Williams: It's a really interesting medium, as an artist.

Seth: I think so. Sure.

Williams: The possibilities are endless.

Seth: Personally, I think it's a more exciting medium than painting, because so many people get to see your work, as opposed to just a gallery show. Unless you're a huge painter, world famous. Otherwise, you're getting only a few hundred people to see your work, when in comics, even in a worst case scenario, you're getting a thousand or two.

Williams: Yeah. Does that feedback help you grow as an artist? Do you do things in stories, then people point it out?

Seth: Sometimes. I think that feedback is important. You've really got to feel like you're communicating with people. It really helps. I think that the main reason you do art is the desire to communicate something. So you definitely want some feedback.

Williams: That's a big debate with me and my friends about communications with comics. I feel like you should be making people think, and that's sometimes even more valuable than communicating.
Seth: I kind of think of them in the same level. Communicating should be something that makes people think; otherwise, there's not much point in communicating it.

Williams: Like Fiona's stuff, a lot of them, are just single images, I guess they do kind of tell a story, but it's also . . .
Seth: Fiona and I disagree on a basic point. She has stated that she doesn't believe plot is important. This runs completely diametrically opposed to how I view telling a story. I feel plot is extremely important. Plot meaning, basically, storytelling, to me. What draws me to comics is the storytelling potential of it, and if I wasn't interested in storytelling I'd probably be more likely to just do illustrations or drawings. So, I know we disagree on that point. Even so, I feel like you can't string a series of images together without telling some kind of a story. It's just a basic thing about cartooning. If you've got panels, a story develops.

Williams: People rationalize the meaning in it.
Seth: But, of course, I feel planning that at first is the most important thing.

Williams: Did you read the part in the Chris Ware interview (in *Destroy All Comics* #1 [1994]), where he says he doesn't even really plan his stuff out ahead of time?
Seth: Yeah, I was actually kind of disappointed when I read that.

Williams: But I think he's an exception, because I think his brain works at such a furious pace that he actually is planning it out, I just don't think he's planning it out on paper.
Seth: Yeah, you might be right . . .

Williams: From interviewing him I know that he's really meticulous about everything . . .
Seth: I feel that he must have some kind of a grand scheme of some sort when he's working on it. That's kind of how Chester works. He does things

panel by panel, and whereas he doesn't plot out exactly what each panel is going to be, he does have a bigger picture of where it's going. Maybe Chris is doing that, he kind of knows where it's going, but doesn't know what's in the next panel. At least I hope so.

Williams: Do you write your stuff ahead of time?
Seth: Yeah, I do a pretty tight script.

Williams: Do you set up the shots? Do you describe the shots at all?
Seth: I do a rough breakdown for the whole issue, but it's very rough. Like I might very well change things around when I'm going, but I really like to know exactly what's going on the page, and the next page. When I'm thinking compositionally, for telling the story too, it's important for me how the pages fit with each other and how they balance each other, and of course, it's really important for me to figure out how I'm telling the story. So, it's important for me to take a shot and plan it out for the entire sequence so I can see how it flows, whether this is the right choice on how to tell it, stuff like that. I think it's very important to plot this stuff out.

Williams: It's weird to me that you actually compose each panel separately, too. That's something I wouldn't do.
Seth: It's very expedient. It's probably why I do it. The light table makes it easy, but it's really important for me that the composition be as simple as I can get it, yet still convey whatever information has to be conveyed. If I felt I could get away with it, I would throw out perspective entirely, but I don't feel like that kind of approach is really good for telling a story, unfortunately. I really like folk art, the way it's really flat. If I was to just do illustration, I would probably gravitate towards that approach, of removing perspective entirely. But, when you're telling a story, you find it's almost impossible to tell a story realistically if you don't have that level of perspective in the drawing. That kind of holds me to a more realistic approach.

Williams: Fiona totally gets rid of everything.
Seth: Exactly, and I think that works, with when she says she doesn't think plot is important, but I think as soon as plot becomes more important, and you have to have a character walking from his apartment down to the train station, you really find that that kind of so called perspective, of reality, is a necessity. You can't convey the same feeling . . . maybe you could . . . maybe I just can't do it. I feel like it's really important for telling that kind of story.

Reworking early stories; unpublished revision of the story from *Palookaville* issue 2.
© Seth, used with permission from Seth.

Williams: It just depends on what kind of feelings you're trying to convey.
Seth: Exactly.

Williams: If you want reality and human experience, then those backgrounds and those buildings really help.
Seth: I find I can't break away from it.

Williams: I do it, not only because of that, but I like old strip artists so much, and I just respect the idea of having learned how to draw perspective flawlessly, like Roy Crane does. I just think that's such a valuable thing as a person, to know.
Seth: Well, if I could draw as well as Roy Crane, I would, but I just can't reach that level. I think you have to work within your limitations. I just don't ever draw that realistically.

Williams: How often do you draw?
Seth: Every day probably.

Williams: And how long?
Seth: It all depends. It really depends on what I'm working on. With illustration and comics I'm probably drawing every single day. No, that's not true. I get some days to goof off, but if I have a lot of illustration work I might be drawing all day, or I might be drawing for just a couple of hours. When I'm working on the comic book, usually though, I'm drawing like a really long day. Like from about ten in the morning till about midnight. That's because it takes me a lot of work to get the comic done. It's really pretty concentrated work, usually. With illustration, I can slack off a bit, and maybe only draw for a few hours a day.

Williams: Wow, that's amazing. That's a lot of time.
Seth: I feel it's really good for you, though. I'm amazed how after doing illustration for five years, it really improved my drawing ability. I found the working out of a pose for a character is effortless, compared to how much work I had to put into it five years ago. It really does start to become second nature, and you can approach much more difficult drawings a lot easier. I never thought I'd get to that point. It always seemed to be a struggle.

Williams: That's the thing about doing a newspaper strip that would be so great, that you have to do it every day . . .

Seth: Unless you're drawing *Cathy*, and then you just get worse. These modern strip cartoonists don't really have much in drawing ability anyway, so . . .

Williams: That's the thing, me personally . . . I feel like you have to push yourself to do that and to get the subtlety of a Fiona Smyth emotion kind of thing, combined with the really knowing how to draw, too. I think that's the future of comics.

Seth: I think once you can really draw, you can move off into any form of stylization you want, but you still have those technical abilities to fall back on. I think this is exactly the opposite of what modern fine artists are doing. Once you have those skills you really can legitimately move in any direction, but you're held back, your options are much too limited when you don't have those skills, when you're drawing in a primitive style because that's the only style you can draw in. I think it never hurts to be able to draw well. If once you can draw well, you move into a style that doesn't display any drawing skill at all, well, that's fine. It's just a matter of having the option to choose, one way or the other.

I think so many painters I see around in the galleries and stuff, I look at it, and I can really tell that they can't draw any better. That this is the best they can do, and that's why they're doing it this way.

Williams: It's almost insulting to me, as a viewer, because it shows me that they don't really care about what they're doing. "Why do I want to look at this, you didn't put any effort into this at all?"

Seth: I agree. I think art should be a struggle. You really should have to struggle to make it good. When I'm doing illustration work, I don't struggle with it. I do the simplest approach I can. I create a composition that's effective and simple and then I can get it done in a certain amount of time.

Williams: Do you usually illustrate articles? Is that the kind of stuff you're doing?

Seth: Yeah, Yeah. Like editorial stuff. But when I'm working on the comic book, I always make it a point that every single panel that I'm working on, I try to do something more complicated than I would normally do. Because I want it to be better. I want to push myself, and that's the only way your drawing really does get better, if you keep pushing yourself. If I was just doing illustration, then I'd be a hack, but comics keeps my integrity and forces me to try to do my best work.

Williams: That's really cool.

Seth: I think you can only do that if you love something too, 'cause otherwise it's just a job, and in any job you want to goof off. You don't want to have to mop the floor if you can just stand there, unless you own the place and you love it.

Williams: Exactly. That's totally how I approach comics. I do things just to make myself learn how to do things. In comics I'll do the same shot over and over again just to make myself learn how to draw it.

Seth: It's important. I think probably the medium in the last twenty or thirty years has had its first group of artists who are really just doing it because they love it. It doesn't mean it's all good, but it is good to have a group of artists involved in something that's just not a commercial venture.

Williams: That's the thing, comics have been this really weird beast that hasn't existed before. It's almost commercial, but then there's this creativity to it.

Seth: I think it's pretty exciting. Even if we never do develop a large audience, I really do feel like I'm involved with the very beginning of a really exciting art movement.

Williams: I hope so.

Seth: Yeah, if it lasts.

Williams: I think it will, because it seems like everybody just wants to do it, regardless of money.

Seth: I hope it will last. There's always the danger that it's a complete anachronism, like radio plays, or something. I mean, there are people out there who collect old radio shows, but there's no market. If you really want to do great radio plays, you might be able to do some, but there's hardly any audience and I'm afraid that in forty years, that's what comics will be like. There will be like two hundred people in North America who are sending their little copies to each other. It's sad that it could happen. But I'm really hoping it doesn't. I'm hoping it goes the other way, or at least stays like this.

Williams: I think it can't help but go, as long as there are people who really believe in it, and preach the virtues of it.

Seth: I hope so, I really do.

Williams: That's my mission.

Seth: I'm hoping it will grow too. I think we're in a stage now where people who would never have even done comics are considering it as an option. People who have a lot of talent, instead of ten years ago when only a few oddballs would be willing to do it, people who just loved comics. Now, you've probably got some people growing up who are about twenty years old, and might have a lot of talent, and they've seen some good comics, and they might think, "Why not go into comics," instead of thinking, "Why not go into illustration," or film making, or whatever. It's only when you start attracting greater artists, will the medium grow. I think that in a small way that's beginning.

Williams: That's really true. Another question about technique, do you letter with a brush?

Seth: Yeah, I do. I use one brush for everything. I like to use a number six.

Williams: Is that a Japanese influence at all?

Seth: No. I don't know how it started. I forced myself to learn how to use a brush six or seven years ago, and I just got really comfortable with using one brush for everything, like the same size. I don't like to switch to other tools for things, so I just make it a point to ink everything I do with the same brush. I feel it gives a real continuity to the artwork, and with the lettering matching that way.

Williams: Is it really slow?

Seth: I've never gotten my skills down on using an Ames lettering guide or anything.

Williams: Yup, I use one of those actually.

Seth: They're kind of alien to me. I've got one here, but I've never figured it out, so I just eyeball everything.

Williams: Yeah, it gives you a more natural feel. That's the one problem with the Ames thing, it gives you this kind of . . . I don't know, I'm using it on the *Crime Clinic* comic I'm doing [two issues published by Slave Labor in 1995–1996] 'cause I want that fifties comic feel, but on other stuff I don't think it's really necessary.

Seth: Strangely, I didn't even notice until my third issue that I was using upper and lower case, and that's not normal in comics. Chester pointed it out to me, and I realized I never noticed that everybody just uses capital letters.

Actually, just the capital letters is nice. It's very readable, but now I'm real comfortable with using upper and lower case.

Williams: I think with you, it speaks of the gag influence, because those artists weren't into the same kind of formulas that comic artists are into.
Seth: Definitely not. The one thing those guys really excelled at was composition, and that's something that a lot of comic book artists didn't excel at. They were better at their sheer draftsmanship.

Williams: Have you seen Jack Cole's art?
Seth: Sure.

Williams: To me, he's the best comic artist ever.
Seth: Yeah, he's great.

Williams: His composition really works for me. He's one of the few comic artists who actually understood composition.
Seth: Sure, he's got a good compositional sense. [Will] Eisner had good compositional sense too. I think [that's]the thing about comics that's kind of forgotten. I think about ten years ago, I saw, Frank Miller said some sort of a thing about the history of comics was the history of shit. That really offended me, because there really is a phenomenal amount of high quality stuff out there, and so much of it has been forgotten. So much of it deserves reprinting. Like where is that great collection of *Barnaby* by Crockett Johnson [daily strip, ran with Johnson as artist from 1942 to 1947]?

Williams: There were some in the seventies.
Seth: Yeah, there were those Del Rey editions too that came out, but . . . that's great stuff. There's tons of great stuff out there, really forgotten stuff, and it's a shame there isn't a bigger audience for these old strips too.

Williams: I had this humongous argument with Jeff, about whether there [were] any good things done in comics in the past, and I think half of it is that people don't see it. I mean, *Krazy Kat* [George Herriman strip, ran from 1913 to 1944] is going out of print, and that's just a crime.
Seth: It really is. I think too, you've got to look back at the stuff with a certain historical perspective. You can't expect that some of these artists, I mean, they were working in craft, and it may not stack up against the great novelists or something, but it's still very interesting to look at. Somebody like Dan

DeCarlo even, who was really a very skilled cartoonist. Those *Archie* stories or the stuff he did at Marvel in the late fifties may not be great art, but it's certainly worth looking at to study a master cartoonist, showing his skills, and there were tons of these guys. Dick Sprang was a really good cartoonist.

Williams: I got to meet him and talk to him for a little bit.
Seth: Oh, did you?

Williams: He was so nice. He's just the nicest guy.
Seth: I'd like to meet him. I love his stuff. You know who no one ever mentions as a great cartoonist is Raymond Briggs. Do you know him? *When the Wind Blows* [1982]?

Williams: I think I saw something by him. . . he's written a book on how to draw comics?
Seth: I don't know. He's a British guy. He does children's books; that's what he's known as, although his children's books are always in comic strip form. He did *The Snowman* [1978], he did *When the Wind Blows*, he did *The Man* [1992]. *The Bear* [1994] is his newest one.

Williams: He's still doing stuff now?
Seth: Oh yeah. He's an older guy, but you should go into a children's book-store and ask for *When the Wind Blows*. This is one of the greatest comic narratives ever written. It's meant for adults, and it's about nuclear war. It's such an affecting piece, you'll cry at the end of it.

Williams: I've seen a book written by him on how to draw comics, but I didn't get it 'cause I wasn't familiar with him, and I didn't have enough money or whatever.
Seth: He's really one of the all-time masters. You could put *When the Wind Blows* next to *Maus* [1980–1991] as one of the great comics, and you never hear his name, just because he's out of the loop. He's over in the children's book world. That's part of the problem with the big picture, they don't look around.

Williams: I don't know, much to the chagrin of Chris Ware, I even see film as part of the big picture, and I see writing as part of the big picture, too.
Seth: Yes, you definitely can't just look at comics. That's too small of a world. You should hope that people doing comics are reading books and watching movies. That may sound like a strange thing for me to be saying since my

current storyline is so much about comics, but I certainly don't intend to keep doing that.

Williams: What films and authors are you into?
Seth: My favorite authors, well, number one would be Salinger. I've always been a huge J. D. Salinger fan. Second on that list would be Alice Munro. She's a Canadian writer. She's in the *New Yorker* all the time. She's one of the most wonderful writers ever. Her work is so sensitive and so, I don't even know how to describe it, it's just wonderful stuff. It's really well written and really insightful. Raymond Carver would be up near the top. That would probably be three of my real favorites. I usually like books that are non-genre oriented.

Williams: I can see the Salinger influence on your work. I never thought of that before, in spite of the fact that you were reading *Franny and Zooey* [1961].
Seth: Salinger is somebody I've loved since I was in my late teens, and I've read the stuff a thousand times. He's another one of these people, like when I was talking about Crumb I was saying there's certain artists that you don't feel like they influenced you, so much as when you read it they confirmed your own thoughts. Salinger is definitely one, and Woody Allen would be the third of that group. I'm a huge Woody Allen fan.

Williams: Have you read a lot of his writing?
Seth: I've read all of his writing, and it's fun, I laugh, but it's his films that are his great works.

Williams: As far as film directors he'd be your favorite?
Seth: Yeah, he'd be my favorite. I'd probably put Mike Leigh up there.

Williams: Who else?
Seth: I really like Orson Welles, of course. And I love Frank Capra, although I realize . . .

Williams: Do you like Preston Sturges at all?
Seth: The thing is, everybody always asks me that when I say I like Capra, but I don't really know Preston Sturges's stuff very well at all. I think I've seen like one film.

Williams: To me, he's even more poignant than Capra.
Seth: Well, Capra is pretty corny, but he always sucks me in.

Williams: You're right.

Seth: He's always got me going when I'm watching *Mr. Deeds Goes to Town* [1936]. I'm buying into it every time, even though I realize that his humanist philosophy isn't entirely practical, still at the end I'm feeling that "stick-up-for-the-little-guy" attitude.

Williams: That's funny, you also say about how Schulz sucks you in too. There's this one part when you're talking about how some *Peanuts* are kind of trite, but it's true, those guys have a talent that comes through that, and even though I don't agree with everything they're saying, like Schulz was a pretty hardcore Christian for a while, I'm still sucked in.

Seth: I think when you're reading the work of a really talented person, a difference of opinion doesn't matter. I think the talent definitely pulls you through, and you find yourself being much more tolerant than if you were reading a more didactic work by somebody who is just preaching at you. That never sucks you in. I mean, I don't get sucked in to Ditko's philosophy. I might find it interesting that he's doing this crazy work, but not for one second is he sucking me in. He was probably sucking me in more when he was doing *Spider-Man* or *Dr. Strange*. Any sort of Ayn Randian philosophy he was putting across in *Spider-Man* would have got to me more than it would get to me through *Mr. A*.

Williams: Have you seen the new *Dr. Strange* reprint that they came out with?

Seth: Is it the hardback?

Williams: Yeah.

Seth: I thought it was really shitty looking.

Williams: Seriously? I took out the colors and compared them, and they're actually really good colors.

Seth: Oh yeah. Is this on the glossy paper? The *Marvel Masterworks*?

Williams: Yeah, I don't like the glossy paper either, but the colorist was actually aware of what was going on in the work. I hate all the other ones though. *The Incredible Hulk* one is like garbage to me to look at, because I know what it really looks like.

Seth: When I looked at the *Dr. Strange* one, I just thought, I'll keep my little paperback, the one I have from the seventies. I just didn't really like the production values on it.

Williams: It gets to me.
Seth: I do love that Ditko *Dr. Strange* stuff. Great stuff. Really beautifully drawn.

Williams: It's funny, because looking back on it, out of all the work that was done at Marvel, that's the only stuff that still stands up.
Seth: Except the Kirby. Everything Kirby stands up to me. There's no period, except maybe the very last years of his life, like *Captain Victory* [*Captain Victory and the Galaxy Rangers* was published by Pacific Comics from 1981 to 1984], of something that I don't like.

Williams: *OMAC* [Kirby's *OMAC: One Man Army Corps*, published by DC in eight issues in 1975, is essentially Marvel's Captain America set in the future] doesn't stand up. Did you read *OMAC*?
Seth: Well, I don't like the strips. I'm not a fan of *OMAC*, or *The New Gods* [published by DC in eleven issues from 1971 to 1972], but I still think the drawing is phenomenal.

Williams: Yeah, that's true. The problem with the Kirby early Marvel stuff is it has that stupid dialogue on it.
Seth: Well yeah, the stories don't read well.

Williams: I don't even read the dialogue anymore. I've decided it completely doesn't exist to me.
Seth: I find his monster stuff real readable though. That stuff is so stupid, but it's fun. I can read endless amounts of that monster stuff.

Williams: In my opinion, that's where Ditko hit his peak.
Seth: Yeah, he did great stuff there too, and some of the stories are actually not that bad. I read a few of them as a kid that I remember actually frightened me. It's hard to believe now, when you look at them. The stories that frightened me more than anybody as a kid were [Basil] Wolverton's horror stories, and the science fiction stuff that he did. They really freaked me out. There was something definitely creepy under the surface there, more so than the EC stuff that I read. I remember his stories of people turning into crabs,

or those brain bats taking them over. There was something scary about this transformation that almost always went on in his stories, this loss of personal identity. They really did it to me as a kid. They kind of freaked me out.

Williams: The idea of Wolverton's stories really scared me too; actually, as a kid, his humor stuff scared me. His people, like the *Mad* drawings of ugly women, it's all just really bizarre. And it's so funny . . . the more I find out about him, he was just a jolly guy. He didn't realize how scary . . . Did you see the New Testament stuff he did [Wolverton illustrated Herbert W. Armstrong's *The Bible Story*, published in three volumes from 1982 to 1983 by the Worldwide Church of God; Fantagraphics republished the work in 2008 as *The Wolverton Bible*]?

Seth: Yeah, actually I owned it all for a while, then I was foolish enough to get rid of it. I tried to get it back two years ago, then it was too late. I sent away for it years ago and got it all. At some point I was stupid and I thought, "Oh, I don't want this," and I got rid of it, and I've been kicking myself ever since. It's interesting to see how he could control himself and try to keep it to a low key.

Williams: The Revelations stuff is really frightening, though.

Seth: That stuff he's pulling out all the stops. The funny thing about Wolverton is, in a lot of ways I think Wolverton was a naive artist.

Williams: Really?

Seth: I think he had a lot of skill, but I think his approach was very similar to a lot of folk artists. The fact that he didn't realize how grotesque the work was and how affecting it was is really similar to a lot of naive artists. Also there's a real obsessive quality to his work. That hatching style is really similar to folk artists who will put every leaf on a tree, or every single rivet on a train. It's kind of an overkill approach, which is an attempt to do something realistic, and yet it achieves the exact opposite effect. I think, just reading the way Wolverton talks about things that he had a very simplistic approach to what he was doing, unlike a more intellectual artist like Kurtzman, or something.

Williams: I really want to think of Wolverton as a total genius . . . a conscious genius.

Seth: I don't see him that way at all.

Williams: I think you're right, I just have so much respect for it, that I . . . but you're right, I don't think he was aware of it.

Seth: So many of these guys I don't think thought of what they were doing in any higher sense.

Williams: Jack Cole just thought his comic stuff was just crap, and he didn't care about it at all.
Seth: He's a sad story.

Williams: And how. Have you seen his gag cartoons?
Seth: Yeah, I have. They're gorgeous. Man, he could control the watercolors. They were beautifully done.

Williams: He was one of those complete guys to me, who just did it all.
Seth: Yeah, he definitely was a real master when it came to cartooning.

Williams: A problem I have, now that I'm becoming more involved with criticizing comics, I don't know how to criticize these people that I'm friends with and I really respect, but who I don't think are performing at a certain level. How do you feel about criticism?
Seth: Well, I think it's always worthwhile to criticize people who are doing good work. I think the danger is when you start criticizing people who aren't doing very good work, because then there's nothing constructive to say. Like, I can say I really like Dan Clowes work, but I think he's got more potential than he's using. I think when he did that first episode of *Ghost World* [1993–1997], I thought that was a real creative jump in maturity of his storytelling, but then when I see him doing something like "The Happy Fisherman" [*Eightball* 11, 1993], it's just a waste of his talent. He's just fucking around with goofy stuff, trying to please his audience.

Williams: Don't you think he has a weird, kinda sick, fascination with that humor, though?
Seth: Definitely, but I don't think it's his strong point. I think maybe it's funny, I thought "Shamrock Squid" [an open source character created by Clowes, first appeared in *Eightball* 10 (1993)] was hilarious, but in a way I think it's a waste of his abilities. I feel like in many ways, Dan is loaded with talent, but *Eightball* is kind of a catch all to please everyone. You've got some humor stuff . . .

Williams: Have you talked to him about that?
Seth: No. I don't know him very well. I've corresponded with him once or

twice, but I'd be more than willing to tell him. Because of the fact that I think he's so talented, I feel like I can criticize him, but if he was just some guy working at Marvel who showed me some really crappy stuff he did, I'd probably just say, "Oh, that's fine," because what's the point of criticizing him. It doesn't make any difference. Like when Joe shows me something and I don't think it's any good, I'll tell him so, 'cause I think he can do better. I think that story Dan did, "Glue Destiny" [*Eightball* 12 (1993)] left an inkling in there of a real new approach for him. Same with that "Blue Italian Shit" [*Eightball* 13 (1994)],the one with the guy telling about his experiences as a punk.

Williams: Yeah, I remember that, but the story didn't stick in my mind.
Seth: I think there's like a maturity of approach there, that's a little different from his other stuff. I sometimes feel like Dan's trying to be too cool, and I don't like to see cartoonists trying to be cool. I think there's certain things going on in cartooning right now, and one of them is this desire to be hip, because comics are supposedly hip right now, and I think that's a real mistake for any artist to be trying to be hip, and drawing cute trendy girls, I think is like . . .

Williams: The thing is there are a lot of kids like that around here, and I think, having lived in Berkeley, I can understand where that *Ghost World* story is coming from. That's a side of humanity.
Seth: It's perfectly valid to write or draw about anything, but it's just a little too timely for my tastes. I was much more pleased with the first episode of *Ghost World*. I almost wish he hadn't carried it on. It's becoming episodic stories, which I think is the downfall of comics to begin with. This idea of settling on characters, and then you just keep telling stories about them.

Williams: What about *Wash Tubbs*?
Seth: I think, to a degree, that's always been a fault with cartooning. I don't think you should set up characters and carry them on for years and years and years. When you read *Catcher in the Rye* [1951], when you get to the end you might wish there were more Holden Caulfield, but if there were, that would ruin the story. A story should have a beginning, a middle, and an end.

Williams: *Wash Tubbs* is like that for me.
Seth: But it's not, though, because it's not a beginning, a middle, and an end. In a novel you have to know where it's going to end. If Peter Bagge ends the Buddy Bradley story [ongoing character in Bagge's *Hate* comic book (1990–present)] tomorrow, it wasn't a novel, it was a bunch of episodes. I think

that's something cartoonists fall into, because if a character is popular, you just keep doing more of it, but I think things should end. If comics are going to move forward they've got to be like movies and novels. In everything else, if you're telling a story, there needs to be a point, and because of that, you have to be concise. You have to be something that does have a definite beginning, middle, and end.

Williams: I don't know . . . I think those old guys managed to pull it off without doing that. You disagree?
Seth: I don't think they pull it off.

Williams: Okay.
Seth: I can't think of any continuing comic, right now, that I really think pulls it off, for a greater purpose.

Williams: Well, you're doing a continuing story.
Seth: But this is like a book. Six issues is one story. If I didn't have to do it in episodes I wouldn't. What I mean, it's not continuing stories that's the problem. For example, *Velvet Glove* [Clowes's *Like a Velvet Glove Cast in Iron*, originally published in serial form in ten issues of Clowes's *Eightball* from 1989 to 1993 and in one volume in 1993] is one story, even though it was over eleven issues, or whatever. I don't feel that *Ghost World* is like that. Maybe I'm wrong, but I'm really starting to feel that these are episodes, not building towards a greater theme. I could be wrong, he could pull it around and surprise me, but that's definitely not what's going on in *Hate*. *Hate* is definitely becoming like *The Simpsons*, where you have a group of characters that you create stories for, and I think that's a big mistake.

Williams: Actually, yeah, I totally gave up on *Hate*. I was a humongous *Neat Stuff* fan, but . . .
Seth: I think *Neat Stuff* was a superior product, but, I still think Peter Bagge could do better work. I think he's latched himself on to Buddy Bradley as his meal ticket, and I think it's a mistake.

Williams: Yeah.
Seth: Like *Palestine* [1996 collection of comics "journalism" by artist Joe Sacco, originally serialized in 1993] is my example of a great piece of comics work. There's something that's concise and meaningful, and it's got an end, a middle, and it says something.

Williams: You know, I was talking to Jeff [LeVine] about that. I read the entire book; I didn't read them as they were coming out. Jeff said that it lost something because of the format that it was coming out in. I think that's a really valid point, that when something is forced to come out in these chapters that come out over a period of months, like I think your whole *It's a Good Life* story, even though I love it as it is, but I think it will be even better once I can sit down and read it all together.

Seth: That's how I'm planning it. My end goal is the collection, more than the issues.

Williams: You're doing a collection of it?

Seth: For sure.

Williams: With extra pages?

Seth: No, but at the end there will be all the Kalo cartoons I've discovered, but I can't tell you how many, because that would spoil the story.

Williams: That's my point, is it because Drawn & Quarterly is saying it should come out in a serialized form?

Seth: I think it's just because of the basic nature of comics. You can't support yourself working two to three years to finish one story and then just publish it all at once. You've got to have a comic book. First of all, you've got to build reader interest too. If I had just started drawing it last year, and then finished it next year, and then put it out, nobody would even know who I am. You build name identification by building your own series, which means people are more likely to buy the collection. And you've got to have that money by serializing it first, and then getting the extra money when you collect it. It's the only financial way that's logical.

Williams: It's frustrating because books aren't like that. Book publishers will give you an advance to do your book. Actually that is Jeff's big rant for this week; that comics should come out like books. I guess there's not the market for it yet.

Seth: That's the problem. I think if the market could support it, it could happen, but at this point, there's no publisher who could give you twenty thousand dollars to live two years on so that you could turn out a graphic novel.

Williams: Those silly Batman artists make more than that in a year.

Seth: I know. They can clean up unbelievably. I heard about one inker in

Montreal, who inked one issue of *Superman* that sold well, and he made eighty thousand dollars for that one issue.

Williams: Jesus Christ!

Seth: When I heard that Todd McFarlane made a million dollars on that first issue of *Spawn*, I felt sick. It's such an injustice.

Williams: There are a lot of directors who that same kind of thing would happen to. These great directors, like Orson Welles. It's a total tragedy.

Seth: It's heartbreaking, but that's just it, if you're making too much money, you must be doing something wrong. Somebody once said that no work of art that is great is ever commercial, and I think that's true. Even though, that doesn't mean it couldn't make a lot of money, but it's never intended. Nobody ever sits down with the intention of making a lot of money, and then turns out a great piece of art. You have to go the other way.

Williams: What's the circulation of *Palookaville*?

Seth: Right now it's hovering close to five thousand.

Williams: Wow! Last time I heard it was around three thousand.

Seth: Yeah, it's moved up. The last couple of issues alone, it's got about a five-hundred-reader increase each time, I think. So I was pretty happy with that. It's still not quite at five thousand, but it's getting close.

Williams: Do you think it's the ongoing story, or do you think it's just that people are finding out about it, or something like that?

Seth: From the mail I'm getting, I'm guessing that it has a lot to do with the new story. I'm getting a lot more positive response. I think some of it has to do with that the frequency of schedule is better now. I had that really big gap in between issues two and three, where a year went by, and since then it's been really strong in my mind to make sure I could get three issues out in a year, so I'm going to try to stick to that. I really do think it helps.

Williams: It's easier to remember what's going on in the story.

Seth: I think frequency is important; of course if you were getting it out bimonthly, you'd sell even better, but there's only so much you can do.

Williams: Is that one of your goals, to become a full-time cartoonist? Would you want to do it bimonthly? If you could pay your bills?

Seth: Even if I could afford it, I don't think I could ever get it out that fast. But, I would love to be a full-time cartoonist, and get it out four times a year, instead of three.

Williams: Dan Clowes seems to make a living, so it is possible.
Seth: I think it's possible, especially if you can get up higher in the sales figures. I think Dan is definitely selling over ten thousand.

Williams: Oh yeah, I thought he has up to twenty-five thousand.
Seth: Last I heard was seventeen, but if he's selling twenty-five thousand he's laughing. That's good. That's really good! I bet he and Peter probably have the best sales at the moment.

Williams: (joking) Except for all those Vertigo books.
Seth: Except for all the crap.

Williams: Actually, I've heard that Ed Brubaker is going to be writing for Vertigo now.
Seth: Oh really? I don't think that's a great move for him.

Williams: Oh, I think it pays the bills. I think that's why he's doing it.
Seth: I think there's a danger of working for those companies. I think they suck you in. Once you start dealing with that corporate structure you've got to bend to what they want. I just think getting involved with Marvel, DC, or even Image is a big mistake.

Williams: Unless you want to make millions of dollars.
Seth: Well, if you want to make money it's a good choice, but if you want to keep any kind of artistic freedom it's not.

Williams: Do you ever do signings or stuff like that?
Seth: Yeah, I do signings. Usually Chester Brown, Joe Matt, and I end up doing signings as a group, the three of us, because we're so close together. Whenever somebody calls about something we all go. We've done a fair amount of signings.

Williams: In New York?
Seth: Yeah, New York. We went to Albany and Ann Arbor, you know, places

that are relatively close. Here in Toronto we sign at the Beguiling, it seems like at least once a year. I hate signings actually.

Williams: Just because it's such an awkward situation, or what?
Seth: Exactly. I think I'm a fairly social person, but I'm basically antisocial, so I always end up having a really bad headache afterwards because both Joe and Chester are pretty quiet, so it's up to me to talk to everybody, and then I just feel like shit later, because I don't like having small talk with people I don't know.

Williams: As somebody who likes cartoonists, it's always frustrating. When they come to town, a lot of people go to the Hernandez Brothers and stuff, and I want to meet them, but in that kind of situation, I don't feel like meeting them at all, 'cause it's exactly that, small talk, and I'm not good at it at all.
Seth: I don't even go to signings if somebody is in town now, because that's just no way to meet anybody. The only way you can meet somebody is to have a nice one on one conversation with them.

Williams: I feel obligated when it's some old cartoonist. Like Jack Kirby, I had to go.
Seth: Sure. I wish I'd met Jack Kirby.

Williams: I actually got to hang out behind the back counter at Comic Relief where I was working, and talk to him a little bit.
Seth: That must have been nice.

Williams: I had a chance to go out to dinner with him, which I blew, and I'm going to be regretting for the rest of my life. It was a couple of months before he died.
Seth: It's kind of sad. It's hard to connect with people, even if you want to. Especially with some of these older guys. I remember Will Eisner came through town a few years ago, and there's just no way of really connecting, really having a real conversation, but you really can't do anything about it. You can't force some kind of intimate conversation that's never going to happen.

Williams: What old comic book artists do you like?
Seth: I like Kirby, of course, and Ditko, C. C. Beck, Sheldon Mayer, John Stanley would be like top of the list. John Stanley is one of my absolute favorites.

The usuals I guess, like Dick Sprang, and Wolverton. H. G. Peters, do you know his stuff?

Williams: Oh man, yeah, I love his stuff. That's the great thing about working in a comic book store, I get to see all those originals, because those *Wonder Womans* haven't been reprinted.
Seth: Definitely. All I have is that one *Wonder Woman* hardback.

Williams: I wish I had the money.
Seth: I had to pay plenty to get it out of Joe. I like Dan DeCarlo a lot, and Kurtzman, the usuals I guess.

Williams: All the *Mad* guys . . .
Seth: Well, I like the *Mad* guys, I like Will Elder a lot. Probably nobody too obscure or anything.

Williams: Do you like animation at all?
Seth: Not much beyond the thirties. I'm a big fan of the Fleischer stuff, and I'm a big fan of the early Disney stuff, like the black and white *Mickey Mouse* stuff, and the *Silly Symphonies*. Any really early animation I like.

Williams: When you're walking around, you give the impression in *Palookaville* that you relate to a lot of things through comics, but do you really . . . that *Tintin* thing in the new one with the train, that's happened to me before from that same book, so that really struck me.
Seth: That's pretty true. I think I'm so immersed in cartooning that there's a million different reference points that are constantly causing associations. There's always something coming up. I could be eating something, and for some reason it sparks the memory of some old gag cartoon. I feel that in some ways, my life philosophy has been formed by specific cartoons or strips that really spoke to me in some way. In an issue or so of *Palookaville*, I mention a gag cartoon and a strip that I really feel represent my whole approach to the world. That at some point or another they kind of became like personal totems or something. I feel a real connection to cartooning that kind of transcends just an interest in it. It's almost superstitious or something, where you're constantly thinking about it.

Williams: What do you think cartoonists should do to make sure the medium doesn't end up like old radio shows? Or is there anything they can do?

Referencing *Tintin*. From *It's a Good Life, If You Don't Weaken* © Seth. Used with permission from Drawn & Quarterly.

Seth: This is a tricky question. I think the best thing cartoonists can do would be to start approaching their work with a real seriousness of intent. With an artist's concern. I think for a long time cartoonists have approached things from the point of an entertainer, even the alternative and underground cartoonists have had a real anti-art stance. They would rather call themselves pornographers than artists, or writers, or whatever term you want to use. I think if comics are going to have a long lasting staying power, beyond some sort of a youth audience, they've really got to produce some enduring work. I think that comes from a maturity of approach, where you really do aim to tell something with a serious intent. Something that's more complicated than just getting a laugh out of the audience. I'm not saying that they shouldn't be funny, but not just get a laugh, or doing some cheap fart joke, or just being weird or hip for its own sake. I'd like to see in ten or twenty years a body of work of cartoonists that really were trying to produce comic novels, that really had some sort of staying power and could speak to a generation that's older than twenty years old. I think maybe that would produce some hope for the comics medium.

Williams: Do you think there's an audience out there for that kind of stuff?
Seth: I think there could be. I see things grow by word of mouth slowly, and I think that's the only way it's going to happen. I don't think it's going to happen by articles in *Rolling Stone* saying comics are hip or anything. When I get letters from people, it's often like, "A friend of mine showed me your comic, and I don't read any comics, but I really like this one, and I'm going to keep reading it," or whatever . . .

Williams: The *Love and Rockets* syndrome.
Seth: That's the way an audience will grow, beyond just people who read Marvel comics as a kid, or people who are reading them because they're hip at the moment, and stop later. I think you need to have a literate audience that actually likes to read. And it doesn't have to be a huge audience to keep comics alive.

In America, I think hardcover novels only sell about eight thousand copies. That's pretty bad, but that's enough to keep them alive. Of course, softcover novels sell a hell of a lot more. I think we have to have something like *Maus*. It had a hook that brought in the regular public. It was about the Holocaust, but they could read it and they could enjoy it. They might not have read it if it was about Art Spiegelman's relationship problems but if an audience could read something like that then they could read Chester's latest book, *I Never Liked You* [serialized as "Fuck" in *Yummy Fur* from 1991 to 1993, collected edition published in 1994]. That has a wider appeal than just the trendy culture of people in their twenties. It actually does speak to just the basic human condition. I think the more cartoonists produce works that are generally from the heart . . . Jim Woodring's work is another example. I don't think you need to be twenty to read that. Maybe you're not going to enjoy it if you're fifty years old, I don't know, but maybe you are. I think the more mature work that is produced and the more it's collected, and the more of a large base of this kind of work is out there, the better chance we have of building a larger audience. Where they can come in and they can buy *Maus* and then, if they like it, maybe they buy one of Chester's books, you know. Then there's enough stuff to actually keep an interested reading audience. Hopefully a number of good cartoonists will grow over the years to fill that need. That's my only hope for it. I don't think any marketing scheme is going to pull us out. I really don't think things like the hippest cartoonist in the world kind of promo are really going to do anything. Anything where they're trying to align comics with youth culture, I think is a mistake. I don't want to be part of youth culture! Rock and Roll is youth culture, and that means you've got to keep it at a level that seventeen-year-olds can appreciate. I'd rather be in with the jazz crowd. It should be something . . .

Williams: Actually jazz is having a humongous comeback right now.
Seth: I can believe it. But it's not real jazz.

Williams: It's frightening to me, 'cause I've been a jazz fan since I was a kid, and it's strange that there are all these people now who are into Charlie Parker, Dizzy Gillespie, and all those people.
Seth: I look at it like this; I don't care if some idiots buy my book, as long as some intelligent people buy it too. If the idiots keep you going, more power to them. If they're buying Charlie Parker, they're helping to support good music. I often wonder when people are buying things, if I'm in some real hipster's apartment and they've got a Chet Baker CD, I'm wondering if they have it 'cause they like Chet Baker's music, or because they think it's real cool to be a heroin addict. I always wonder about people's motives when things are hip. I think, jazz having a hip resurgence, is just like comics having a hip resurgence, it only lasts as long as it's hip, and if it ceases to be hip you're in trouble. Look what happened to the underground comics when the counterculture dissolved.

Williams: Yeah.
Seth: I don't want to be around when the slacker culture dissolves and suddenly you got no sales. So I kinda hope my work doesn't appeal to people on that level.

Williams: I don't think your work is on that level.
Seth: I hope not (laughs). I seem to get a lot of letters from people who don't seem to be part of that culture, so that's good. I mean, I've got no problems with it. If you want to buy my comics and you're wearing a touque and you've got dreadlocks that's fine with me, but I don't really target market it towards them, or anything.

Williams: What do you think about the future of small press comics?

Seth: I pretty much look at the small press, I don't know if this is insulting to the small press or not, as the training ground before you move into the alternative press. I can't see any logical reason why you would stay self-publishing if you had a choice, unless you're self-publishing in a better format. I can't really get into that whole philosophy of the do-it-yourself thing. It's kind of like the punk thing, where anybody can play an instrument. I think that's only valid to a certain point. I get good mini-comics that come through, and I think, "This is great. In a few years this person might be doing a really good comic." But I look at it as, this is where they can learn and grow before they're seriously published. Like when I see something by Adrian Tomine or Ariel Bordeaux, or things like that, I think these are pretty good.

Williams: Have you seen *King-Cat*? [*King-Cat Comics and Stories* (1989–present), a long-running mini-comic by John Porcellino]

Seth: No, I haven't actually. I usually rely on people sending me stuff. If they don't send it to me, I don't see it, usually.

Williams: He's a genius. He's one of the saviors of small press of real quality.

Seth: Do you have a different opinion of small press?

Williams: My opinion differs wildly. I just got into this humongous argument with Carol Swain, through a letter, and it's basically, I think the whole thing is art. The format of the book, where it goes to sell, is art to me. The whole idea of it is art. When you're working with this format that Will Eisner, or whoever, established fifty years ago, it's just a product. It's like what happened if the pages on *Eightball* were whited out and something else slapped on top of it. The package itself isn't really art. It's a format that people are used to getting their stuff in.

Seth: I think I see what you mean. You're saying that real comics are a commercial commodity, and mini-comics represent a pure desire to do comics.

Williams: Exactly.

Seth: I don't think I can agree with you on that though. I think the only difference is format. Especially when you're talking alternative comics, because I don't feel like anybody in the alternative market is doing it for the money, like in Marvel and DC. I look at it as a difference in professionalism though. I think there may be people in mini-comics that are as good or better, than people working in published comics, so it's not a matter of if you have a real comic then you're better than somebody who is Xeroxing, I don't think that at all, because there's a lot of crap published in the alternative press, but I tend to think, that if you're that good, you might as well move into a larger form of distribution which comes through real publishing (these are all kind of nebulous terms, like real publishing and self-publishing), but it's not the format. It's certainly not the size of the comic; I think it's the fact that when you're self-publishing with a Xerox machine, your audience is more limited. It doesn't mean that if you can round up the money and then publish it, that means it's better. It might still be just junk, or if you were a genius it would still be genius. But I think it's the difference between Xeroxing up some short stories and having a novel published. There's a much larger audience you're more likely to reach, and chances are, if you're being published, there's some level of professionalism involved, not necessarily a level of artistic merit. So I tend to think of anyone who is really good working in mini-comics, that the next step is to move to the larger audience.

Williams: I think people at Drawn & Quarterly are really lucky, but almost everything else I look at, maybe Fantagraphics is finally now, with Acme, learning to finally package it exactly how the artist wants to package it, but that's the thing that bugs me. You guys all have these really quality books, and it looks like you had some input on it basically. Chris Oliveros seems to be a really nice guy.
Seth: He is. It's a dream company. We are really lucky.

Williams: And that's my problem with Fantagraphics, and it just seems to me like an extension of DC and Marvel and this whole thing.
Seth: Why? Because you think the publisher is in a superior position?

Williams: Yeah.
Seth: Well, I think you're right.

Williams: "Welcome to the real world."
Seth: Yeah.

Williams: I think maybe now, with Chris Ware . . . that the stupid shelf-rack kind of format is just wrong.
Seth: I have a feeling that that's not going to happen. With any kind of publishing there's a certain kind of standardization rule that really holds, just like with books. You don't see too many novels that are ten inches tall, or fourteen

inches tall, because of the simple fact that you have to sell through distribution channels, and I think that keeps things within limits of experimentation.
Just like I feel like, you might look at . . . who is a favorite author of yours?

Williams: Raymond Chandler.

Seth: Okay, Chandler for example. He would have had to deal with the same
system of publishers and editors, et cetera, that people at Fantagraphics have
to deal with. Especially in any kind of publishing situation, I think there is a
real sort of give and take between publisher and artist, unless of course you're
self-publishing. Self-publishing is just as valid if you can manage to get it together. Black Eye Press is actually a small publisher that is doing a pretty nice
job of production values, the people who do *Pickle* [comic book by Dylan Horrocks, published by Black Eye Productions, a short-lived small press Canadian
comics publisher, from 1992 to 1996].

Williams: I don't know . . .

Seth: I'm not crazy about everything they publish, but for an artist/publisher
relationship I think it's very easy going there too.

Williams: There seems to be a real interest in quality work in companies now,
and the work itself is really quality, but it seems like the last frontier. It's
the thing that separates us from grandness in art. No matter what, the publisher's taint is still there, except for maybe Chris Oliveros, but for most of the
other people the publisher's taint is still there.

Seth: I just can't be that purist about it. I tend to look at it, is there anyone in
the mini-press, besides Steve Willis [pioneering mini-comic artist], who when
they're given their choice to reach the larger audience through the alternative
press or whatever, would say no. Isn't it a logical step to move from the small
press to the alternative press?

Williams: I think it has been. That's the thing. It's this accepted thing.

Seth: Would you like to buck that system and head in another direction?

Williams: Ideally, yeah.

Seth: Then how would you do it?

Williams: I know it's not financially possible, that's the thing. And I'm trying, even though I have two books coming out from publishers where they've

given me a chance to do it. One of them I'm doing completely my own way, and the other one, I'm doing as a crime comic, because that's how crime comics look.

Seth: But is that your choice?

Williams: Yeah, both of those are completely my choice, and if they started saying things like we're going to have to put this ad in the back, unless it was for something I endorsed, I would start disagreeing with it, and I would be tempted to go someplace else.

Seth: But there you go, you still do have the power. You always have the power to say no.

Williams: I think that's a new thing.

Seth: Oh, of course the comic book industry is a history of crime and abuse against any kind of artist, but I don't think that damns the whole publisher/artist relationship. I do believe, especially working with Chris, that you can have an equal position. In fact, I feel like I get more out of it than Chris does. When I got my first comic book contract from him, I couldn't believe it. There was like three lines, and it said, "You get this, you get this, and you get this," and I was like, "What do you get?" It's gotten a little bit more complicated since then, but basically I think it always depends on the individuals. There will always be sleazeball publishers. Even if you're selling mini-comics, there could be some guy who owns the store who completely rips you off for what you leave there. You go in and say, "Didn't I leave ten copies here," and he says, "Nope. There were only five, and none of them sold."

Williams: That's happened to me.

Seth: And I think that's the basic thing about dealing with people.

Williams: The thing I was talking about with going through all these other publishers, is that in spite of all that, I'm still going to do a mini-comic.

Seth: I can understand that. I've done some mini-comics, even after being published. I still think the mini-comic format is fun, and I don't think it's an invalid format because it's self-published or Xeroxed. I just do really tend to just think of it as a matter of audience, and production values. If you can get just as good production values out of a Xerox machine, for example, that you can get out of real printing, then there wouldn't be any reason why anyone would print at a certain point. I could see a point coming where you couldn't really tell the difference, and at that point it does become moot, as to which is the legitimate publishing method. Especially because of my love of old things, I am attracted to the comic book format itself.

Williams: I am too. That's my frustration. I have these two sides. Part of me wants to be this crazy artist type, and part of me loves the way comics used to look, and . . .
Seth: Sure. I've always wanted publish a comic in that off register dot process. When I look at those old *Little Lulu*s with that really flat color laid over that simple artwork, it's so appealing. And then of course there's the other direction, you've got all these production values now, you could do an incredibly beautiful water, well, not watercolor as in painting the whole thing, but I'd still do black lines. I don't like painted comic books. Those Jon J. Muth . . .

Williams: What do you think about [Lorenzo] Mattotti though?
Seth: I like *Fires* [Mattotti graphic novel published in 1988]. I think he's good, and I think it's perfectly legitimate, but I think the thing was, it's because he's a good cartoonist. Whereas, I feel, almost all the painted comics I've seen are produced by illustrators, who don't have any storytelling skills.

Williams: Yup.
Seth: And if they had great storytelling skills, maybe it would work, but I haven't seen one yet that does.

Williams: I'm a big hater of Jon J. Muth.
Seth: Yeah, me too. And I really hate that *Marvels* [revisionist Marvel limited series published in 1994, written by Kurt Busiek and illustrated in a realistic, painted style by Alex Ross, retelling key events in the history of the Marvel Universe from the perspective of everyday people] thing. I opened that up expecting it to be some incredible thing, the way people are talking about the artwork, and I just thought it was kind of half-assed looking.

Williams: What got me was the characters, and the way they were represented, like "Oh, I remember these guys," and I tried to read it, but after looking at that art for like five minutes, I was just like, "Ugh."
Seth: After seeing the Harvey Awards last year, that thing cleaned up . . .

Williams: Oh really?
Seth: Yeah, it won almost everything. I will no longer be voting in the Harveys

anymore. Those awards have just gone down the toilet. They don't represent anything anymore, if that thing can win, and you're not giving any awards for like, Chester Brown or Peter Bagge, any of the bigger cartoonists who are at least producing valid work, then forget it. That's just another crappy award. It always happens. They set up an award, then it just devolves after like four years, into something that just votes Stan Lee into the Hall of Fame again. I'm so sick of that.

Anyway, I think too much of the pseudo-realistic painting style is totally inappropriate to cartooning, because it slows down the natural movement between panels and turns it into series of stills, like fumetti [a comic book utilizing still photographs instead of drawings]. Fumetti never worked. Why should we turn cartooning into it?

Williams: I think *Fires* shows the potential, though.

Seth: Certainly I agree that any technique could be used, but I seriously do think that if you were going to paint a comic in a photorealist style, you'd need to be a genius to pull it off. It's just like if you were going to do a comic with a series of photographs . . . there's something about that still quality that comes from too much realism that slows down that natural progression between panels, and it ends up looking like a bunch of film stills.

Williams: Have you ever thought about adapting books into comics, and what do you think about that?

Seth: I've thought about it. I suppose it could be successful. It depends; it's kind of like adapting books into movies. Occasionally someone will do a great movie out of a book, but I guess it all depends on the individual too. You'd have to be a pretty good artist, if it's a great book, to do anything with it. I think things belong in their own medium. I think, probably the best movies were written for the movies, and the best books should probably remain books, but there's certainly no rules. But who knows, maybe somebody out there could do a great adaptation of some book and it would be brilliant. I probably wouldn't do it. Maybe a short story would be a better subject. To really do a novel justice it would have to be like six hundred pages. They're just totally different mediums. I don't think the strengths of writing are the strengths of comics, just like the strengths of film are not the strengths of comics. They all have different things of what subject matter they're best suited to, and it's not superheroes in comics. I've heard a lot of people say that comics are best suited to superheroes, because it's the most believable medium for them, and that may be true, but I certainly don't think that's what comics should be all about. I think they're suited to an awful lot of different things, but we need to explore further to see how well comics handle different types of narratives.

Williams: I think the potential is so unlimited.
Seth: I agree.

Williams: There's everything. You can just do so much.
Seth: In a way we're lucky that comics were relegated to a children's medium for all these years, because it's left a real opening up of it as an artistic medium until we were around. Otherwise, if comics had started to expand along with film, we'd have a much harder time getting in. What's exciting about comics is that it's a small field, and you don't know who is going to be the geniuses and who is going to be awful. It's so small that you really have a chance to do it.

Williams: But what's always daunting to me is the drawing ability of the guys in the past.
Seth: Well, sure. The further you go back, I really believe, the better the draftsmanship ability is. If you take a look at *Punch* cartoons from 1900 or 1910, you see a level of draftsmanship that no one on the planet right now is capable of. Because nobody is trained in that way any longer or has that sort of discipline to really learn how to draw like that. All us comics artists are basically self-taught, and we reach a certain level where a certain competence sets in, but there's a level of draftsmanship that has disappeared from the world, and I think it has a lot to do with the progression of modern art and modern taste.

Williams: The school system too. I read about the old guys taking classes in New York in the thirties and stuff, and it sounds like they were so rigorous, they made them learn so much. I have a book written by a teacher from around the turn of the century, on art, and it's so intense.
Seth: I know. These older guys definitely had a much firmer grounding in a real understanding of how to draw, than is really going on anywhere right now. If you look around at comic books, you'll see some people who really can draw very well, somebody like Dan Clowes or Chris Ware, with a real technical ability, but then there are lots of people who are doing well, who really don't have that much drawing ability at all. People who, if we were back at the turn of the century, wouldn't be able to get a job sweeping the floor at one of these magazines. I think maybe it had something to do with the apprenticeship system even, of apprenticing under a really good artist first.

Williams: Do you feel obligated to try to learn that level of draftsmanship?
Seth: I feel obligated to push myself to draw better and better all the time. I don't know if I have that much skill.

Williams: To aspire to it at least.
Seth: I'm certainly aspiring to always get better, but I don't think I have any illusions that I'll ever be able to draw with that kind of perfection of draftsmanship. I think Crumb pushes himself really. He really is an amazing draftsman. And there are a few you can name, a few people who really are incredibly skillful. I think since the advent of the camera the desire to be able to draw that realistically, that's not photo-realistically, has really declined. Even somebody as cornball as Norman Rockwell had an incredible draftsman ability.

Williams: I really love him actually.
Seth: I think that he's great, but I think that his subject matter is real middle-brow stuff, but I look around the world of illustration now and I don't see anyone who really represents that level of craft.

Williams: How autobiographical is your comic?
Seth: It's pretty autobiographical. I tend to think of autobiographical comics as meaning that they're true, but it doesn't mean that it's some kind of factual account though. I will regularly change events around, if it makes the story better. I would say, the first issue of my comic was 100 percent true, and the second and third were 90 percent true, and working up from there the level of truth has certainly dropped. It's true, that anything I'm thinking reflects my actual thoughts, but who the hell knows what I was thinking that day, I was walking around after meeting Ruthie, or whatever.

Williams: Is she actually your girlfriend?
Seth: She's not the girlfriend I have now. She's more of a composite of people I once knew, but the events depicted are pretty true. This series is much more of a composite of different events. Everything in it is probably 80 percent true; they're shuffled around in time, or whatever makes the story work best dramatically. I think probably most people who are writing autobiography are doing that.

Williams: Changing stuff around. . .
Seth: Like, say, Chester's recent storyline, I'm sure everything in there has

happened, but maybe not in that order, or in that level of importance, or whatever.

Williams: It's funny, Adrian Tomine manages to make his stuff seem auto-biographical, even though it's not.
Seth: Yeah, same with Lynda Barry. She always felt that way, but of course she was making it all up.

Williams: I haven't seen much of her stuff.
Seth: I used to be a huge fan of Lynda Barry, and when I was first developing an interest in autobiography, it was Lynda Barry more than anyone, that made me think it was the thing that was the truest, for the best writing. Then later, I found out it was fiction.

Williams: That's great. You said that after you finish the story you're working on right now, you're going to be doing a fiction story, and I was wondering, what's it going to be about?
Seth: I've got an awful lot of stories planned out. For example, I was planning out this cartoonist story even before I started *Palookaville*. It's just that it was a much different story, back then, in my mind.

Williams: Were you planning it out in your head or on paper?
Seth: In my head. That's how I always do it. I just keep it in my head, then, as the years go by, I find, things naturally get better, 'cause they start to re-combine with other ideas. When I first planned this cartoonist story it was nothing like it came out. It was really much more boring.

The fiction I want to do is the kind of fiction you can't put a label on, be-cause it's just stories about life. I guess if you want to call it slice of life . . . I don't really like that term, because that tends to mean nothing of importance happens. I don't want to do any genre fiction. For example, I think the next story I'm doing will probably revolve around the life of an old woman in her house. That's the best synopsis I can give of it. Nothing is going to happen that makes it a dramatic event.

Williams: Is she going to feed the birds?
Seth: Yeah, things like that. Actually, there will be no bird feeding in it, but you know what I mean. It could take an entire issue of her cleaning the house, as an introduction to the story.

Williams: That's the kind of stuff I love. I eat that stuff up.

Seth: That's exactly where my interest is going. When I was talking to Dylan Horrocks, he was telling me he'd read a Japanese comic book where they'd put forty pages in to show one kiss.

Williams: Wow!

Seth: And I thought, man, that's exciting. Hopefully those were forty great pages that really worked, but to have that space to really explore the story-telling, I think is important. Nothing really dramatic happens in my life, so I don't want to do that, because it becomes melodrama if you're making it up. I don't want to do any scenes of people bursting in and beating up some guy because he's sleeping with the girlfriend. Not that that's not real, but it doesn't ring true of my life experience. So even though it's fiction, it will be all based on my life experience, how I imagine this or that, and it will probably be pretty low key stuff. I just want to try to do a wider variety of stuff than just autobiography.

Actually, I was planning to do a biography of Grey Owl [assumed First Nations name of British author and conservationist Archibald Belaney], but Collier beat me to it, but I'm still thinking I might adapt . . . you might call this a crime story actually, there's a famous case here in Canada, back in the sixties, in the town where I grew up, actually, of a fourteen-year-old boy named Steven Truscott, who was accused of the rape and murder of a twelve-year-old girl. It's a really interesting case, because I think he was innocent and so sometime or other, I've been thinking, I might like to put ten or twelve issues into telling that story, but that's down the road. This is the kind of stuff, I have about eight of these stories in my head, different stories I want to do, but I'm never sure which one is going to be the next one. When I get to the end of this story right now, I'll know for sure which one I'm going to go into. Just like, I wasn't sure I was going to do this one when I started it.

Williams: You had a bunch of other ideas you were choosing from?

Seth: Yeah, it was a couple of other autobiographical stories that were going through my head at that point, and I'm glad I didn't choose them actually, because this one feels right for me, for my push towards my move to fiction. I feel like I'm learning a lot in storytelling as I'm going through this one, but I might not have learned as much if I'd done one of these other stories.

Williams: I really like how you work in what's actually going on in your head while you're doing these things.

Seth: That was a real conscious choice that I wanted to do that with this. I felt that in the first three issues, I'd almost made a mental decision that I didn't approve of narration, that stories should only be told from the outside, and I made a pretty conscious effort to do it that way. Then, when I hit the fourth issue I reevaluated why I was thinking this. Sometimes I'm very systematic in how I think. I can remember I was going through a point in my artwork when I thought, "Artwork must only be black and white, with no shading. No grays. Grays pollute the whole thing." Then, at some point I reevaluated that and thought, "Hey, my artwork looks much better with grays on it." So when I hit the fourth issue, I thought that this is the kind of story that almost demands an interior monologue, and how can you get away with that. I thought, "I don't want to be walking around with thought balloons," so I just thought, "narration is the logical choice."

Williams: What do you think lies ahead for the future of the medium?
Seth: What do I really think, or what do I hope?

Williams: What do you really think, 'cause you kind of already talked about what you hoped.
Seth: Well, right now, it looks pretty bad. Have you heard about the big problem with the distributor that's going on right now?

Williams: With Marvel buying Heroes World . . .[1]
Seth: Yeah. There's a couple of ways it could go. My worst case scenario is that Marvel could succeed in destroying the medium. Basically, they want everything, so I could see them trying to squeeze out everybody, and if twenty years down the road, Marvel was a smart enough business to get rid of all the other businesses, even DC, I think that would be the end of comics. I think that would be the thing that pushes it into being an anachronism, like radio plays, with one product, that only is one thing, superheroes or fantasy, and I think that won't be able to sustain itself. But if we're lucky, and the alternative market continues to grow, I think the diversity that will come with that, could, and I hope, and I think a part of me really does believe, that we will open up a larger, not a much larger audience, but a large audience, who is a

---

1. When Marvel purchased Heroes World to convert it to its exclusive distributor, the result was to reduce the comics available to other distributors significantly and therefore to lead these other distributors—as well as publishers—to seek other exclusive arrangements. Marvel's strategy failed, but the result was the destruction of the multiple distribution system, leaving Diamond the only distributor left standing in North America.

more literate audience. That's the kind of thing that I'm hoping, forty or fifty years from now, when the time comes for me to die, that I will see a more exciting medium happening with wider range. But part of me also says that it could just stay like this. This could be the best it gets, with this number of people reading, and you just continue to eke by. It's really hard to say. Those companies like Marvel and DC really have worked towards destroying the medium. They killed off every other genre of comics when they saw superheroes were selling well, and that kind of nondiversity . . . look how much less the sales of comics are. You need diversity for any medium to grow. If there were only one type of book, and they were all romances, sales on books wouldn't be too good, and I think that would be the downfall of the publishing industry. These guys are greedy, and they don't care. They only care about the short term. So, I think the alternative market, or whatever you want to call it, is really important to the medium surviving, because that's the only place where you'll find the diversity that keeps any art form alive.

An Interview with Seth

BRYAN MILLER / 2004

Bookslut (June 2004). Reprinted with permission.

Bryan Miller: In *Clyde Fans* Simon obsessively collects penny postcards. Not so dissimilarly, the protagonist of *It's a Good Life* collects cartoons and books of cartoons. What draws you to the theme of collecting?
Seth: It is hard for me to even envision a character who doesn't collect things. Collecting is such an integral part of my life that it seems natural that any character I write will collect. I have tried to keep this tendency in check when writing, but as time passes I am beginning to embrace the idea that all my characters might very well be collectors. The things people own and why they want to possess things say a lot about them as people. Also, searching for things is such a direct metaphor for searching for meaning . . . and that is just so clearly what most of my stories (most stories, in general, really) are about.

Miller: What is the mindset of the collector?
Seth: Collectors are interesting because they seek out things that no one cares about and find out the vital information regarding those items. They catalogue and interview related creators, manufacturers, et cetera. They preserve important cultural items. Later, when these things are considered interesting or important, the academics come along and benefit from the work of these outsider collectors. But people don't like collectors because they can be a strange lot—greedy, secretive, rude, socially awkward, et cetera. I have met more than my share of collectors who I found personally hateful. I don't really care for collectors myself, though clearly I am one of them.

People seem to collect for a variety of reasons. Some are accumulators (they just need lots of things), some are trying to get back their past (specifically childhood), some strongly need to possess things, et cetera, et cetera. I have all of these tendencies . . . but mostly I collect as a way of exploring the

Simon's collecting habit. From *Clyde Fans, Book One* © Seth. Used with permission from Drawn & Quarterly.

past. By buying the cultural items (especially books, movies, and records) of the past you begin to get a deeper understanding of the times. There are so many surprises to be found. It's a constant process—there are so many layers of the past to dig through. But it is such a pleasurable experience. I just love the objects of the past and looking for them (and possessing them) brings me the most happiness in life. I like nothing better than looking through some dusty pile of magazines in an out-of-the-way store with the hope that something great is at the bottom of that unpromising pile.

Like other collectors I am also trying to recapture the feelings of childhood. A lot of my life of drawing and making things is simply an attempt to re-create the feeling of being a child and doing those same things. I don't collect a lot of things from the era of my childhood, but occasionally I will seek out some item (or totem) from my childhood. Recently I tracked down a wrist-radio on eBay that I owned as a child. Holding it in my hands again was a beautiful moment.

Miller: Your work often feels marked by a sort of longing for the past. Do you really think the world was so much better then? Do you consider yourself a particularly nostalgic person?

Seth: I have no illusions about the superiority of the past. People have always been miserable and life has always been difficult. However, I can honestly say that I don't think much of this present time. Certainly, here in North America, things couldn't be cheaper, uglier, or more vulgar than they currently are (well, they could, and probably will be—in the near future). I think that the early to middle twentieth century was an aesthetically more pleasing time period. While I personally have no desire to live through the Depression or World War II, I do think that culturally the quality of many things was superior, especially design. Things were created for actual humans (with genuine care and effort). You cannot look at a popular medium-priced radio or clock from that period and compare it with the same popular medium-priced item from today and not come away convinced that things are just much shittier today.

The modern world is very ugly and the pop culture is so mind-numbingly dumb that you have to make a conscious effort to shut it out. That's why I'm considered a "nostalgia guy." I just like things from the past better. I don't want to live in 1932, but I sure wish some of the elements of that time had survived into this time. Though obviously, their fascination with "progress" is the worm in the apple that created this shitty culture we inhabit. It's a complicated question. And believe me, no one is more confused about his feelings about the past and the present than I am. I find, as each year passes, my understanding and feelings about the twentieth century are more muddled. The only thing I can say with real certainty is: The mass culture of our current age makes me feel like I need a shower.

Am I nostalgic? Can you feel nostalgic for an era you never lived in? I am interested in the time before I was born, but I feel the most nostalgia for the era of my own childhood. The 1960s and early '70s was the last vestige of that old world . . . elements of it were still hanging around everywhere. I didn't think about it much as a child, but now I realize those old businesses and products and movies et cetera that were lingering into the time of my childhood left a deep impression on me. All that stuff seems very sad to me. I'm not really a nostalgic type so much as a melancholic. I spend a lot of time alone, and most of it is spent in a fog of self-pitying melancholy. It sounds pathetic, but it is so true.

Miller: When you conceive a story, do you write it out in script format or sketch it out in panels? Is there a particular process when you begin plotting your work or does it differ?

Seth: Well, most of it goes on in my head and then there are various note-taking stages. But when the actual work of the comic book comes, I usually write out the scenes I want to include in the issue and then type out whatever dialogue (or narration) is to be included. Then comes the real planning—working out thumbnail breakdowns of the comic. This is where the real writing happens (in my opinion). In comics, so much of the story is told through the pacing of the story. For me, this process is where it comes together. After that, it's just the laborious process of drawing and inking the comic book.

Miller: The first three segments of *Clyde Fans*, the ones dominated by Abe, are very chatty while those centered around Simon are wordless for long stretches. Did you find one more challenging to work with than the other?

Seth: When I am writing, I am generally not thinking in terms of quiet or talkative. Instead I am making a distinction between "inside and outside." In both the first and second parts of *Clyde Fans* the story is told from the outside. Generally, we don't get inside the characters' heads—instead we view everything from outside, voyeuristically. Viewing from the outside can be either quiet or talkative, depending on what you are viewing. The narrative approach of these two parts are different—monologue versus cinematic (I suppose), but both share an outside viewpoint. In part three I move inside and we have Simon's thoughts. There is a bit of the inside approach in part two, but not much.

I like both wordy and quiet comics; however, my characters tend to be explainers so I think I enjoy writing the wordier stuff more. I think I place a higher value on the quiet approach though, because it is always more interesting to hint at things than to explain them. Inevitably I end up doing both.

Miller: Do you often work with photos or other references?

Seth: I have tons of photo reference around the house and I certainly use it for background details, et cetera. Old catalogues come in very handy for drawing household items. I must say though, as I get older I find that I have

The allure of the past. From *It's a Good Life, If You Don't Weaken* © Seth. Used with permission from Drawn & Quarterly.

absorbed a great deal of this visual information into my brain and often I can just make the background stuff up out of my head pretty easily now. But if you want to freshen up your drawings, it really helps to study some new photos. It helps refresh your compositions and make your "details" more interesting. I almost never use any reference for figures any longer (although I may flip through books, et cetera for character types if I am drawing a crowd scene).

Miller: I once read an interview with Chester Brown in which he said you think so many indie comics centered around autobiographical stories because the rest of the medium was intensely focused on fantasy and autobio is as far removed from that as possible. Has autobiographical work become a kind of cliché of its own in the indiecomics world, as dominant in more literary comics as fantasy/sci-fi in mainstream books?

Seth: Not really. There is a fair amount of autobio in comics but honestly not that much. If you're not writing genre fiction, I think it is a pretty natural response to use yourself as the main character (writers certainly do it all the time). We are just so used to genre conventions in our media that we tend to find autobio more of a sore thumb. The current trend of "diary comics" seems more of a genre because it seems to have a form of some sort (the four-panel strip form) and that can create a group of simple, unwritten rules on how to make these comics. I haven't seen that much of this stuff firsthand so I may be off-base here. I still think fiction is the primary force in underground comics. I also think cartoonists, in general, are becoming less uptight about all the genre stuff. We've created more distance between what we are doing and what the mainstream guys are up to (certainly a lot more than back in the eighties) and so we are less concerned about reacting against it. Dan Clowes is using a superhero in his next comic—I think that is a sign that we don't really feel any reaction against that stuff anymore. A superhero is just another symbol to be used now. Ten years ago it was a more charged issue.

Miller: Do you plan to return to more directly autobiographical work at some point in the near (or far) future, or are you no longer interested in that subgenre?

Seth: I do autobio strips in my sketchbook. It seems a natural form. I will publish some of that stuff eventually. I have no real plans for more "finished work" in the autobio form, but who knows. I haven't ruled it out.

Miller: Peter Bagge's *Hate* used to sell in high volume a decade or so ago, relatively speaking, and now nobody does those kinds of numbers. At the same time sales have diminished, the profile of literary comics has been raised. Is the market for literary comics like yours getting better or worse?

Seth: The comic book market is certainly in decline (or so it seems to me), and the book market seems to be in the ascendancy. For myself things are just getting better and better. I feel that "graphic novels" are coming of age. Who knows though, things are always going up and down. I'm dedicated to doing my work no matter what the situation, but I obviously prefer things to be good.

Miller: Is the bookstore market really a viable outlet for graphic novels on any large scale? For that matter, is the direct market a viable outlet for such work?

Seth: Nothing seems overly viable. Thank God for publishers like Fantagraphics and Drawn & Quarterly. It is always a struggle to make ends meet when you are publishing work that is outside of the popular trends. I don't know how I would carry on without Chris Oliveros—just knowing that he is there ready to publish my work and willing to help in any way to make the process perfect just makes life worth living. He is a saint.

Miller: Disregarding the obvious answer of marketability, what advantages does the graphic novelist have over the prose novelist and vice versa?

Seth: Comics and prose have some things in common but not as much as people think. In fact, instead of comics being a combination of drawings and literature, or film and literature, I think that comics are closer to a combination of poetry and design. The drawings in comics ideally should be used as design elements. They are not there simply to be pretty—no, when used well the drawings act as symbols to direct the eyes and the emotions (in a way, they are language symbols much like the letters of the alphabet). Clearly the drawings are trying to be attractive and to create evocative images—but also clearly they are being placed on the page as elements in an overall design that leads you (the reader) through the comic. As for the poetry element—well, comic writing is all about rhythm. You are not writing poetry in the traditional sense, but the way the writing is broken down in the panels and then how it is run through a page—the way it is paced in general—it is just all about how it sounds in the mind. The brevity, the rhythm, the breaks for silence. These are elements that probably have more to do with free verse than they do with the traditional novel. Not that novelists aren't concerned with the sound of their work, but it is not so clearly linked to pacing in the way that writing and designing a comic page is.

So, end of digression. Prose and comics are quite different. The ends though are the same—telling a story. The strength of prose is in the description (which in comics is generally handled in the drawing) and in the ability to do a very sustained inner dialogue. It is nice in a novel to carefully describe a room, for example, and have the ability to go on for pages about it, drawing the reader's eye to certain objects and lingering on them. In comics, this is usually drawn and therefore can be a bit obvious if you take the effort to point out descriptive details by focusing directly on them. I use this obvious ploy myself, all the time. You are often limited in your ability to capture the richness of the detail of real life (limited by your drawing and the simplicity of cartoon style) which a novelist can describe in minute detail. Conversely, description as drawing is one of the great strengths of comics, freeing the writer from dealing with the use of words for description's sake, allowing the reader to take in setting, et cetera, in a less direct manner. It's a matter of opinion—sometimes a strength, sometimes a weakness.

You can certainly do a sustained inner narrative in comics, but it is hard work. In a novel, we can just slip entirely into the inner world for scores of pages, but in comics, since you are constantly drawing the outer world it can be a real chore to keep the visuals exciting when you are drawing forty pages of a person having an inner monologue. One of the tasks I am well acquainted with in my *Clyde Fans* book. Undoubtedly, there are lots of pros and cons for both mediums, but these are the two differences that pop into my head.

Miller: How intensive is your work on the Fantagraphics collection of *The Complete Peanuts*?

Seth: The most intensive time was the designing of the first book. All twenty-five of the books will follow a fairly rigid design sense, so most of the work was done in the initial stages. However, each book probably takes about a month's work—which is plenty when you are doing two of them a year (and you have soooo much other work to do to!). Essentially, each book will look like the others in the series, but elements like covers and titles page and endpapers must be updated for each volume. Also, certain elements will change for every decade of the strip.

The biggest element of work for each book is a series of double-page strips I have been doing, which are reconstructed landscape drawings made up out of Schulz's drawings but cut apart and recomposed into new scenes. These are challenging and pleasurable to do. It is a bit like drawing with Schulz's hands.

Miller: Designing a book is something most people probably don't give much thought to beyond what the cover looks like.

Seth: True, most people don't think much about book design . . . a shame really. A well-designed book is one of the most perfectly beautiful things in the world. The arrangement of cover to endpapers to title page, et cetera is such a marvelous set of elements to play with. When done well they are a terrific model of things in balance. I love a well-designed book.

My wife, Tania, gave me the perfect metaphor for my role in the *Peanuts* books. I am like a jeweler. Schulz's strips are the gems, but it is my job to create a beautiful setting for them. Hopefully a setting that makes them even more beautiful, yet doesn't overpower the gems with its own garishness or self-importance. That is what I'm trying to do—give Schulz's work the dignity and sophistication it deserves. Whether I have succeeded or not depends entirely upon the readers' response. Probably no response at all is the best sign that I have succeeded.

I've tried hard to steer away from the cheerful pop designs that have almost always hindered Schulz's books in the past. I want the reader, when they see the book, to realize that this is an adult item, something meaningful. God knows the strip is subtle and rich enough—people need to be reminded of that.

Miller: What exactly is your process and to what degree are you trying to channel Schulz? Do you feel pressure to, in some way, please Schulz?

Seth: I felt no pressure to please Schulz. My obligation was to the strip. The strip deserves a proper presentation, and I've tried to give it one. If it fails, it's entirely my fault. The strip clearly needs no window dressing, just its own dignity. Schulz himself, obviously, wasn't that interested in the design of his books while he was alive—most of his books look pretty tossed together by the various companies that reprinted them. I'd like to think Sparky would have been happy with our books, but probably he wouldn't have cared all that much. I'm trying (within reason) to create the *Peanuts* books I would like to own myself.

Seth Interview

DAVE SIM / 2005

Following *Cerebus* 5 (August 2005) pp. 38–45. Reprinted with permission.

This interview is part of a series of interviews Dave Sim conducted entitled "Advise & Consent" dealing with comic creators' use and nonuse of editors. Dave Sim interviewed Seth on April 21. Dave did the transcription; Dave, Seth, and Craig Miller edited the text.

Sim: I guess the first question that I have is—since we already have the Chester [Brown] and Joe [Matt] interviews pointing out that you're not a great one for input creatively—was that always the case? Was there ever a time when you asked other people for advice on your work?

Seth: Yeah, I would say when I was first starting out, a couple of times, I guess. Before I was working on *Mister X*, I was trying to work up some comic books of my own at that point, and I had just come through a period when I had really stopped working entirely. To put this in context, this would be after I went to art school—then after I dropped out—I decided to try and do some comics. And around this time I met up with an old girlfriend of mine—actually the woman who later married Bill Marks of all people—and she was interested in comics, and I started meeting up with her and showing her my stuff: mostly for encouragement, really. She was someone who was giving me a lot of positive feedback, which I really needed at the time. Not much criticism— she was trying to do her own comics at the time, so I'd say what was going on there was actually a mutual support system. Then after I started on *Mister X*, I would have to say that the only time since I started working professionally that I was involved in showing work to other people would be with Chester, when I first started doing *Palookaville*, and he was working on *Yummy Fur*, and a little bit when Joe came along, too. But even at that point, I wasn't looking for feedback as much as for reassurance. Because I pretty much always felt this desire to stand or fall by what I did myself. And to some degree I've always resented getting comments, even if they make the work better.

Sim: Let's double back a minute to *Mister X*. You were doing that for Bill Marks at the time. Did he have much input, or did you just turn the work in?
Seth: There wasn't much input. The place was so unprofessional. They basically gave me the book—a person who had never done any professional work—and Dean Motter was really not involved enough to be critiquing anything. He gave me a couple of pieces of compositional advice that I think of to this day—things like varying the head sizes on the page and watching out for odd shapes in your composition and things like that. But generally I was sort of left to my own devices. One of the things that galled me was that they wouldn't let me do the cover, and there was this kind of implied criticism that I wasn't up to the standard of doing the cover. That seemed to me like the perfect scenario for deflating whatever feeling of self-worth you might have.

Sim: It was like a vote of nonconfidence.
Seth: So there never were any specific criticisms addressed towards me, but there was a feeling of judgment going on there. It wasn't like an apprenticeship system where I was being taught anything. An apprenticeship system by myself, because that was where I learned by seeing the work in print, but that's really all it was, an opportunity to figure things out on my own.

Sim: So there was a time when you were showing *Palookaville* to both Chet and Joe?
Seth: Certainly I showed the first issue to Chester. I probably showed the first four or five issues to Chester prior to publication. And I can't really remember any actual criticism that Chester gave me. Certainly there were instances where I could read his reaction. He was generally always pretty positive. I think he recognized—as anybody does—that when you put that in their hands, it's kind of a vulnerable position. You just spent months working on this thing, and the last thing you need is to sense someone's disappointment. I didn't really come to any understanding about how to change my work, but I did come to understand how to see the work from the outside a little more clearly. The whole process of creating a comic book, as far as I'm concerned, is like being lost in a dream world while you're working on it: a dream world that fluctuates between "I'm a genius" and "This is a piece of crap." So putting it in someone else's hands and watching them read it was an enlightening experience: by watching their reactions to things.

Sim: But there did come a point where you cut that off.

Seth: I think at some point I just felt uncomfortable with the process, be-cause I just felt like I had already committed myself to the book in a finished state when I put it in their hands. So to place it in their hands and then sense that they weren't very thrilled with it—I wasn't really going to say, "What can I do to fix it?" All it was doing was setting up a sort of emotional disappoint-ment for me, putting it in someone's hands and *expecting* a reaction of some kind. And I just wanted to remove that whole element from it, to stand or fall by the finished product and put it out there. If it was any good, I just wanted it to be good as a result of my own decisions.

Sim: My assessment was always, "It's still just another opinion."

Seth: Exactly.

Sim: I mean if you have an audience of three thousand or six thousand or however many people you've got, there's going to be such a spectrum of reac-tions anyway that it might as well be, as you say, "This is my hill to die on" if I'm making a wrong choice or I'm making an unpopular choice.

Seth: Exactly. I would say that the only time it has not been true was recently when Chester made some criticisms to me after publication that I took to heart. The end of Part Two of *Clyde Fans*, the sequence where the character Simon is walking out of the town, and there are memory flashes of the people he's been talking to. Now, after the book came out, I didn't show it to Chester, but after it came out he was talking to me about it and saying that he felt that whole sequence was really like hitting people over the head with a hammer. He felt there was no need to repeat these lines [of dialogue] again. My first reaction was, Well, I don't know if I agree with you on that, because I chose the other direction. But as I thought about it, over time I thought it did seem kind of "unsubtle" to me. And I think what bothered me about the comment and the reason that it stuck in my brain is that I did think that it had fallen into the category of a kind of cliché. And if there's one thing I hate, it's to feel that I'm regurgitating some clichéd technique that I've picked up through too much viewing of other work—like pop culture crap—and the more I thought about it, the more it really struck me that that was the case with the "voiceover" experience of the character revisiting these traumas from earlier in the story. So I did give it some serious thought, and when I republished it in book form, I reworked that sequence and actually removed the dialogue and added in a couple of pages and just turned it into a couple of mental flashes of a couple of the characters he had been talking to.

A rare instance of Seth modifying work based on feedback; Simon's modified departure. From *Clyde Fans, Book One* © Seth. Used with permission from Drawn & Quarterly.

Sim: It seems to me that's very much an *avant-garde* kind of problem. It's al-most—from the stories that Chet and Joe were telling me—that's really what you guys are watching out for in each other's work: the "trite and the cliché."
Seth: That's probably true. The biggest embarrassment as an artist is when you produce something that you think is earnest, and to have it seen by oth-ers as representing some kind of cliché. Because you can't help but see it on some level as—well, it's not even really a criticism so much as a realization of personal failure that you're stupider than you thought you were.

Sim: Well, I think it's also because comic books are so much more condensed and so labor intensive that it's not like a half-hour television show or some-thing. "It's trite and cliché"—well, so what? It's just there to sell soap. Where-as if you're putting several months of time into your book and years of time into the overall collected version, the last thing you want it to be is the same thing that you can get just by switching on the television.
Seth: It's what you're setting out to try and avoid by trying to do something honest, and that's really the hardest thing, especially when you're working in a medium that was composed of clichés from the beginning to some degree. You're trying to get away from that, but you know that somewhere inside you [are] the thousands and thousands of superhero comic books you've read and you don't want to be regurgitating that stuff, but that is the language that you're working from, so it makes it, I think, especially disappointing when you've failed to tap into something Real and instead just regurgitated some-thing else that you weren't planning on regurgitating. In the first issue of *Palookaville*, I had one panel where there's a punch thrown, and it was a very difficult panel for me to draw, because I only knew how to draw someone throwing a punch from having read millions of comic books. I had never given any consideration in real life to what it was like to throw a punch, so it was very difficult to draw that. And even with that in mind, I don't think I gave it enough thought. I look back on that now, and I still think that falls too closely into "what a comic book punch looks like."

Sim: Yeah. Well, it is "a punch inside a comic book" so it is kind of difficult to step outside that construct. One of the things that I did think was interesting was when Joe was talking about his recent experiment with trying to do the James Kochalka thing of "four panels a day." And he said he gave up after a week, because it was just pointless. And I said to him that I thought that one of the problems that you've got on the avant-garde side is that you're trying to be so Authentic, so True to Life, and a lot of times life is very trite—life is very clichéd. So you're always on that borderline between documenting life accurately and possibly just ending up with a very trite observation at the end of the day and coming up with something genuinely new, something that does cut to the core of human experience.

Seth: I think it's really difficult *to* do that. In any medium it's difficult to do that, but certainly in comics it is because you're dealing with, as you say, a lot of condensing of material—you're dealing with "condensed reality." And so to try to re-create the multileveled experience of being alive by sitting in your basement drawing a comic book—it's an extremely complicated process. And certainly, trying to boil it down to a four-panel epiphany every day is a process that I can't imagine trying to engage with for more than a couple of days myself. I think Kochalka is a perfect example of someone who has bled the life out of any attempt at reality by creating this really fake approach to reality, by trying to make everything into a "cute" moment. It's funny that from the outside fringes of the so-called avant-garde, he's approaching life without much more complexity than a "Love is . . ." cartoon.

Sim: I also think that there's the problem of influence. You can see that guys like Chris Ware and Dan Clowes must be really trying to avoid turning into each other, but you end up having a lot [of] the same problem[s]. There are guys drawing comic books who have obviously read "way-too-much-*Eightball*," and that's how they see life—through Dan Clowes's eyes.

Seth: True. However, I think it's true that of all the artists I know, Chris is the one person I have the most faith in approaching it honestly, because I think from the outside, people may look at what Chris is doing and see a certain kind of "system" in how he's working, but he's really one of the few artists I know who approaches each attempt at the board with such a strong, self-motivated sense of analysis on why he's making any decision on the page, which I would say is kind of unusual among comic artists. Certainly there's a lot of innovation that's gone on, and a lot of people have made really remarkable choices in how they choose to tell the story, but people tend to have—like myself: I have an approach when I come to the work. I sort of know what I *want* to do and how I'm going to *attempt* to get at a story. And I have a way of going at it. And I'd say that that's certainly true for Chester and several other people I could name. But Chris, I think, more than anyone is trying to reinvent the wheel every time. I'm not sure that he—I mean, you can't reinvent the wheel every time. Like any artist you're going to recognize that it is a Chris Ware piece. You can't start fresh every time. But he's got the right attitude. I think in any medium as stylized as comics, you can easily get locked into a system. And I'm certainly aware of it in my own work.

Sim: Well, and you also end up "raising the bar" on yourself—if you have reinvented the wheel every time—just the variety of formats that he tackled and the different themes and the different approaches.

I guess the concluding question would be: How comfortable are you critiquing somebody else's work if you've arrived at that point where you think—I mean do you think that critiquing is an intrinsically unhealthy thing and that Chester, as an example, would be better just getting everything out of himself? Or do you think it varies from person to person?

Seth: I guess my answer would be "Whatever makes you comfortable is fine with me." But, from my personal point of view, I prefer the idea of an artist struggling to learn on his own and figure it out on his own, rather than, you know, being part of a gang that's supplementing each other's work with critique. I guess that's just because my own inclination is, I'm attracted to the image of the artist working alone and producing this complete work. For example, I don't know how anyone can stand to work with an editor. I don't really know how fiction writers have become used to that idea. I can understand working with a proofreader: *that* makes sense to me. But even working as a prose writer, if there was someone changing around all the sentences in an article I had written and as a result of that it turned out to be a better-written article, I'd have to conclude at the end that I really wasn't much of a writer. You could maybe say that you were a good "idea man" or something, but if I can't craft it myself given the skill required, I guess it would be like having an inker, basically—which is another situation I've always disliked: the idea of working with other artists. I guess an actual collaboration is a different story, but I've never been much *for* collaboration. I could imagine saying: I'm going to write this, and you draw it. But I wouldn't want to have someone drawing it while I'm looking over his shoulder. I can certainly understand a level of self-doubt that would cause you to appreciate having someone there who can actually give you the reassurance you need by taking control. It would be nice—at the last minute—to have somebody you respect saying, "Here are the right decisions." I'm always surprised that there are artists who have the ability to accept that with a limited amount of ego. I'm just not one of them.

Sim: One of the things that Peter Birkemoe brought up on the panel is the situation of people bringing up artwork at conventions to be critiqued, which does put you in an "editor category." They're coming to you to get the help taking the next step, and I have found that I'm not interested in other peoples' opinions on my work, but I'm perfectly happy to give someone else an opinion.

Seth: Oh, I have no *shortage* of opinions. The problem is I find—it's tricky. I really think that the whole portfolio review situation is one that's fraught with problems. First, no one is actually there for criticism. Everyone is there for positive feedback. So, you are generally dealing with people who are looking for reassurance, which is fine if you want to go to one of these things and present yourself as an emotional support system for these people. If they really wanted honest criticism, I would probably feel more comfortable with it, but in that situation, what is actually happening is that you are dealing with someone's fragile ego, and I find that really uncomfortable. Even if I were there to give honest criticism, I would probably start with the positives. But when you feel that people aren't there for actual criticism, you can't really move on to much of the honest criticism beyond telling them something vaguely encouraging. There are times when you see people's artwork where you feel like to help them in any way you would really have to be brutal. And I just feel that nobody's there actually asking for that.

Sim: Well, I always tell them at the same time that if they were bringing up the artwork that I was doing at the time that I was seventeen when I dropped out of high school to draw comic books, I'd say, "Don't be crazy. Go back to school—you don't draw well enough."

Seth: If I saw my own artwork presented to me that I was drawing at the age of twenty, I'd just think, "Oh, this poor fool." So you really can't tell who's going to be any good. And at the age of twenty I really wouldn't have been ready for that kind of harsh criticism either.

Sim: I mean there is the danger that you're just going to discourage them so dramatically that they'll give up, or there's also the danger that you're going to change their decision-making—they'd make a really good Seth, but they'd make a lousy Dave Sim.

Seth: Obviously, you have people bringing work to you that really has nothing to do with your interests or even what you consider to be good art, whereas they could just walk one table over and be considered a genius.

Do you think that you would enjoy being an editor?

Sim: You mean, like a full-time job?

Seth: Yeah, or even for just a period of months, editing a variety of others' works, say.

Sim: No. I think—well, maybe in the way that Archie Goodwin was an editor on *Epic Illustrated* magazine.
Seth: What was his approach?

Sim: Basically, I don't think Archie ever accepted a piece of work that he didn't think was already at least 98 percent of the way "there." He might "tweak" it a bit or "nudge" it a bit or offer a few suggestions, but if you rebelled at all at any of his suggestions, that was fine, he would leave it exactly the way you wanted it to be published.
Seth: That's because he felt simpatico with the writer's sensibilities?

Sim: I think that he had such a level of expertise—having worked with all of the old EC artists at Warren, and having done a lot of work on newspaper strips and what-not—that he had a good working knowledge of what it was that went into a good comics story, so his criticisms were usually valid. There you get into the problem, however, where you would have to ask, "If Joe Blow were making this same criticism, would I be taking it the same way, or am I saying, 'Well, he's got to be right because he's Archie Goodwin?'"
Seth: I think one of the secrets of criticism is that it has to come from a source where you actually place any value in the criticism. I mean, it's got to be someone whose opinion I'd respect before I'd even give it the consideration of whether they might not have a point.

I think I tend to write off other people's opinions, because my own tendency is to go with my own opinion unless I'm presented with something that strongly counters it.

Sim: It's been interesting in doing this piece, in talking to all the different guys about the degree to which they allow and encourage criticism, where they get it from. Will Eisner, as an example, didn't show his work to his wife, Ann, for the first twenty-five years of their marriage. Then, in the graphic novel time period, she became one of his surrogate readers. I asked Frank Miller if he shows his work to Lynn [Varley, his wife and oft-collaborator] and, no, he doesn't show his work to Lynn. Do you show your work to Tania?
Seth: No. Mostly because, to be perfectly honest, I don't think that she's that interested. I think she's interested on a certain level, but I don't think that comics are a big interest of hers, and I actually feel that she would

probably—I don't trust her to be honest enough, in truth. I think she'd be too "encouraging"—um—

Sim: And you're past that point now. That mutual admiration society thing.
Seth: Yeah, exactly. With my own work with her, I put it in her hands and let her decide whether she wants to look at it or not. That's *after* publication.

Sim: So it's pretty much after publication?
Seth: Yeah. I'm trying to think—I think one of the reasons that I don't show people the work before publication is not that I'm so convinced that I'm right, [it's that] I'm more concerned about being influenced to believe that I'm wrong.

Sim: Well, that was the same reaction that I had with the example I used on the panel—and a couple of times since then—of the text pieces in *Jaka's Story*. I would never have asked anyone's opinions on that because I'm pretty sure everyone's reaction would have been, "No, text doesn't belong in a comic book."
Seth: And you already *knew* that, so you had to fight it out to begin with.

Sim: Exactly. So I think it's one of those—as you said back at the beginning—situations of choosing to stand or fall based entirely on what I perceive to be my own merits. I would hate to think of changing a work of mine to accommodate those opinions and then ten years later be rereading it and going, "No, I think I should have stuck with my first choice."
Seth: I think, too, that as I'm getting older, that I'm getting less concerned with—I think initially I had some worry of putting something out and feeling foolish. Like, maybe it would be nice to get an outside opinion to make sure that it isn't absolutely stupid before I let it go into print. I think I'm more comfortable with the idea that this is what I do. My attitude now is: if it's stupid, then I guess I'm stupid. I'm not going to be able to reinvent my mind just before publication, to make sure that everyone thinks well of me. If I want this to be a reflection of how my mind works, then I've got to have some faith that I know what's right. That doesn't mean that I couldn't be making serious mistakes in the crafting of the story. Obviously, I'm always going to be looking at the story later on and saying, "Maybe I should've had two panels here instead of one," or "I have to add another page in here [in the collected version] to slow this down" or something. But when it comes to the basics of the story *itself*, you've got to have some confidence to be able to—certainly

as time goes on—to just be able to put it out there, and to be able to say, you know, my opinion has to be the most valid opinion about my own work in the end.

Sim: I picked up on that when I was doing the interview with Craig Thompson and—he's only been in the business for a few years at this point—he was talking about that level of anxiety at the end of the working day of looking at what you've written and wondering if this is even a story, or is this the sort of hen-scratch that the average college student would produce just sitting in a coffee shop? And I think you're going to have those concerns for a while until you've produced enough material so that eventually you can just look at the finished work and say, "This is how I tell my stories."

Seth: I think when you're young, you have a lot more things in your mind of what you're looking to do, the people whose work you've read that have had an impact on you, and you kind of have an idea of What Work Should Be. You don't know what your *own* work is yet, but once you've done enough of your own work—you don't really pick your style. It picks you.

Sim: It doesn't matter what you do, your work comes out on the page.

Seth: Your only hope is that whoever you are turns out to be any good. I have a question that's kind of unrelated to this. Do you feel that living in Kitchener has had a specific effect on your work itself? Not to imply "regionalism" of any sort, but do you feel that the physical place that you live in has had an effect on your work, or that the work has been separate from "where you are?"

Sim: As with just about any question along those lines, the problem that I have with it is that there's no "control group." If there were a Dave Sim that lived in Toronto or a Dave Sim that had lived in New York instead of just traveling to those places infrequently, I could look at his work and look at Kitchener Dave Sim's work and say, "Okay, here are the differences." I think probably the fact that I was the only comic-book artist around here in town probably made a difference. In all likelihood it probably made me—just tying it in with what we're talking about—made me less inclined to seek out criticism. All of the reaction that I got because it was at conventions or in the mail was so "far after the fact" that I was always working on different stuff and wasn't really that enamored of what I did three months ago anyway.

Seth: I think it's kind of interesting—the differences between cartoonists and painters—in that painters, even if they're working toward the international stage, they tend to be involved in some sort of local scene. They still have a place in town where they hang their work, and they're connected to the area that they're in—at least in the early stages—and have a connection with their peers, whereas with cartoonists it seems like a more strangely solitary profession. Your work goes out into the world independently and has little to do with the actual environment that you live in—in the way that other art "scenes" do. Still, I think that when you're dealing with life, you can't help but have the place that you live be an integral part of the work, somehow. But in the case of cartooning, it's not as obvious what that is.

Retro Man

GERALD HANNON / 2006

Toronto Life (January 2006). Reprinted by permission.

He wears forties suits and hides away in his basement concocting a comic book town called *Palookaville*. For Seth, it can be hard to tell where the fantasy ends and the real world begins.

When the telephone rings in his apartment, it actually rings. It doesn't warble or twitter electronically, or give you a blast of the latest hip hop hit. It rings the way telephones used to ring in the movies—a jangling, insistent bell that would cue the camera to pan down to that squat, black, suddenly ominous instrument with its worn dial. A hand, perhaps with chipped nail polish, would settle on the receiver, hesitate, and the music would swell. Part of you would think, Answer it, answer it, and part of you would think, don't, don't. It's him.

Seth's telephone looks exactly like the ones in those forties movies. It's ringing this afternoon, but he doesn't answer it. He is a well-mannered man of forty-three whom you might easily mistake for thirty and just as easily mistake for a character in an exercise in noir. He is slim, smooth faced with slightly chubby cheeks, possessed of luxuriantly black hair haphazardly parted in the middle in a vaguely Edwardian fashion. He wears round glasses. He is very pale—he is not a man who sees a lot of sunlight. When we met at the Guelph bus station, he was dressed as he always is: in a vintage suit, white shirt, a period tie, and a fedora; but now, in his apartment and in deference to the room's warmth, he has removed the jacket and, of course, the hat.

He shares the first floor of a small brick house in downtown Guelph with Tania, his thirty-year-old wife of three and a half years, and three cats, Orange, Greyboy, and Little Lulu. It is perhaps the strangest apartment I have ever been in. On the outside of the door, there are two small signs. One reads, "*Palookaville*: Central Depot. Please Knock Loudly." The other reads,

"Headquarters of the Honourable Northern Brush, Ink, Pastepot and Beef-steak Society." That door opens directly onto a small living room that is richly, exuberantly, voluptuously eccentric. There are shelves of dolls and figurines. There is a horse from a merry-go-round. There are many, many books. There is a stuffed dog and a stuffed squirrel. There is a plastic nurse doll. There are framed cartoons on the walls. There is a fire chief's hat. There is a whole shelf of trophies, all of them awarded by Seth to himself, the brass plates on the bases recording one disappointment after another—"Never Called a Boy Wonder, Seth, 1962–1987" is just one of them. When I tell him that, as a child, I was a great fan of *Little Lulu*, he points out that he has a complete collection of those comics, in reprint in fifteen volumes, plus 135 originals. When I mention that I loved Plastic Man, he shows me a *Plastic Man* comic. When I tell him that I can't remember the name of Plastic Man's fat sidekick, he replies that it's Woozy Winks. Of course.

Guelph, in all its happy banality, may be just outside the door, but I'm in *Palookaville* now, a town where the telephones still ring, where disappointments have the luster of success, where men wear hats and marry late, where the only time of day is twilight; a town where a man can live his life twice— once in real time and again in the hyper-real time we know as art.

Seth, born Gregory Gallant, is a cartoonist, a comic book creator, a graphic novelist, an illustrator, an artist. Your choice—he'll answer to any of them. Since 1991, he has produced eighteen issues of the comic book series *Palookaville* and three graphic novels (*Clyde Fans, Book One*, *Wimbledon Green*, and *It's a Good Life, If You Don't Weaken*), and has published a collection from his sketchbooks under the title *Vernacular Drawings*. The Art Gallery of Ontario featured his work in an exhibition that ran last summer and fall and which opens at Guelph's Macdonald Stewart Art Center this month. It includes panels from his graphic novels and an obsessively detailed model he built in cardboard of a town he calls Dominion, which appears in *Clyde Fans*. He also designed and illustrated *Bannock, Beans and Black Tea* [2004], a memoir about growing up in Depression-era Prince Edward Island that he encouraged his father, John Gallant, to write. As far as magazine illustration is concerned, Seth has reached the peak of the profession—two *New Yorker* covers and a two-page spread in the August 29 issue. The National Film Board is preparing a documentary on him. He designed and illustrated Toronto writer Derek McCormack's new book, *Christmas Days* [2005] ("an Advent calendar in words and images"). *Wimbledon Green* was published in October. He'll be designing and illustrating a book about cocktails [*Classic Cocktails: A Modern Shake*, published in 2006] by Mark Kingwell. He is on contract to design the collected *Peanuts* and has already completed several volumes.

Readers who have avoided comics since an adolescent obsession with *Spider-Man* or *Archie* will find much that is familiar—and much that is decidedly different—in the world of graphic novels. Both, of course, tell their stories largely through pictures, though in the case of comics, the cartoonist would most often be illustrating someone else's storyline. Graphic novelists like Seth produce both text and art, and the resulting "novels" take on themes that comics, with their focus on gags and teen fulfillment fantasies, could never address. *Maus*, by Art Spiegelman, about his father's experience of the Holocaust, was published in the early eighties and is one of the first serious graphic novels. Long a coterie interest, such works are gaining a wider fan base—Daniel Clowes's novel *Ghost World* became the basis for the well-received 2000 film of the same name. Peter Birkemoe, owner of the Toronto comic book store The Beguiling on Markham Street, notes that buyers, once largely male and young, are now almost as likely to be female and well beyond university age. Partly, he says, it's because comic novels have matured and now attract serious reviewers in the mainstream press, and that has drawn a whole new audience willing to experiment.

Among graphic novelists, Seth has emerged as a poet of the dispossessed, a man who brings an adolescent fervor to the attenuating joys of the old and disappointed and infirm, to the plight of the hapless and bewildered young. The *Palookaville* series was heavily autobiographical for most of the earlier issues but now is devoted to continuing the story of the world-weary Matchcard brothers, Simon and Abraham. It is an exercise in the terror of lives writ small—as the realization slowly dawns on the brothers that they are responsible for their own sadness. The series isn't, for all that, a depressing read—there are too many flashes of wit, too frequent a nod toward a Charlie Brownish resilience of the human spirit.

Seth works obsessively, in a small, cramped studio in the basement. "Work," he says, "is what my life is about." He rises at seven most days and is at his desk by eight. He works until four, then takes a break until seven, when he returns to the basement and stays at it until eleven or later. There is a computer in the room—though he does not use it for drawing, which he does in the old-fashioned way, with pencil, pen, and brush, using overlays for the color effects he wants. It can take him thirteen hours to produce a single page. He expects that he has a good two more years of work before *Clyde Fans, Book Two* will be done.

He's been drawing since he was a child. Born in Clinton, Ontario, a small town west of Stratford (notable, he points out, for being both Alice Munro's home and the town where Steven Truscott was accused of raping and murdering twelve-year-old Lynn Harper), he grew up mostly in Tilbury, near Windsor (his father, he says, loved to move, and even in Tilbury they would change houses every year). The youngest of five children, he has three brothers and a sister. John Gallant had only a Grade 2 education (*Bannock, Beans and Black Tea* makes it clear how heartbreakingly difficult John's life was), though after the war and some thirty years in the military, he returned to school and upgraded himself to the point where he got a job teaching technical studies in high school. Seth's mother, Violet, is English—she and John met during the war. Though his parents separated when he was twenty and his father remarried and has moved back to [Prince Edward Island], Seth is sweetly tender about them both, particularly about his mother, who was ailing and suffering from dementia when Seth and I first spoke. "It is the great sadness of my life now," he says. "I really love her so much. Back when I was in my twenties, I would wonder how I would deal with my mom's death, and I couldn't imagine it. Now she's dying in bits and pieces. There's this feeling that when your mother dies you're truly alone in a way."

I did not meet her, nor see them together (she died as I was writing the final pages of this article), but I feel I glimpse his love, and his resignation too, in the way his character Simon Matchcard deals with an aging mother who is weary and prey to strange and terrifying delusions. In *Palookaville*, he gently removes her glasses when she falls asleep in front of the television. He guides her upstairs to bed, she in her housecoat, muttering incoherently, fearing the beings that come out of the light socket every night. Then he dreams of drowning. The panels sometimes show only the characters' shadows. The only color is a muted grey blue.

Seth describes himself as a child as "a crybaby, a mama's boy, picked on, someone who took a long time to learn socialization skills. A typical comic book kid, over-sensitive, not good at sports, without many friends, so I spent a lot of time by myself." Much of that time alone was spent reading comics. "His room was full of them," his father remembers. "All he seemed to do was sit in that room and draw—I think he was only six or seven when he began, and he'd figure out stories all by himself. That was his main pastime—drawing."

He kept many of them and has had them bound in hardcover, along with diary-like entries about his life at the time. The text he keeps private, but the illustrations display a young man's preoccupation with superheroes. As he says, "Superheroes play into the loser teenager fantasy so well, the sense that

Simon dreams of drowning. From *Palookaville* issue 17 © Seth. Used with permission from Drawn & Quarterly.

you have special powers inside that no one can see. It's so baldly revealing, it's kind of embarrassing. But I made comics as a way of entering the portal of a fantasy world, and it gave me a rich interior life and focused my imagination." No one looking at them now would recognize Seth's distinctive hand or his current obsessions. The superheroes he created then looked like standard comic book characters and had the usual adventures, though one of them, The Bobcat, became a stand-in for himself, lived in a tiny town not unlike Tilbury, and had the most comically unappealing costume—a mask that appears to consist of a small, furry animal that had crawled on the hero's head and died. This was not a life he shared with others. "Nobody knew at school," he says. "Being a comic fan was not a road to being more popular, so I kept it to myself. I also did separate comics involving sex but destroyed them. I found out later that every cartoonist did that—created sex comics and then destroyed them."

His own sexual initiation would become the subject of the third issue of *Palookaville*, published in June 1993. In it, Greg Gallant is in his final year of high school in Tilbury, beginning an affair with an older, married woman who works in the same restaurant as he. It's completely charming and deftly executed, with the cinematic pacing that informs all his work. It no longer pleases him, though. "I have long since written them off as bad work," he insists. "It lacks in the detail of real life and feels too falsely constructed."

That issue of the comic more or less ends with his leaving home for art college in Toronto. "I knew I was going to be an artist," he says, "and if you wanted to be an artist, you went to art school. I turned up for my portfolio review, and I showed them my 'art,' watercolors and things like that, and the guy said, 'OK, show me your real stuff.' So I pulled out the comics. That's what got me in the door."

If Gallant left Tilbury in 1980 a shy, comic-obsessed nerd, he was soon a dazzler at the Ontario College of Art. Maurice Vellekoop, a stylistically different but equally talented artist and illustrator, was at OCA at the same time and remembers being awestruck by him. "He wore lots of leather and silver, had bleached-blond hair, wore makeup. He knew so many freaks and went to nightclubs filled with cross-dressers and drug addicts."

Gregory Gallant had discovered punk culture. "It seemed exciting and super-modern," he says. "So I made the transition, but it was private at first, and I didn't know there was a whole punk world until I went to a punk bar for the first time, and suddenly I felt completely at ease and made friends—it freed me from all those feelings I had as a teen." It led to his reinvention as Seth. It also led to being queer bashed.

The very first issue of *Palookaville*, published in April 1991, is devoted to an incident years before, when the very heterosexual Seth—in a flouncy long coat, his man-purse over his shoulder, his hair, goatee, and eyebrows dyed platinum blond—took the subway (clearly the Toronto subway; one of the delights of Seth's work is recognizing local landmarks). Unfortunately, he happened to share a car with a group of homophobic goons who began calling him a fuckin' faggot and cocksuckin' freak, and he made the mistake, as one frame delicately puts it, of blowing kisses at them as he left the car. They followed. He ran. They caught him just outside the toll booth and beat him very badly. The TTC fare collectors just watched. There's more to the story, told with much verve and self-deprecating humor. The frames move from close-ups to long shots. There is a sense of rhythm and cadence, action panels alternating with quieter, more reflective scenes. According to Vellekoop, who remembers the incident, "The characters in the nightclub section were all friends, and he caught their essence and every detail perfectly." There is a wonderful epilogue—one page, nine panels, all of them focused on Seth himself as he smokes a cigarette (he still smokes, though intermittently and somewhat guiltily) and sums up the story for us, but those nine simple panels are a small masterpiece of concision, elegance and variety within brutally tight and self-imposed limits. And the whole thing, except for the front and back covers, is in black and white.

He can't remember the exact date, but Greg renamed himself within three years of his arrival in Toronto. Changing his name was a conscious effort to create a new identity. "I picked the most pretentious, scariest name I'd heard, and it was Seth. I liked the Egyptian connection, too; Seth was the brother of Osiris. I was very determined about it. I always corrected people if they called me by my old name, and within a year I was Seth. It worked well for separating myself from my younger self, but it's not the name I'd pick if I were choosing now. It really seems pretentious to have a single name."

The name change also came with a new look—the now trademark vintage suits, hats, and ties. He is never seen without them. I asked Peter Birkemoe, a longtime friend of Seth's, whether he'd ever seen him in mufti. "I've shared a hotel room with him," he says, "so I've seen him in a T-shirt. But never any other way." That sartorial eccentricity began with a developing interest in the jazz and big band music of the twenties, thirties, and forties. As Seth puts it, "I'm an obsessive, and I wanted to extend that interest in the mid-twentieth century to all aspects of my life. And I did extend it to everything. If I wanted a tea kettle, it had to be the right kind. For a long time, the way I dressed was deliberately anachronistic, but now it's mostly a habit."

A masterpiece of concision. From *Palookaville* issue 1. © Seth. Used with permission from Drawn & Quarterly.

For an artist who made such a confident personal debut with the first issue of *Palookaville*, it's surprising that he never graduated from art college.
"I dropped out near the end of third year," he says, "because I lost direction
completely. I entered school a hick, small-town boy who wanted to draw superhero comics, but by third year I was more interested in taking drugs and
screwing up. My schoolwork declined terribly—when I did it—and I no longer had any idea what I was going to do art wise." By then, he had also discovered the comic book worlds of Robert Crumb and Los Angeles's Hernandez
brothers. Superheroes didn't cut it anymore.

What he did was take a job with the Vortex Comics company on Queen
West in Toronto, where he slugged away for three or four years in the mid-
eighties producing *Mister X*, a comic he calls "a quirky sci-fi mystery set in an
art deco city of the future." It was not a job he loved, though he did end up
meeting Chester Brown there, a fellow cartoonist with whom he quickly became friends. Brown remembers being a little afraid of him when they met—
this was Seth of the white makeup, a big cane (acquired for self-defense after the bashing), and the white hair. Brown got past that, and they regularly
hung out together, but he remembers that Seth "hated working on *Mister X*,
hated working with writers. He was just too slow, and he hated work that he
found so uninspiring. The publisher finally fired him, and he turned to illustration to make ends meet."

I met him then, in the late eighties. I'd taken my first freelance job, editing
a union magazine for television producers at the CBC, and used him several
times for illustration. It didn't pay very much, and I'm pretty sure the editorial board didn't appreciate the bargain they were getting, but he scrupulously
delivered brilliant stuff, on deadline, no complaints. Even today, he provides
charming spot illustrations for *CA Magazine*, the magazine for chartered ac-
countants that he's contributed to for years. "Somewhere in the back of my
mind, I think I might still need the money, so I don't burn any bridges. And I
tend to be loyal to people who are loyal to me."

He has certainly been loyal to Drawn & Quarterly, the Montreal-based
publisher that has released all of his graphic novel work since the first *Palookaville* in 1991. Chris Oliveros started the company sixteen years ago, when
he was just twenty-four. He says Seth sells well. *It's a Good Life, If You Don't
Weaken* has sold 15,000 copies to date, and has been translated into Span-
ish, Italian, and Dutch. *Bannock, Beans and Black Tea* has just sold out its first
printing of 6,000 copies. Those numbers may seem small, but in the world of
graphic novels, Seth is a John Irving. Only a couple of American superstars
like Crumb and Clowes sell more.

His AGO show was something of a milestone—the first time that the gallery exhibited a comic artist as a contemporary artist in full stature. "What caught my attention," says Ben Portis, the AGO's assistant curator of contemporary art, "was the extent to which young artists in galleries were doing this. Take a walk along Queen West and you'll see work by artists under thirty for whom this was the formalism they were drawing on."

When Seth married Tania van Spyk (they met in Guelph at a life drawing class), the wedding was the cartoon world's social event of the decade. Chester Brown was there, of course, along with Maurice Vellekoop and Joe Matt and Chris Ware and Daniel Clowes and James Sturm and other top names from the world of comics. Peter Birkemoe threw the stag and remembers it as "the lamest, tamest stag ever. We went bowling and then back to my parents' rec room to watch vintage nudie reels, but no one was interested, so I quickly switched to old *Betty Boop* and *Bosco the Clown* cartoons from Fleischer Studios." The wedding itself took place in an old country church. Seth wore a top hat and tails, and their families arrived in vintage dress. The other cartoonists chipped in to supply handmade decorations. The scene became quite magical, with little paper stars and moons hanging over everyone. The bride's mother did a belly dance. It was a *Palookaville* wedding.

It will be something of a *Palookaville* life. It is clearly possible for their home to accept another resident. But it's difficult—in this room of shadows and slanting afternoon light, with its nuzzling cats and its forties couch and its stuffed animals and its row of gently glinting trophies—to imagine that there's room for any other personality but his. That doesn't seem to worry Tania, who says she felt at home the moment she walked into the place: "I'm not the housewife type, and I come from a family where my dad worked all the time. So I'm used to a man's being busy."

Lucky for her. Her man will be very busy. He is the perfect exemplar of the Wildean dictum that life imitates art, though he has carried it one step further, weaving art and life so inextricably together that he is presenting us with something new and enticingly strange. It is a life that sometimes seems a boy's fantasy of what being an adult is all about, rendering it sadder, more vexed, more helpless than it really is, yet a life that is nonetheless fully mature in its assessment of itself as at once introverted and shy and ostentatiously flamboyant. It isn't easy for him. He often seems tormented by the sense that the real Seth is the work-obsessed introvert huddling over his basement drawing board, that the real Seth is perhaps still Greg Gallant, and that the endlessly conversational charmer I know strikes him as "baldly desperate, sad, pathetic. At the end of today," he tells me, "I'll say to myself,

You just never shut up, do you? I'm always fighting with myself—wanting attention and ashamed of wanting it at the same time. It's the artist's dilemma: what you're doing you're supposed to be doing for yourself, but you're always wanting others to love you, too."

He's talking real time, though. He'll get another chance. In *Palookaville*, you always live twice.

On Cartooning

REBECCA BENGAL / 2006

American Documentary/POV, PBS.org (June 29, 2006). Reprinted by permission.

POV: The ligne claire ("clear line") style Hergé employed when drawing the iconic characters of *Tintin* contrasts with the unusually realistic landscapes and backgrounds of the worlds Tintin visits and inhabits. As Scott McCloud pointed out in his book *Understanding Comics*, this contrast gives the effect of allowing the comic reader to "mask themselves in a character and safely enter a stimulating world." "One set of line," he writes, "allows readers to see; the other to be."

Your style is extremely distinctive: evocative and impressionistic in its use of light and shadow, with a compelling urgency of movement through the story. Describe your own illustrative strategy as you see it. How did you arrive at it? How do you feel it's been most effective? Did you struggle to find it or did it come naturally? When does it not work?

Seth: Style is a funny word—we all think we know what it means because we look at a cartoonist's work and we see the evidence of it there. It is right on the surface. However, the funny thing about style is that it is a misleading concept. Many young artists (myself included when I was younger) have the mistaken idea that you pick a style and draw in that style. Some people manage to do it this way. However, in my own experience it seems more likely that the style picks you. It is something that grows out of a series of choices when you are learning to cartoon. If, for example, you decide to simplify the drawings down to their most basic shapes (to aid in clear storytelling), then those choices in simplification decide your style. Perhaps you chose circles for heads and blank backgrounds—there is your style. Maybe you preferred a more atmospheric approach and you used a lot of crosshatching to define your figures—another style. Ultimately, a million choices are made in trying to figure out how to tell a comic story and these little choices (e.g., How do I draw a nose simply?) add up to a style.

This is the process that evolved my style. I certainly didn't realize it at the time, but the way I draw now is the result of thousands of such choices over the years. When I was in my early twenties, I didn't really have a clear drawing style and I was worried about acquiring one. I drew one strip in an Edward Gorey style and another in a clean line approach. I didn't know what I was doing. A few years later I was surprised to discover that I had developed some sort of style of my own by simply trying to learn to draw a comic book. It happened while I wasn't paying attention. If I was talking to a young cartoonist, I would certainly tell him/her not to worry about style. It will take care of itself. Instead pay attention to the details of your craft.

On the matter of "masking"—I'm not so sure I accept that idea. I don't think I experience this effect when I'm reading a comic myself. I simply enter into the reality of it in the same way I would a prose novel. I don't need an iconic representation in a novel to enter into the world of the story. I merely need to decode the words and have them unfold in my mind into pictures. I believe a comic does exactly the same thing, except with the comic book you must decode both the words and the pictures and combine them in your mind into a single unit. I believe this is why Hergé's clear line approach is so effective. The drawings are really a series of simplified picture symbols that are as easy for your reading brain to decode as the words are. They are remarkably clear. He is never deliberately trying to create any ambiguity in the drawings. If you had to pause to figure out the drawings in a *Tintin* comic, I would be surprised. Hergé has done a masterful job at making the storytelling clear. This straightforward approach to storytelling is exactly what I am aiming at myself in my own work, and Hergé was a large influence on my thinking back when I was young and trying to figure out how to tell a story.

POV: Among your most well-known characters are traveling salesmen and comic book collectors. How do you feel about your recurring characters? How real do they become to you as you work and live with them over the years? Do you imagine them having a life independent of the comic?
Seth: Writers often say that the characters come to life for them but sadly, that has not fully been my experience with them. Perhaps if, like Charles Schulz, you have drawn them for fifty years they come to life for you. I find that I have a good understanding of my characters and I know how they would "act" in a certain situation, but they are too fully made up out of bits and pieces for me to think of them as real. They are stitched together from

parts of myself and other people and things I have read in books or imagined; Frankenstein monsters more than real people.

I suppose, in a vague sense, they live outside of me. I do feel that with a character like Wimbledon Green, that he carries on somehow after the book is finished. If I wanted to, I could sort of squint and take a look and see what he is "up to" and then write another comic story about him. But that all seems to be happening in some dark, rarely visited back corner of my brain.

Generally, I am not much interested in continuing characters (for my own work). I like to come up with a story that has a beginning and an end. However, I don't impose that restriction on others. Sometimes a continuing character works. As a reader, I often want more of a character after I finish a book—so I am no different than any other reader. The temptation to return to a character who has been well received is a difficult one for a cartoonist—and it is easy to make a mistake and return to that well one too many times and find it has run dry. The history of cartooning is mostly the history of famous cartoon "characters"—not powerful or meaningful stories. As an artist—I am not overly concerned with creating characters. Mostly I am trying to capture something about life itself and convey it through the person who the story is about. Hopefully they become interesting people rather than great cartoon characters.

POV: Describe your working process. Do you work daily? When you begin a comic, do you start with image, or with text? What are the raw materials of a story? Do you always know what is going to happen, or does the story take turns that surprise you?

Seth: I work every day. Though I work on a wide variety of projects and some days I don't get to do any cartooning—I may just be drawing or designing for a commercial project. I find that the longer the period is between actually working on a comic strip, the more likely I am to be depressed. Something about cartooning is just more satisfying to me than any other artistic pursuit (though it is also more difficult). Usually my ideas come to me in a vague form—just a feeling or a situation or a setting—and then as I develop the idea it constitutes itself into a comic form in my brain. Not that it becomes anything complete, merely that I start to see it with a kind of structure or rhythm. In other words, much like a writer might start to put together sentences in his mind to describe the scene he is imagining, I start to imagine comic panels and the sequences they may flow in. When I actually sit down and start drawing little thumbnail sketches of the strip, it may take on an entirely separate narrative flow, but it usually starts with at least one simple sequence—say, a character rising from his bed while recalling a dream. It never starts as a series of words that then have pictures added to them. I would imagine a filmmaker thinks in a somewhat similar way—imagining scenes with movement rather than just characters' dialogue which will then need some visuals.

A lot of my story ideas take years to develop, usually starting with something very nebulous, like an interesting building I might see on a drive somewhere, and then over time other little odd bits and pieces will be added to it. Perhaps I will read a book and it will mention some occupation that interests me (a trainspotter for example), and I might then imagine that this fellow lives in that house. Eventually these things come together into some sort of an empty skeleton. I often have many of these skeletons rattling around in my brain. What changes them into real material for me is if something human from my own life gets added to them to make them vital. Perhaps this guy will become the vehicle to discuss the relationship I have with my father (or some such thing). When this alchemy happens I am often surprised. The stories themselves are always a bit of a surprise to me because I never really try to come up with "plots" for them and so I don't really know what they are about (in some ways) until they are up and running.

POV: You've said that comic writing is much like poetry because so much depends on rhythm; you also said you believe comics are closer to being like a combination of poetry and design than drawings and literature, or film and literature. Can you talk a little more about what you mean by that—and how cartooning is different for you as a creative process than working in other genres like illustration and design?

Seth: Illustration and design are almost purely visual activities while comics is mostly a storytelling medium. That makes them very different right from the start. While working on those activities I am merely thinking of trying to create something aesthetically pleasing that treats the viewer with some kind of respect. I try to get some sort of sense of humor into it too—and some beauty. All of my art has a real hand-done feeling to it so I want it to be beautiful in some fundamental way—it should look human and warm.

Now comics—that is a lot more complicated. In comics I am trying to be an "artist" in the bigger sense, and I'm trying to convey something of real life experience. Every day I go down into my studio and I feel a real variety of human emotions—the whole experience of spending so much time alone (which a cartoonist must do simply to do the work) engaged in introspection and memory really fires my entire purpose as an artist. It is very frustrating

Interesting buildings lead to stories. From *Clyde Fans, Book One* © Seth. Used with permission from Drawn & Quarterly.

to me that this deepest [level] of feeling is the hardest thing to get down on the page. I don't feel I have ever managed to get even a tenth of it into anything I do. I think as a human being there is a strong desire to communicate to others all that turmoil of emotion that is locked up inside of us. The experience of inside and outside is so profound—we live in this exterior world but everything is understood from inside our minds. We really live in here and not out there. That interior landscape is so difficult to portray—but that seems to be the thing most important to try to share.

As for comics and poetry: The connection between the two is fairly obvious if you've ever sat down to write a one-page comic. The entire process is concerned with rhythm and condensed language. In many ways, the restrictions placed on a cartoonist when he writes (amount of text that will fit in a word balloon or caption) and the very nature of how reading panels creates a rhythm, a cadence, in the reader's mind makes a pretty good case for comparing the two disciplines.

POV: Marshall McLuhan, author of the 1967 book *The Medium Is the Massage*, wrote about the differences between what he called "hot" media versus "cool" media. Hot media, like movies and radio, he said, were dense with data and therefore demanded only a passive audience, whereas "cool" media, lo-fi and utilizing iconic forms, required active, involved audience participation. His examples of "cool" media are television and comics. Do you agree with McLuhan's assessment?

Seth: Being a fellow Canadian, I agree with McLuhan on nationalistic terms alone. Seriously, though, I think McLuhan is dead right. It could be simply self-interest but I do think that comics (like prose) require a more active involvement of the reader. As I mentioned earlier, simply reading a comic book is a process of deciphering the words and images simultaneously. That sounds rather impressive, but of course, if you've read any comic (even *Garfield*, for example) you realize that it is a rather natural process and doesn't require any study. Whenever I hear someone say they met someone who doesn't know how to read a comic book, I am always perplexed. It seems pretty easy to me. If you are having too much trouble reading a comic, I suspect the cartoonist has done a poor job of his storytelling.

Simple or not, I do believe comics are an inherently fascinating art medium. In the hands of a talented and ambitious cartoonist the work can be an extremely layered reading experience and can involve as much analysis from the reader as they wish to put into it. I think the electronic media of film and television can be as richly layered—but I would agree with McLuhan that the viewer is mostly in a passive state while taking it in. They are both more clearly group experiences, too. Reading remains a more intimate process—one to one. That one to one relationship between artist and reader appeals to me.

POV: You're redesigning *The Complete Peanuts* as a twenty-five-book series for Fantagraphics; you've also said that you were significantly influenced by *Tintin*. How have these comics found their way into your work, consciously or perhaps unintentionally? What about other influences of yours, like the short stories of Alice Munro?

Seth: Personally I am a sponge when it comes to influences. I have been influenced by an endless stream of other artists and writers and filmmakers.

At some point the word "influence" seems to be a poor choice, because after a certain age you are less being influenced than simply outright stealing from your peers (which I have certainly done). Generally, when I consider my influences, I tend to go back to the "seminal"—the ones I was drawn to at a young age and had tried my best to absorb whatever I could from them. Schulz was the most powerful. His work interested me at an early age and has continued all of my life. I didn't understand as a child why I was drawn to his work (I just thought it was funny) but later, in my early twenties, I began to go back and reread all of those *Peanuts* books I had loved as a kid. I came to really see and appreciate the sensitive genius he was. Unlike any other cartoonist working in that commercial venue, Schulz managed to infuse a very personal and idiosyncratic vision into what was essentially a kiddie gag strip. The work had a lot of black humor, and it was sad, poignant, and dark, but not in a calculated way. Schulz was simply fusing his own inner life with the characters. It touched people even if they never understood why they were responding to it. He really was one of a kind. Funny, smart, subtle, mean, and emotional. A rare type to find working in newspaper strips in those days.

Later, I discovered Robert Crumb. Crumb is surprisingly like Schulz in that he used comics as a natural outlet for his own inner life. Unlike Schulz, he was not restrained by the conventional media, nor was he from the same generation as Schulz. Crumb's self-expression was markedly bolder and more startling, but essentially, these two artists are not that different from each other. Both of them are amazing examples for a young cartoonist—neither compromised their vision in any way. They both took what was a straightforward commercial art medium and used it as a very personal method of self-expression. These men were great pointers for a young artist to follow.

When I was about nineteen or twenty, I began to be interested in the three artists that would hold my interest in that first half of my twenties: Crumb, J. D. Salinger, and Woody Allen. The last two have slipped somewhat from my radar over the last decade, but in those years these men were very influential in my thinking. In retrospect, it tells me a lot about myself that I was drawn to these three artists and not others. All of them were somewhat introspective and backward-looking and none of them were artists with a capital "A." I certainly wouldn't put myself in a list with these men, but these are the qualities that I was clearly looking for in them.

There are many artists who have been important to me since then, and out of those a good number of artists I am most drawn to are oddball loner types—somehow I really admire these characters who produced art for such personal reasons (often getting little positive feedback from the outside world). That purity is very appealing. And certainly in the last decade I have found myself responding heavily to a handful of Japanese writers from the early twentieth century ([Jun'ichirō] Tanizaki, [Yasunari] Kawabata, [Yukio] Mishima, et cetera) whose slow and patient interior storytelling appeals to me greatly. Alice Munro is definitely among my very favorite writers simply because she has such a deep, deep understanding of the inner life. I would never list her as an influence because what she does is mysterious and is something beyond my ability to incorporate or even outright steal.

As for *Tintin*: Hergé came along at just the right time for me. I started studying his work in my early twenties, and this was when I really needed some examples of how to tell a story clearly and cleanly. That brilliant clarity of line and design in *Tintin* was the object lesson I needed.

POV: Although some have approached its widespread popularity, there is no exact parallel to *Tintin* in American comics. Why do you think this is so? What in American comics comes closest to *Tintin* and approximating the cult of *Tintin*? In other media?

Seth: It probably has something to do with national character. America and France/Belgium are such different places, and I think the popular media of these two cultures reflect something on the character of the countries themselves. America adopted the superhero as its model (eventually) and this seems to have filled the same role for young children that *Tintin* filled for much of the rest of the world. The difference between a *Tintin* and a *Superman* is an interesting comparison, and I think it says an awful lot about how Americans view themselves vs. how Europeans do. I don't think it is a coincidence that both of these iconic figures rose to popularity during the thirties and WWII. I won't bore you with an essay about what these two characters represent. I think it is pretty obvious right on the surface.

Certainly Hergé's example was a better model for producing lasting cartooning. The very format of the hardcover Tintin albums vs. the disposable pamphlets of the American comic books meant that the North American artists would naturally be viewed differently than their European counterparts. It has made for a longer steeper climb for cartoons to find an adult audience over here in America.

POV: Pop artists like Andy Warhol and [Roy] Lichtenstein, and other artists like Raymond Pettibo, have certainly been influenced by comics and have incorporated elements of them into their paintings. (Warhol was particularly influenced by Hergé.) And of course, Art Spiegelman really struck a nerve with a literary and a mainstream audience with *Maus*. In the last few years, a number of literary journals have been devoting space to comics; the *New York Times* magazine began serializing comics in 2005, beginning with Chris Ware's. Although for years comics have been denigrated as a so-called "low art" category, it appears they're becoming not only more popular and widely accepted, but perhaps even validated as a form of art and a long literary narrative. Would you agree with this? Is "form" the right word here? Do you think that this kind of validation is inhibiting in any way, that comics are in danger of becoming less rebellious or creatively free because they're more accepted and being published in the mainstream?

Seth: It has been a long uphill climb for the lowly comic artist. Lately, it seems as if we have finally gotten our heads out of the water and have made some important steps to get out onto the beach. Personally, I think this is great. I have no desire to hang onto any kind of outsider status. I would like the comic book (or "graphic novel") to be a perfectly legitimate medium for artistic pursuit. We are much closer to people perceiving it that way. I think there are currently a handful of cartoonists working today at a level that is equal to any other group of artists in any of the other mediums. I can't control how the work will be perceived or labeled—I simply know that the comic medium is like any other medium. It has its own strengths and weaknesses and it is only as good an artistic tool as the artists who practice it. It has a lot of negative baggage as a junk medium—but film and photography were once in this camp also. I have faith in it. However, the outside attention that comics has been receiving in the last few years has been very gratifying. I've noticed a large change in how my own work is being received. Things have changed significantly in a pretty short time period. I have no worries about the rebelliousness of the medium being squashed—already a new generation of cartoonists has risen up behind me that seems to be rebelling against all the directions we took. It appears to me that this new generation wants to get some "fun" back into the medium and that they aren't all that interested in producing "long and complex" narratives like the "old farts" of my cartooning generation. The comic book has real roots in the junk culture and no matter how much highfalutin acceptance it gets there will always be a contingent of cartoonists waiting to remind us of its origins. Which is also a good thing.

POV: Do you think it's also fair to say that a division or tension exists within the world of American comics, between the mainstream daily syndicated comic strip world or, say the *New Yorker* cartoon world, of which you are a part, and the comics underground/graphic novel world, of which you are also a part?

Seth: They are all part of some kind of a continuum because they are all forms of cartooning. But—the intentions of the artists in these various camps are quite different. I can respect and enjoy cartooning that strives for more traditional goals (e.g., simply going for a laugh) but I don't feel a great affinity necessarily with these cartoonists. I would probably feel more of a connection with another artist (of any medium really) simply based on what their artistic intentions are. For me it is a desire to communicate something of the inner life. In some ways this is probably closer to a contemporary fiction writer than a newspaper comic strip artist or a *New Yorker* gag cartoonist. That doesn't mean I don't feel any connection to these artists—I do. But it is often based more on a shared cartooning history rather than where we are heading.

POV: Hergé underwent a period of despair and anxiety during which he suffered recurring nightmares filled with whiteness—certainly iconic dreams for a cartoonist! Eventually, after psychoanalysis, he emerged with a new direction: *Tintin in Tibet*, with its stark alpine landscapes and minimalist cast and story, was a major departure for Hergé. Do you have periods when you lose faith in your work? How have you handled them? What do you feel is your greatest creative or artistic accomplishment?

Seth: "Do you have periods where you lose faith in your work?" Yes—those periods are called "every day." I find the process of cartooning a genuine struggle. You must have the confidence in yourself to pursue your work and publish it (you've got to have some faith in it to send it out into the world) but you must also have enough doubt about what you are doing to constantly try to tear it apart and try to make it better. It is a tightrope walk that is never very pleasant.

A cartoonist has a very isolated job. You sit in a room with yourself every day, all day. You have to come to some sort of truce with yourself. It is difficult to do, and easy to become depressed or melancholic. When I first read of Hergé's troubles, years ago, I was not surprised. It seems an archetypal cartoonist story. The fact that this depression became fodder for his work strikes me as just what I would expect. You work it out at the drawing board—I could relate to that.

As for my greatest creative accomplishment—that is the work yet to come. I like some of what I have produced and others, not so much. The work that most holds my interest is the work-to-be.

POV: How does politics influence or impact your work in comics (or not)? Has it had a lesser or greater effect over the years?

Seth: I am really not much of a political person. I have political beliefs, but they don't occupy a large part of my daily life. I am so utterly self-obsessed that my main artistic concerns are generally informed more by my inner world than the political realities of the outer world. Clearly I am a typical product of this pampered North American affluence in that I can afford to be complacent and contemplate my own navel. When the end of the world hits (any day now), I am sure I will suddenly find out what a sheltered cry-baby I was. But it will be too late then to have made any effort to prevent what I am currently ignoring.

POV: What are you working on now?

Seth: I am plowing ahead with the second part of my book *Clyde Fans*. I hope to have a good chunk of it done by the end of this year and the whole book hopefully finished up in another year after that (with luck). Look for the next issue of *Comic Art Magazine* (no. 8) for a small hundred-page book (titled: *Forty Cartoon Books of Interest*) that is shrink-wrapped in with it. This is a little book I recently produced that explores some of my collecting interests over the last twenty years.

It looks like there may be a strip in the works for a high profile magazine—but the negotiations have just begun on this so I am not naming any names just in case it doesn't happen [Seth is referring to *George Sprott*, later serialized weekly in the pages of the *New York Times Magazine* from September 24, 2006 to March 25, 2007].

Talking to Seth

THOM ERNST / 2009

Toro Magazine (March 4, 2009). Reprinted by permission.

Q: Gregory Gallant is a sophisticated and respectable enough name—why change to Seth?
A: I wouldn't change it now, if it were up to me. It was a decision made long ago. Like most comic book people I had a relatively isolated childhood. I was a kid who spent a lot of time by himself, didn't get along well with the other kids. I grew up in a small town, and when I hit the big city, it was a chance to start a new life—to rebrand myself. I think sometime in my early twenties, along with trying to put my entire childhood behind me—I mean, I didn't sit down and say to myself, "Here's a chance to create a whole new identity"—it was part of a process I was going through of trying to be somebody else, I think. At some point I just picked a new name.

You see, for the first and the only time in my life I felt connected to the youth culture. I was involved with the punk scene and the nightclub scene and I got heavily involved in creating a whole new persona for myself and eventually that also involved coming up with a new name. And the new name stuck around long enough that when I began my career as a cartoonist I was still in favor of that idea. Eventually, by the time I established myself as a cartoonist the name was connected to it. I wouldn't have done it, in retrospect. My own name is fine. I don't have any real problems with it any longer, but going back on it now is as lame as having a fake name.

Q: It would be like Prince changing his name to a symbol.
A: Or even worse, John Cougar going back in that long process to John Mellencamp, which was mortifying to have to phase it in through three different stages.

Q: How do you convince people your name is no longer Gregory but Seth?

A: You do it very aggressively is how you do it. Once you've decided you're changing your name and it's not like someone's given you a nickname, it's up to you. You tell everyone your name has changed and you force them to use it. And every time they use your old name, you correct them until eventually it becomes second nature.

Q: Unless, of course, they're your family.

A: Family too.

Q: Really?

A: I made my family change my name too. They don't call me anything but Seth.

Q: So if you want to be called Seth, how is it possible it was so easy to find out your real name?

A: Initially I tried to bury the name. So I wouldn't tell people my real name, but at some point I no longer cared about it. The whole thing seemed silly. So at some point it was a non-issue. If anybody asked me my name, I would tell them. And now it always appears in my book somewhere—in the copyright or somewhere. It's just an old affectation now. I don't give a second thought to the fact that the name is available. I think a lot of people assume that Seth is just a professional name and in my real life I go by my old name, but it's not true. I've been Seth for so long it is like a nickname that has stuck. It's the name I'm used to.

Q: What does your wife call you?

A: She calls me Seth. She never met me in any other guise except Seth. The name Gregory would seem totally wrong from her.

Q: It's a great name. I won't ask where you got it because that's your little secret. But I wish I thought of it myself.

Now, how do you respond to this statement: "There is no such thing as graphic novels, only comic books"?

A: I would agree with the statement. "Graphic novel" is a red herring name—something that was come up with to provide a more respectable term for comic books.

I think comics are a lot like movies in that they are both twentieth-century art forms, primarily. And that they started out as popular forms and that they had funny names: movies, comics. But movies always had the word "film" too, which was the more sophisticated term you could use. But comics really had nothing else, which is one of its problems. "Comic" or "funnies," these kind of terms, much like "movies," were popular names that came up to basically describe the overall effect of them: movies move, comics are comic.

But the problem with "comic" is that it's not a very effective term. It really doesn't describe much of what goes on. And once you get away from humor it is pretty much a misnomer. But "graphic novels" is not a better answer. At this point, much like my own fake name, you should just say, "Well, who cares?" They should just be "comics," and people should just be used to it. But the term "graphic novel" has stuck. I didn't think it would have any legs, but it seems to have caught on and now it's an effective marketing tool, so I've gotten used to it.

Q: The term "literary comic book" gets tossed around too.
A: Yeah. That's a bad term too. They're all Frankenstein constructions. "Literary comic book" is also very limited in that it implies there's a literary purpose to it. A lot of the comics for adults aren't very literary in nature. Some of them are purely surreal or almost non-narrative. There are a lot of young cartoonists around that I certainly would not call their work literary. But it is clearly art—it's not just popular work or genre work.

"Art comics" has started to come up in the last few years as a term. Which is also an awkward term but it does cover a lot of ground in that it implies these comics were produced to be art forms rather than commercial forms. I just usually stick to the term "comic book" or "cartooning." I almost call all my books "picture novellas," but that started out as a joke. I stuck with it because it's got a nice antiquated sound to it.

Q: If titles alone could sell, everything would be called *It's a Good Life, If You Don't Weaken*. What inspired such a perfect linking of words?
A: It's an old saying, though it's not the exact old saying. The actual saying is "It's a great life, if you don't weaken." But my mother use to say it to me all the time, and she naturally lessened it. I grew up with the lesser version which is, "It's a good life," which just seemed the natural title to me at some point when I was working on that book.

Q: Do you believe it's a good life if you don't weaken?
A: I do. I believe it very firmly. If there's one thing my mother taught me, it's a certain stoicism. I do believe that it's a beautiful world but you must have

an inner resolve to appreciate life. It's a combination of both recognizing the beauty and also having the ability, at the same time, to remain firm enough in the world to be able to enjoy it.

Q: I have no problem believing that an ex-punker could become a successful cartoonist, but I find it fascinating that an ex-punker and cartoonist has such a positive outlook.
A: Yeah, well, I think I'm basically a positive person. Even when I was a punk, I was an enthusiastic punk. I wasn't a "no future" punk.

Q: So this seemingly endless meeting of movies and comics—is it natural that the two should collide?
A: Only commercially. I don't think the forms have much to do with each other. People associate them with each other a lot because they're a combination of word and image, so it seems natural that you would connect them somehow. But I don't really think comics and film operate in the same manner at all. In fact I think they would almost be completely disconnected if it weren't for what happened in the 1940s.

Let me digress for a moment:

The earliest phase of commercial cartooning would be the newspaper strip. And the early newspaper strip was not in any way connected to what was going on in film. It was probably more connected, if anything, to what was going on in vaudeville. It focused on the simple idea of telling jokes—a lot of times using stereotypes, a lot of ethnic humor aimed at a new immigrant class. If you look at those early comics, almost all of them take place as if they are on a stage with the panel border being the proscenium arch, and the characters are almost always the same size. You never change the frame, you don't have any close-ups or any establishing shots—all these film terms.

It's in the forties that people like Milton Caniff come along. Also a lot of the early comic book artists—these were the first generation to grow up with film—and they start to employ film techniques in cartooning. That's when you start seeing things like close-ups, establishing shots, crane shots—all the language of film. And this stuff is very connected to cartooning. People still use all those terms. Cartoonists will say, "We'll cut to a close-up," which is clearly directly related to film. But the truth is the media don't operate in the same manner. Film is about capturing some quality of motion in the world and comics is a still medium entirely.

In the way that film is connected to photography, comics is not. Comics are a drawn language. If anything, they're very abstracted. Cartooning is trying to get away from a realistic portrayal of life. I mean this in the visual sense. If you really think about it, even what you might call realistic styles of cartooning are actually very abstracted. They're all symbols.

Even guys that drew superhero comic books and tried to make them look like real people—well, we only think of it as realism. It's actually not very realistic at all. Look at how they've chosen to portray a nose, an eye or anything of the details in human life. They are just picture symbols. Noses and eyes don´t really look like that. We just accept them as realistic because some cartoon styles are less abstracted than others.

Superman appears to be more "real" in his depiction than Andy Capp. But really they are both equally composed of symbols we have learned to recognize as noses and feet. They're symbols much like the way a written language is composed of symbols—symbols which you put together to create words and sentences. A picture language is composed of symbols that you put together to create an imagined reality.

And it's a very still form. If anything, what comics are most related to is a combination of graphic design and poetry. Because poetry is about compression of time and it's about rhythm, and comics are very connected to those two ideas. Almost everything in comics is about how you choose to deal with time and exactly how much you control a visual rhythm on the page. And graphic design, because obviously you're trying to move around images that are shapes. You're trying to move eyes around, trying to teach people how to move along the page, how to speed things up, slow things down. It's all very much a graphic language as opposed to film, which all takes place on one flat picture plane in which the story unfolds over actual time—it is clearly a real visual language based entirely on motion. They have areas where they cross over, of course. I think the big reason people connect film to comics is because of the storyboards people often use to make film.

Q: The drawn symbols used to illustrate your book *It's a Good Life, If You Don't Weaken* might well serve filmmakers intent on translating that story to the screen.

A: I think the content alone is what's being used when a comic is translated to film. What you wouldn't really be translating into film would be the actual cartooning language. I think, for example, that *Ghost World* was a good film, but it has nothing really to do with the comic. It has to do with the content of the comic. You don't even need to know that that ever was a comic. Because the language that's employed in making the comic is a different language—much like a prose book to a film—it's all about taking the story as opposed to how the story is told.

You don't usually see a film that tries to translate the actual narrative structures of a novel, like how the dialogue is structured or an interior monologue or that sort of thing into the film. What they do is they take the content, the story of *Catcher in the Rye*, say, and then they figure out a screenplay for it on how you can portray it onscreen. And you can easily do that with *It's a Good Life*—it's just a story. The actual mechanics of how you tell a story in comics only relate to film in the sense of whether you want to use the same filmic terms, again, like long shots and close-ups.

But the real mechanics of how comics work is all just symbol-based, and that's really just the technical stuff that doesn't matter to anyone except the artist. The reader isn't supposed to be paying attention to that. Let me put it this way: When I draw a person walking down a street, I'm drawing a series of symbols that you recognize as these images of a person and a street. But it's really more about how I'm choosing to place all these images on the page that matters. It's all done for the compositional effect. These decisions affect how the reader reads the story and what emotional or intellectual effect it has no them.

This is what cartooning is all about; it's about storytelling and it's about stylization. The actual content is from a different part of the brain—that's the story I'm trying to tell and that I then take and I cartoon it. It's like how you stage the play. That's where theatre comes in. The story itself is something else. You can certainly take a play and turn it into a movie, but it's not the same thing as the play. And that's how I feel about cartooning.

Q: So, is animation closer to comics?
A: No. Animation is closer to film. Animation is all about motion. If you watch animation, even the artiest animation, it's almost always about two things: transformation or motion. Animators love to transform one image into another. It's probably the most common effect you see in animation. If anything, it's just a way to do drawn film. I find that a lot of people think animation and comics have a lot in common, but when you really sit down together you find cartoonists and animators have very little to talk about.

Q: And you've run into a few?
A: Definitely. The fields cross quite a lot.

Walking down the street. From *Clyde Fans, Book One* © Seth. Used with permission from Drawn & Quarterly.

Q: Does one form trump the other in terms of artistic merit?
A: I wouldn't say so. I think all popular art forms are in some sort of competition for legitimacy. At different points different ones have a leg-up on the others. Film has a high leg-up on all the other art forms because film turned into the art form of the twentieth century, surpassing everything else.

Comics were kept in their infancy for so long that for the longest time they would have definitely been secondary to animation. Even in animation you always had a serious wing around the world that was trying to produce work that wasn't just meant for laughs. And up until the late sixties, comics had none of that. So comics have been a very late bloomer. But I would say that now, today, I believe that comics is the more exciting field than animation. Animation seems to have pretty much lost the battle. Except for the odd interesting work, they seem to have taken over as a second-string movie industry—mostly producing children's crap. The real gems of animation come out of the National Film Board [of Canada] and Eastern Europe. Places far from the commercial marketplace.

Q: Eastern European animation is scary.
A: They are.

Q: We all remember when *Itchy & Scratchy* were canceled on *The Simpsons* and replaced with a European cartoon. . . .
A: Yeah. Actually, *The Simpsons* may be the greatest achievement of commercial animation. It was pretty successful and a pretty smart show.

Q: Are you anticipating the upcoming release of *Watchmen*?
A: It's of no interest to me in the sense that the book is of no interest to me either. It's no different than if they were filming some other book that I read and didn't care for. The fact that it's a comic doesn't connect it to me the way people expect it should.

When [*The Dark Knight*] came out, the guy at the Xerox store I frequent kept asking, "Are you going to see it?" And just to be polite I'd say, "Oh yeah, eventually I'll get around to seeing it," though I had no intention of doing so. And then for the next three months every time I came in, "Have you seen it yet?" And I had to keep making an excuse. The truth is I'm just not interested in those kinds of films. It doesn't really matter to me that they're from the world of comics.

Q: Do you prefer your comics and film to be rooted more in reality than the fantastical?
A: No, not at all, although I do tend to think that the works I find most moving are works that are about real human life. But that doesn't rule out the fantasy world. There are lots of films that fit in between those two worlds. The primary thing is it has to have some sense to me that the artist is describing something meaningful and real from their life. And that could come through in something like *Alice in Wonderland*, for example, where it's an entirely absurd world. Generally, I find that is not the case with a lot of fantastical work.

This is not always true, but when people do something with a genre film, say, a horror film, and it turns out to be a really great piece of art, they tend to say it transcended the genre. And I think the reason why they say this is because we tend to think of genre works as being a set formula that people work within—sometimes they do a great job of working within the formula, but the formula is what is predominant. That's why fans of genre work return to the same genre, because they want the stuff that makes up the genre.

Q: What does your friend Chester Brown have to say about his experience trying to get the film of *Ed the Happy Clown* off the ground?
A: Well, I'm not even sure what's current anymore. It seems as if that film's been optioned as long as I've been alive. Is there any movement on that project?

Q: The little I know is that it's still above board.
A: Yeah, well, I expect to be hearing just that as I'm going into the old folk's home. I think it could be a really good movie because it's got a lot of great visual stuff in it and it's very funny and it's very black. But I hesitate to imagine it in a modern context with a lot of CGI and stuff. I could see that being pretty awful. I would personally prefer if it was very low-tech.

Q: So you wouldn't want it to go the way of Pekar's *American Splendor*.
A: I actually didn't see *American Splendor*. When the time came I just couldn't work up the energy to see the film.

Q: Are you a movie fan?
A: I love movies, but I must say I'm very arbitrary in what I choose to see. By all rights I should have gone to see *American Splendor*. People said it was OK. I just didn't really care. I wasn't that enthusiastic about Harvey's work at that moment in time. It just didn't excite me to see it, and I felt as if I'd be going to see it because it was based on a comic, like required viewing.
This is the thing about what we were talking about with *Watchmen*—there's almost this sense that if you're a cartoonist you're required to see all these films that are somehow connected to cartooning, but it's not in my contract.

Q: You might remember that I once cornered you at a party and tried to convince you to take King Vidor's movie version of *The Fountainhead* and make it into a comic. The German expressionism seems tailor-made for illustrating.
A: A movie to comic book? You mean like a comic version of a film? Well, I'm not a big one when it comes to the idea of translating one medium to the

other. I tend to think it's not really necessary. It's not a fact. I've seen tons of great films based on other pieces of work, and sometimes, as you know, a good film is better than the book. But personally I have little interest in translating one form into another. But it's not a rule. I wouldn't say it's never the case.

I certainly wouldn't be interested in translating *The Fountainhead*, though, because I have such deep hatred for Ayn Rand and objectivism. As much as I like the idea of Howard Roark as the incorruptible architect, I can't stomach any of the objectivist ideas behind it.

Q: It's a book that falters with age.
A: I liked it when I was nineteen. I was very susceptible to the ideas at the age of nineteen, but time has not been kind to the ideas of objectivism.

Q: I was happy to find out that you have a real appreciation for Charles M. Schulz.
A: Schulz, more than any cartoonist of his generation or the generation that followed, succeeded in infusing that commercial medium with his own inner life. That was a great achievement at that point. It's still a great achievement.

I think *Peanuts* is an unsurpassed work that really spoke to me, and showed me that what any art is about is about the inner world—the personal life of the artist. It's not about trying to come up with a good concept or trying to create something flashy to get attention. It's about trying to create something meaningful.

Q: Was he subversive?
A: In many ways he changed the whole world of cartooning. His earliest work would have been seen as very adult, very black, very sophisticated humor that was cutting edge in the fifties and sixties. Too much marketing changed that. In the first twenty years I don't think anyone would have thought to give it to kids. Schulz is almost universally celebrated across all the different areas of the cartooning world from the people I consider my peers working in modern, adult cartooning to people working in Spider-Man comics.

Comics Reporter Sunday Interview: Seth

TOM SPURGEON / 2009

Comics Reporter (June 7, 2009). Reprinted by permission.

I'm a great fan of the cartoonist and designer Seth, whose comics I've come to enjoy more and more over the years. He has what would be for many artists a decade's worth of projects either recently out or imminent: *George Sprott, 1894–1975,* a book-length expansion of his *New York Times Sunday Magazine* novella and a work that features some of his best cartooning to date; *The Collected Doug Wright, Volume One: Canada's Master Cartoonist* [2009], which he designed and I believe edited; various volumes of *The John Stanley Library* [2009–present] for Drawn & Quarterly, featuring his design work; a short comic for *Kramers Ergot Volume 7* on Thoreau MacDonald [2008], a two-page comic on a giant canvas that shows off more of his cartooning chops; and two more volumes of *The Complete Peanuts,* a series on which his design work has set the standard for this new era of deluxe strip reprints. I'm probably forgetting like five things.—Tom Spurgeon

TOM SPURGEON: I think most people are aware that *George Sprott* began as one of the *New York Times Sunday Magazine* serial projects, and more than a few are aware that this is the potential project you offered the *Times* that had the least amount of initial interest for you. What led you to include the *Sprott* idea at all?

SETH: That's a valid question. It does seem like a poor idea to toss in an idea that you don't particularly wish to be picked (though that overstates it—it was merely my least favorite idea of the three submitted). I have learned, from years as a commercial illustrator, that you don't submit any rough drawings you don't like because it is a fact that the art director will always pick the one you hate. The truth is, I tossed in *George Sprott* because I felt I needed to present them with a third option. Let me explain.

I gave them three choices. Choice number one was to continue and finish a story I had begun in *Toro Magazine* but had left unfinished due to a conflict with editorial. Choice number two (my favorite at the time) was a quiet, meditative study of a block of abandoned buildings. I looked over my first two choices and instantly knew that I needed to give them a third. It was pure strategic thinking.

They were not going to pick number one—they wouldn't wish to continue something begun elsewhere—I just knew that. And number two was a shot in the dark. Probably too "poetic" for them. Too artsy. It seemed obvious that there had to be a third option that was a more traditional story and had some human characters in it. *Sprott*—a rather unformed idea at that point—was what was currently floating around in the back of my brain and therefore, *Sprott* it was.

I actually kind of figured they would pick it, but I was still hoping against hope they would go for the second option.

As I have said elsewhere—in the end—they were correct. Working on *Sprott* was the more challenging choice and ultimately, the more rewarding for me.

SPURGEON: Also, as it began to develop, where were you creatively at the time and what was going on that had an impact on your general approach? I've heard people mention a number of things that might have had some effect: an approach you learned by doing *Wimbledon Green*, the Dominion City project, the theme work in *Clyde Fans*, even.

SETH: Well—at the very moment they called I was working on *Clyde Fans* (naturally) and I had just made a solemn oath to devote all my energies to finishing it up immediately. Sigh. How could I say no to the *Times*? It was too good of an opportunity to turn down—though I did consider it.

Creatively, *Sprott* follows naturally out of *Wimbledon Green*. In many ways, I took the lessons I learned making *Wimbledon* and applied them directly to *Sprott*. I suppose *Sprott* is clearly *Wimbledon Green* meets *Clyde Fans* . . . but, really, all my work is pretty interchangeable. It's all of a piece. I don't really think of each book or project as something new, I simply see it all as part of a continuum. I'm working my way down a very specific path and each work is a refinement of what has come before. It's all towards a goal of trying to put down on paper the very specific feeling I have of being in the world—trying somehow to get my inner reality communicated to the outside. In the end, every project fails but I get a little closer to understanding how to approach things in the next work.

When I did *Wimbledon Green*, I made it a point to mention in the introduction that I was trying to emulate a narrative approach I had come to enjoy in the works of Clowes, Ware, and [David] Heatley [Xeric grant winner for his series *Deadpan*]. The use of short, separate strips that build up to a bigger picture when read together. And that was perfectly true—that is what I was doing—applying what I had seen and liked in their works to a little sketchbook story of my own.

But the funny thing is, after *Wimbledon* was published, I remembered something. Back in the eighties I had heard John Cage's *Indeterminacy* [1958] on the radio—ninety unconnected stories told in ninety minutes. This work had had a huge impact on me, and for years I had thought about trying to do something similar in comics form—perhaps fifty unconnected one-pagers that the reader would put together in their own mind. It was an idea that sat on the back burner so long that I forgot all about it.

I can recognize now that seeing these other cartoonists using a similar narrative approach (to *Indeterminacy*) is what drew me over to emulate them in the first place. They had actually put into application this old forgotten notion of mine—done it so brilliantly that I had failed to recognize why I was so attracted to it. I had forgotten the Cage connection entirely. In fact, I hadn't thought of *Indeterminacy* even once while working on *Wimbledon*.

But, by the time *Sprott* came along, I had remembered this youthful notion and I thought, "Here is an opportunity to apply what I have learned from Ware, Clowes, Heatley, and *Wimbledon Green*—and John Cage—to a new story." A piece that was less centrally organized—more fragmented—closer to my original Cage idea.

SPURGEON: I haven't heard too many people talk about the experience of having that platform. What was that experience like, appearing in the *Times*? Did you hear back from a different kind of reader with a different kind of reaction to your work?

SETH: I wish I could give you an exciting answer to this question—but the reality of a cartoonist's life is that you sit in a studio all day and you send the work out and you never hear a damn thing about it again.

I had an excellent working relationship with the *Times* and it was a very valuable experience doing the strip—I learned a lot about editing my own work while doing *Sprott*. But I cannot say I received a great deal of response to the work while it was running. Since it finished, I have received a smattering of remarks here and there, nothing much worth commenting on. As an artist you like feedback but I have learned not to expect it. That's one sure

Wimbledon Green, man of mystery. From *Wimbledon Green* © Seth. Used with permission from Drawn & Quarterly.

way to be disappointed. I must say, though, that the high profile venue was a "feather in my cap," and I have "felt" some vague effect from having serialized a strip there. Hard to explain what I mean by this, though. The lack of direct feedback may simply be the nature of newspaper and magazine publication— I mean, *George Sprott* (the book) has only been out a couple of days and I have received significantly more feedback than during the entire run of the strip.

I think, sometimes, people think a high profile "gig" of this sort is like appearing on the Broadway stage or something—excitement and applause. The sad reality is that you are just sitting in the basement, the same as any other day. You don't actually see anyone read the thing. The Prime Minister of Canada doesn't phone you up and say "Good Show."

I resisted Googling the strip for its entire run but when it ended I typed in the title. The very first "hit" said: "Thank God, *George Sprott* is finally over." And people wonder why I dislike the Internet.

SPURGEON: What was your relationship like to the work while you were doing it and how has that changed since? Was there ever a point where you struggled with or simply didn't like the work? When did it click for you?
SETH: Like any work, it's an up and down process. Some days you think it is the best thing you've ever done and other days you think it's a piece of drivel. I was on this roller coaster the whole time I was working on it. I think initially, after I started working out the first few installments, I was very enthusiastic about the strip. I thought it had a lot of promise. Certainly, at that early stage I felt real genuine confidence that this was going to be the best thing I had ever done . . . but somewhere in the middle I recall feeling quite blue that something was missing from the finished work. Some nebulous quality—something I couldn't put my finger on—was failing to appear. I recall sitting down and doubling my effort there, to bring it to a higher level, and by the end, I recall, I felt pretty good about it. *Sprott* was actually pretty tightly planned from the word go—but there were points where inspiration was stronger. I felt I was getting at something when I did the strip titled "The White Dream."

That same roller coaster of emotion carries on for me after the work is finished, as well. This is true with all my work. Some days I think fondly of some creation and others I grimly accept that it's not very good. It's hard, you want so much to produce good and meaningful work, but it can never possibly live up to your own expectations. Every work is ultimately a failure. How could it be anything but? The only work that ever succeeds is someone else's.

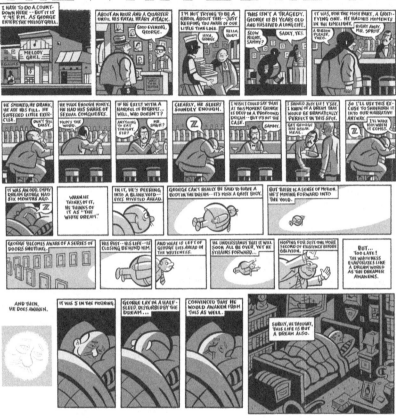

"The White Dream," from *George Sprott (1894–1975)* © Seth. Used with permission from Drawn & Quarterly.

I will say this. I was enthusiastic to expand the work out into a book, and at a couple of points during that process I really liked the work. When I received the printed copies a couple of weeks ago, I couldn't make up my mind if I liked the book or not, but I was genuinely happy with the printed object. Last week, for a few hours (maybe even the whole day) I thought it was a pretty good book—but, of course, that never lasts.

SPURGEON: This is kind of a related question, but did you always know that it would be a book? Did your perception of it in another format have any effect with how you approached the serial aspects of the work? I think that's maybe been the most interesting factor about all the *NYT Magazine* projects, how each one has dealt or not dealt with the serial nature of the assignment. **SETH:** I did not have any concrete plans for it to be a book while I was working on it. Oh, I knew I would republish it at some point, but I assumed I would just include it in some kind of *Art of Seth* book, or some such thing. It wasn't long enough to be a book on its own, I figured.

In fact, while I was working on it, all I was thinking about was how it read in the magazine. Immediately upon agreeing to do the strip I sat down and planned out just how the work would best read. I knew right away that I did not want to do one straightforward narrative, broken down into pages, with a "continued next issue" at the end of each page. I made up my mind that the best way to read something like this (which is naturally fragmented by the serial publication) would be to have twenty-five self-contained single-pagers. Since I couldn't count on the reader dutifully following it week to week, I hoped I could at least make each page satisfying on its own. For the faithful reader who actually followed the strip, they would be free to tap into the bigger narrative.

I had a lot of story ground to cover so that meant each strip had to be pretty dense—twenty-five or thirty panels a page. It might have been smart to design the pages to be cut in half for later republication (like *Ice Haven* was) but I needed to design the pages really tightly to make all those panels read simply. It was a bit of a tightrope between clutter and cleanness. I like to keep things simple and I edited these strips mercilessly—often cutting half of the story material out of each strip. It hurt. I'm used to having as much narrative space as I want to ramble on or use silent sequences.

Anyhow, it was only after the strip wrapped up that Tom Devlin at D&Q suggested I republish it as a book. It seemed an unlikely offer, at first. The story was only twenty-five pages long, even if they were dense enough to equal a hundred of my regular pages. But I gave it some serious thought, and the more I tossed the idea around in my head the more I came to appreciate the challenge of converting this material into a complete book and how much pleasure that process was sure to bring me. I really did like shaping and expanding the work into its present form. It was a very different process than the assembly of any other book I've worked on.

SPURGEON: Did you go away and come back to the material for this book? When there's time between the book and the collection, is there an active reconsideration of the work, or is it all there from the start and coming back to it is basically production work? You changed the overall work quite a bit, actually, through at least the inclusion of some other elements.

SETH: If memory serves, I think there was about six months between the publication of the last strip and my beginning the work on the book. Enough time to mull it over and think of just what could be done with the raw material of the original run.

What immediately excited me was the possibility of further fragmenting the original story. Even in its original run I was able to digress off with a strip or two to describe the history of certain buildings or to give the TV schedule listings, et cetera . . . but the story was still pretty A to B in its construction. Making it into a book would allow me to break that apart somewhat.

Fortunately, because of the structure of the original story (self-contained single pagers) it was very easy to simply insert new material in between the old. This new material would allow me to "diffuse" that directness of the original narrative. A few years ago I played around with idea of a life story told only in eight or nine short segments—a brief episode from each decade of a character's life. A little incident, picked almost randomly from each decade would make up each installment. I wondered, when you put all these incidents together, would they add up to anything? This seemed a natural place to try out this technique, dropping these incidents between the preexisting material. I hoped that the inclusion of some new strips, along with these decade-by-decade incidents (plus some other purely visual material) would make the work more of a jumble for the reader—encouraging them to organize all the material in their own minds when they reached the final strip. I tried to keep the feelings for George somewhat ambivalent so that the reader would be forced, in the end, to try and sort all the facts and decide for themselves what they felt about him.

SPURGEON: I wanted to ask about a couple of techniques employed in *George Sprott*. The first is your use of color. The easiest way to look at it is as a rudimentary designation of present and past, but it does seem as if there are gradations within those choices, and perhaps not even 100 percent regularity as to each color's symbolic meaning. Is there a full range of effect you're trying to communicate in the color? Also, how hard is it to make choices for color as a narrative effect in terms of making it work as design? Do you have to craft pages and sequences with that in mind?

SETH: The use of color is not as complicated as you might have hoped. While working on the *Times* strips, I employed a pretty broad set of color schemes. I was using the magazine to try out color combinations just to see how they looked. Some of them worked well and others came out garish or just plain ugly. When the time came to do the book, I knew I would have to simplify the colors. You don't want a book with a hundred different colors in it—you have to start narrowing things down to create some kind of visual unity. I narrowed it down to the few schemes that had worked well. The final book has only a handful of individual colors in it—and while there are relational connections between the strips that share color schemes, they are not used with any strict methodology. I mean, yes, the strips that show George's direct narrative on the night of his death tend to be all of the same color (green-gray) and the strips involving dreams are usually in a blue tone—but there are plenty of examples of less clear relationships. Color was mostly picked intuitively and for emotional effect.

The "flashback" strips are tan-colored but this was not planned to suggest the sepia tone of the past. In fact, this didn't even occur to me until someone pointed it out and then I regretted I had made this color choice. It had been a toss-up between tan and a pale aqua and I picked the tan purely because the warmer scheme made these pages stand out from the other material of the book. That's all I really wanted there. That's why those pages are done in a watercolor wash style as well—just to separate them out from the other stuff.

SPURGEON: The other technique employed that I thought noteworthy was the use of illustration-only spreads at certain points throughout the story. Can you talk about the effect you're trying to communicate with those drawings—they're abstract, for one thing—and also how they might change the book as a reading experience, the rhythm of how someone moves through the book.

SETH: Rhythm is the key word here. The book is made up of a hell of a lot of starts and stops. That can't be helped, but you can try and control the rhythm of those reading patterns. The big double page spreads serve the purpose of long notes in a series of single beats. They are placed to break up the staccato rhythm of the reading experience. That's somewhat true for the blank pages and the photo pages as well—but less dramatically. Despite what I have said above about *Indeterminacy* and fragmentation, the book is really carefully planned. I am sure the pages could be juggled in a dozen subtle ways, but this incarnation was put together to read with a careful eye toward that underlying rhythm. In my more traditional graphic novels I tend to change rhythm by shifting from dense narrative sequences to quieter ones. This book didn't offer that opportunity as directly. The spreads were an attempt to do something of the same thing but with an entirely different technique. I liked using them and I expect I will employ this technique more and more. I'm already putting them in my newer *Clyde Fans* chapter that I am working on right now.

You are quite right to point out that those arctic landscapes are abstractions. They don't represent actual arctic scenes so much as interior landscapes (of thought and memory and feeling) inside George. Those landscapes, and the gate-fold section, are really the only time in the story that you actually see/feel anything from inside George's perspective. Everything else is an outside view or secondhand experience.

SPURGEON: Did you shoot the building models as they're used in the book? What made you bring that work back into the collection? If I'm remembering correctly, and please correct me if I'm wrong, you worked on the Dominion stuff up to a year before starting on *Sprott*.

SETH: I hired a photographer to take the pictures.

Dominion is an ongoing project and will probably continue, in dribs and drabs, for the rest of my life. I actually included the photos of the buildings as a lark. It just popped into my head and I thought it would be simply fun and "neat" to put the cardboard facsimiles of these places right there next to their comic strip histories and when I thought about it, I liked how it further fragmented the narrative a bit by reminding the reader that the whole thing was "just a story" in my cardboard metropolis. It's funny that showing the 3D model of the building actually makes the place seem less real than the little drawings of it in the strip itself. Plus—I love decorative things and it was a very decorative touch that would "pretty up" the book.

SPURGEON: Do you have any specific interest in or sympathy for the kind of public figure you made Sprott, either the explorer or the public lecturer/ TV personality parts of his life? I think every community had the latter, but other than the horror hosts and maybe George Clooney's dad, they're kind of a forgotten figure even just three decades past their ubiquity. I wondered if you were actually interested in that type of person enough to want to write about them, or if it was a convenient framework for you, or if something else led you to that choice . . . ?

SETH: In a way, George's life story was chosen almost arbitrarily. It didn't matter who George was or the specific details of his life. What was important was that it was a life coming to an end. I wanted to create a situation where the reader feels kind of lukewarm about the person who has just died (as we often do unless they are someone we deeply love). I wanted the reader to then decide for himself just how much sympathy they had for George. I personally

One of the Dominion models. From *George Sprott (1894-1975)* © Seth.
Used with permission from Drawn & Quarterly.

had a lot of empathy for George—he's like all of us—a human being filled
with contradictions. But I tried to keep my directing hand out of it as much
as I could. Is George a good person or a bad person? It's not easy to decide. All
we can say of ourselves is that we are the central character in our own little
stories. We are the star. Others decide whether that is "true" or not.

I was also interested in what makes a person. The choices they make? The
personas they take on? How others see them? Is there a core person beneath
all that? A person underneath the personality?

But, that aside—the simple answer is that I do like that old world of local
television and its celebrities. I picked it because it is a phenomenon within
recent memory yet it is also something that is already gone and antiquated.
It disappeared fast. It was a little world that suited the tone of the story. Plus,

the simple fact that George was something of a local celebrity opened the door to a wider range of "interview" subjects than just those who knew him well. Still—it wasn't a crucial element of the story. Just window dressing.

I grew up around Windsor/Detroit in the seventies. It was a very active area for local TV. Those local television celebrities were visible signs of an active local culture that, in some manner, has vanished (or has certainly diminished) from our more globalized world. They represented an entire local stew of nightclubs and sports facilities and restaurants and department stores et cetera that made up a more cohesive regional culture than exists today (not everywhere of course, but in the smaller or more blue-collar cities). I wanted to reflect that a bit in the story as well, and that is why I focused on places that were central to George's life and work. I wanted to emphasize that George was part of a specific eco-system. He couldn't really live without it. George was patterned on a type of individual that seemed to thrive within that old culture. A kind of man who might be perceived as overblown, or a stuffed shirt—or all bluster. The kind of man who didn't have a good understanding of his own emotions. In retrospect, some of these "characters" ended up looking like buffoons—or at least caricatures. The kind of figures you don't see as often any longer in the media (Though in Canada I can think of a couple—do you know who Don Cherry is in America?) I've known a few old men like George and they fascinated me. There is a lot of "false-front" on them. I was interested in what's behind that front and how you become that guy.

SPURGEON: How did you conceive of the narrator's voice that you use throughout *Sprott*? It's a weak voice in certain ways, not entirely omniscient, and looking back, doesn't appear as much as I thought it did.
SETH: Truthfully, I took the germ for the narrator's voice from the introduction to *Don Quixote*. Cervantes doesn't have "all the facts about Quixote" and that struck me as so utterly brilliant and modern—especially coming from the "first" novel. I just took that outright—it served my purposes. I wanted to further muddy the water about the details of George's life. Because of the narrator's uncertainty the reader doesn't have to take anything as the truth. Another attempt to fragment things—put the decisions in the reader's hands.

The device doesn't appear all that often because a little of that goes a long way. I used it sparingly—just bringing it in when I felt it added the right touch. I needed a narrator simply because there wasn't enough space in each page to let the story tell itself, but, as you guessed, I wanted to keep the narrator from becoming too omniscient. Plus, it seemed like it might be funny.

SPURGEON: I apologize if this is too broad or maybe even too obvious a question, but was it satisfying for you to work with the spread of an entire life with this book? It seems like it's the first time that you've had that many points in time to play with, and I was struck a few times at the effect you got by showing the effects of accretion over a longer period of time.

SETH: I think I would love to work with that sweep-of-an-entire-life in every story, but I haven't approached it in the past simply because I figured it would take too many pages to tell such a story in any depth. *Clyde Fans* is the model—look how feebly I have plugged away at this story and it only represents a few days in the characters' lives (albeit over a span of several decades). I love the more naturalistic approach (moment to moment transitions rather than big jumps in time) to storytelling, like I am using in *Clyde Fans*, but I have to admit, it is the laborious way to tell a big story. What I did with George allowed me to cover a lot of ground economically.

The culmination of a life—that really is what I am most interested in as a writer. I think that is the underlying theme of all my work. *George Sprott* simply gave me the chance to deal with that in a rather perfunctory way. The effects of the accumulation of time is a topic that is endlessly interesting to me. It's the stuff of life. I wish I had the drive and gumption to create a ten-thousand-page comic novel that could get to the heart of that experience. It's not too likely though, is it? What a shame we often cannot accomplish what we know would be the very perfect work. It's just not in us.

That said, I think, as soon as *Clyde Fans* is finished, I am throwing my brushes away to start drawing comics in some simple manner (perhaps markers) so that I can produce more pages. I do believe that the accumulation of detail is the only way to truly capture the real life experience on paper and that means producing lots of pages and I cannot do that in my current methods. So—goodbye urge for perfectionism.

SPURGEON: Did you intend any part of the work as commentary on self-mythology? There's the unreliable narrator, the contrast with the horror host, the failure of the niece to publish her uncle in a manner she felt befitting to him, certainly Sprott's own efforts at distraction and persona-building.

SETH: I'm a guy who has a fake name. I used to have long silver peroxide hair. I used to walk around in a judge's robe and welder's goggles. I now walk around in a gabardine overcoat and a fedora. I named my house.

Clearly I am interested in persona and self-mythologizing. Like I said above—who are we and what makes us that person? That is a central element of most of my work. You can see it as a main theme in *Clyde Fans* and in *Good*

Life and in *Wimbledon*, even. These choices we make determine who we end up becoming—but there are also roles (both chosen and unchosen) that add layers of meaning onto us. Person and personality. Always interesting. I don't claim to have any great answers about it, but I am "exploring" it in just about everything I write.

God knows, sitting alone at my desk every day—I contemplate my own life and who I am, endlessly. I'm sure you do as well, Tom.

SPURGEON: No comment. Do you think it's fair to say the precision with which you told this story is at odds with the kind of fractured, incomplete portrait you're painting? What do you think is the considered effect of these tight grids in terms of the poetry of the piece, the rhythm you're trying to create for the reader?

SETH: I don't know. As the creator it's hard to judge. The shape of the work was largely determined by the needs of serial publication. I probably would not have structured it so rigidly if I had created the book of whole cloth. I often think my choice of drawing "style" is at odds with the stories I am pursuing. The cartoonists that influenced me (Schulz, Hergé, Arno [H. M.], Bateman, et cetera, et cetera) were drawing in those styles for entirely different purposes. Perhaps I am trying to perform Hamlet in a clown suit. It's hard to say—it's beyond my control. I couldn't draw differently if my life depended on it.

However, as you mentioned, the rhythms are within my control. I like those rhythms. That I like.

As I mentioned above, that was pretty well considered—if you take into effect that I was "stuck" with a lot of starts and stops to begin with.

Let me step back, though, for a moment. Those *Times* strips are really tightly controlled for their internal rhythms in the first place. You mentioned poetry and that was a perceptive thing to bring up. When you are writing a one-page strip, it is pretty much the same as what I imagine the writing of a poem must be like.

You become very concerned with condensing time—and to setting up word patterns and rhythms. The thing has to "read right." You have to constantly pare the speech and the images down—boiling the thing down into a reduced form where it is simply more potent—more distilled—than a comic narrative told over a series of pages. In essence it becomes a "block" of comic storytelling. When you have twenty-five of those to deal with, you are simply forced to think about rhythm in designing the book. Almost all the decisions made in putting the book together were made in an attempt to soften these "blocks."

SPURGEON: Can you talk about how the Doug Wright material went from a shared passion that you and some others shared to becoming not just a book, almost a sustained effort to re-impress Wright into our consciousness? At what point did you see this kind of project as possible? Why now and not a few years back? Because you've been reading and collecting Wright for years.
SETH: Wright has somehow become a cause in my life—but I didn't set out to make him so. It all sort of evolved.

Throughout the eighties and nineties, I underwent a long process of attempting to educate myself on the general history of cartooning. I started broad and worked my way down to the specifics. By the end of the nineties I was mostly interested in pursuing the work of a handful of largely forgotten Canadian cartoonists. Wright was up near the top of that list. But he wasn't necessarily at the very top.

By the turn of the century I had collected about seven scrapbooks of Wright's *Nipper*—perhaps half of his actual output. It was a tough uphill climb to get that material. I was also piling up the work of about five or six other Canadians then, too. The ultimate goal of this collecting was really just to get to know their work and to learn from it. The secondary plan was a hope to publish a collective book on the group of them. I didn't think anyone would ever let me publish a book focused exclusively on Wright, for example. I didn't know if there was an audience for such a focused book. I assumed an overview of them all was the best I could hope for. The current market really didn't seem to exist at that time. I never would have even proposed such a book as *The Collected Doug Wright*. Not even in softcover. Times have changed.

I think the turning point of when Wright become more specifically "connected" to me was when Brad MacKay came to me with the idea of creating an award for English Canadian cartooning. It wasn't a foregone conclusion that Doug Wright would be the namesake. I recall we discussed Jimmie Frise as well—but somehow Doug just seemed like the correct choice. I believe it was in the creation of these awards (both the organization and the physical awards themselves) that I first began to realize that it had become part of my "mandate" to bring Wright some of his due. The book just naturally evolved out of this sea change in thought (though this account is seriously selling short the drive and generosity of Brad and Chris [Oliveros] in the development of this project, and I don't intend any slight here to their efforts).

Wright was a terrific cartoonist, and I do want to see him recognized in Canada as a national treasure of some sort. I feel that the Awards and the book are making real steps in that direction. I would like to hope that some future artist would feel a proprietary interest in keeping me alive when I am

Doug Wright's Nipper, by Seth. From *Vernacular Drawings* © Seth. Used with permission from Drawn & Quarterly.

gone as well. Perhaps this is some sort of a trust that artists owe each other.

Anyhow—I have some hopes of this kind for popularizing the works of a handful of other Canadian cartoonist from the past, as well.

SPURGEON: I've talked to a few people about Chris Oliveros's assertion that Doug Wright is a talent on a level with Charles Schulz and Robert Crumb, and the reservations I hear are that they don't have a sense of what Wright was trying to communicate or reveal or explore that sets him apart—that he obviously drew magnificently well and there's an element of how he sees the world in that drawing, but he's not as psychologically piercing as Schulz or bravely confessional as Crumb. Is that an assessment with which you agree or disagree? Is there a case you would make for Wright's work in terms of that kind of depth?

SETH: I think I understand what Chris Oliveros was trying to say when he made that comparison—I think he was merely expressing his enthusiasm for a top notch cartoonist that few people know today, and he wanted to impress on them what it was like stumbling upon a cache of "unknown" work by a legitimate master cartoonist.

However, I wish he had not used the names of Kurtzman or Crumb or Schulz. Almost no one is in the same category as these great cartoonists, and it actually brought an unfair negative comparison onto Wright.

Let's face it: Wright is not in the same camp as those guys. They are in that rarified, top echelon of cartooning—work that really transcends the medium.

However, it is no shame to Wright to be down a peg from these fellows. We all are. But, nonetheless, Wright was a fantastic cartoonist. Much superior to those he might naturally be compared to in the commercial world of kid strips. He's much superior (in my opinion) to [Frank] Ketcham [creator of *Dennis the Menace*], to whom I have seen him recently compared. He may not have infused his work with the psychological depth of Schulz's *Peanuts* but he did actually create a strip of much subtlety (especially evident in the work near the end of the first book and throughout the second volume to come). Wright's best work has two factors worth holding up for study:

1. Obviously, his great ability as a draftsman to capture the real world. His work, in its precise use of observed detail, is a window through time. I am always amazed at the "sense of place" evident in his strips—more so even than photographs—in re-creating in form and feeling a specific place and a specific time.

2. His focus on "the slight incident" as a subject matter for his "real life" strips. The *Nipper* strip starts out as a *Dennis the Menace* type gag strip, but it evolves. If it had stayed in that mode, it would only be of interest for my first reason, listed above. However, the strip changes as time goes on. He eschews the gag format (to a large degree) focusing less on getting a laugh than presenting some quiet aspect of family life. As time goes on the strip is remarkable for its unsentimental view of childhood. He's still aiming for a chuckle, but it's not the most important aspect of the strip. His subject matter is the tiniest of moments—in the best of his strips it is often something we would barely comment upon. Truthfully, I can't think of any other comic strip like it.

This aspect of his work really takes precedence in the second book—but you can see it strongly enough from about 1960 onward.

I love Wright's work and I don't think it needs any defending. He infused the strip with his life and that makes it interesting. Sure, he didn't infuse it with his deepest inner soul like Schulz did. I regret I even have to compare them. It's true that Schulz's name comes up in the book a few times, but I believe we only compare him to Schulz in terms of popularity and child-baldness. Yes, they were on different levels . . . but Wright deserves the title of Master Cartoonist. Schulz, more likely, is in the realm of the demi-gods. Crumb and Kurtzman as well.

SPURGEON: You did a fairly remarkable-looking strip in *Kramers Ergot 7* on Thoreau MacDonald, and that's not someone I thought of you having an interest in before that strip. Can you talk about your interest in MacDonald and what elements of that interest drove the creation of that strip? Because part of it seems to be your capturing something about his art, and another seems to be about understanding this text in front of you. One basic question, too: why the difference in the presentation one page to the next, where you shift to journal pages?

SETH: I have been interested in Thoreau MacDonald for about eight or nine years now. This might've been more apparent to you if you lived in Canada because I gave a lecture about him at the Art Gallery of Ontario several years ago and I also published that modified essay in a Canadian magazine [*Devil's Advocate*, issue 60, published Spring/Summer 2007]. If you came to my house you'd know it as well, because there are examples of his beautiful work all over the place.

Thoreau MacDonald is always up there in my mind as a potent life example—along with Glenn Gould and Robert Crumb. People I admire enormously and think about almost every day. He was modest and hard-working and had a profound connection to the world—specifically the fields and farms of Thornhill, Ontario (now a depressing Toronto suburb). He was smart and had exquisite, austere sensibilities, and I wish I were more like him.

His book designs have had a deep and lasting impression on me. I've studied them all with laser-like intensity and have learned so much about good design just from trying to figure out why he made each of his simple choices. He was like a Shaker in his visual quietness: his regularity of beauty and form: and his austerity of presentation. TM's designs might just be the equivalent of a Bach [composition played by Glenn] Gould . . . I look at what I am doing and seriously worry I may be Liberace.

Anyhow—I admire him greatly, and it was probably inevitable that I would do a work connected to him at some point. The opportunity came up when Alvin [Buenaventura] called me about doing something for *KE7*. TM leaped to mind instantly. His writing has always appealed to me in its directness and its honesty, and I figured this would be a good opportunity to "appropriate" it. It was especially gratifying to work with his diary entries. I have read the two published books of his diaries multiple times, and the writing is extremely soulful—especially considering the economy with which they are written. The two pages are drawn in somewhat different styles in *KE7* for the simple reason that I wanted to contrast the bio with the diary pages. The bio page was drawn with one eye on TM's own drawing—not strictly emulation but . . . with him in mind. Across the gutter, in some vague manner, I was trying to lessen my "voice" in the diary pages, and so I put forward the conceit that they were drawn in a "diary-style." One reviewer (in the *Village Voice*) actually thought those pages really were from TM's own hand-drawn diary (of which there is no such thing)!! Somehow I figured the subject matter was suited to that grand avenue of a two-page spread in that giant book. I had a feeling too that the life of an old Canadian book designer would be the perfect subject matter for that anthology. I was especially worried that several of the young artists involved in the project might tackle the same topic. (This is a joke.)

In some ways, TM has been as overlooked as Doug Wright has. He's certainly been overshadowed by his father's (JEH MacDonald, of the Group of Seven [a group of Canadian landscape painters active in the 1920s and 1930s; the original group expanded to ten members in its later years]) legacy. It's a shame—he's an enormously important Canadian artist in my opinion.

SPURGEON: Are you constantly finding new sources of inspiration, new artists with which you wrestle? What are you passionately interested in right now? Are you able to tell what's going to stick with you?
SETH: Yes—I think that is pretty typical of me. I'm culturally hungry—always on the lookout for new fascinations. I wear interests down. I get passionately interested in something and then focus deeply on it until I burn it out. Some interests last and some don't. I'm not sure if I always know what is fleeting, but I always know what will last. With artists, I have a pretty clear pantheon of personal greats—why one might be on the list has nothing to do with building a hierarchy of merit. A lot of it is simply personal—how something strikes you. When that certain special artist is discovered—one who will be added to the pantheon—it doesn't matter where they sit in the grand scheme of "art". . . it's just intuitive. They hit the right chord with me.

Perhaps Duchamp, Picasso, or Warhol are greater artists than Lawren Harris [one of the Group of Seven painters]. It's clearly true. But Harris is in my personal pantheon and they are not. Who can explain such things? (Perhaps I am just a middlebrow).

Typically, once an artist enters that pantheon I never tire of them but very occasionally someone falls out. It always surprises me. A few years ago I was kind of horrified to discover that I no longer cared for Woody Allen. I cannot tell you how important Allen was to me. I wasn't horrified because I had no interest in his current films (why would I?)—what bothered me was I had mostly lost interest in all his old films which I had loved so deeply. Perhaps that love will resurface. I hope so. I feel pretty indifferent on the matter right now.

Current interests. *Last Year at Marienbad* (1961). William Christenberry. Stephen Shore. Thor Hansen (a decorative Canadian designer) . . . I've been on another Norman McLaren kick (comes up every couple of years) . . . for the last several years I have been reading an enormous amount of classic ghost short stories (mostly from about 1850 to roughly 1940)—a real pleasure. I read a fascinating "ghost" story called "The Great Return" (1915), the other day, by Arthur Machen—an odd story that really stuck with me for some reason. Just today I could feel the excitement rising for a book I read a review of in the *National Post—A Progressive Traditionalist: John M. Lyle, Architect* [written by Glenn McArthur, published in 2009 by Coach House Books]. I could go on.

SPURGEON: I wanted to ask you a couple of questions about Charles Schulz, from the point of view of your design work on *The Complete Peanuts*. First, is it more flattering or annoying that the sum of your design choices on that series has become the Original Eve for this latest wave of modern strip reprints?
SETH: Imitation is the sincerest form of flattery. Seriously. It doesn't bother me in the least.

I design books with my own taste in mind. I wish more books imitated my designs because then I might like them more.

That's meant to be a mean spirited joke—not a compliment to myself. What I really mean is that I have very specific tastes and often modern book design doesn't really fit those tastes. I find a lot of modern design to be too busy. I wish a lot of books were designed more with simplicity, order, and beauty in mind. To be honest—when I look at my own designs, I see the right intentions, but I also see the glaring failure to achieve them (well—some I like better than others).

It's funny that our *Peanuts* design has come to be seen as "classic" because we've only been working on the series for a few years. I've actually seen the design described in those terms—"classic." I'm not complaining—that's very flattering. I mean, who wouldn't like to hear that? That's the dream scenario for me, isn't it? To have this series of *Peanuts* books, with my design on it, to be the definitive collection of the master's work. As a child I so deeply loved *Peanuts*, and as an adult I have such respect for Schulz—I am proud to be linked with him—even in the most insignificant way.

I recall when the first images of the design were released on the Internet, I was directed to go over to *The Comics Journal* web site to see a long thread of complaints about how the design was all wrong—too dour. Too much Seth—not enough Schulz. A complete misunderstanding of *Peanuts*, et cetera.

Strangely, the criticism didn't bother me. I had a gut feeling that I knew the work so well and had such deep respect for the man that I could make my own decision on the books. I still feel I made the right choices for the series. They were really the only choices I could have made. When I sat down to design the books, that design almost immediately developed. The design represents how I feel about Charles Schulz and his masterpiece. It's not a calculated "graphic design"—it's one artist responding to another.

SPURGEON: Second, this is a question I wanted to ask anyone working with the seventies *Peanuts* material after doing the fifties and sixties. Have you noticed the kind of visual change that everyone says started to happen in the 1970s with *Peanuts*? Do you feel the strip with which you're working is different than the one with which you started working? If so, how so? And if not, is there a different quality you get from the work just paying this much attention to it as a designer?

SETH: *Peanuts* undoubtedly goes through some profound changes in the seventies. In a lot of ways, it's another strip ("The Snoopy Show"—or perhaps, "Peppermint Patty's World"). However, that sort of change is pretty true of every decade of the strip. Yet, in my opinion, those shifts are not that important—the whole strip is a continuum. I love the seventies material as much as the earlier stuff (and, to a large extent, the later material as well). Every decade of *Peanuts* has its charms. I am anxious to reread all the eighties material again. I expect that we will be hearing interesting reappraisals of that work as soon as it's in print again. The thing is—as the decades roll along, the characters get older. Not in the actual ages of the *Peanuts* kids themselves but in their voices. Schulz gets old and so do the characters. He's in his fifties in the seventies, and you can see the reflective voice growing deeper in the strips. You can feel the accumulation of years in the voices of the characters.

By the time you reach the end of the strip in the nineties the "gang" are all old people. Just look at Lucy—she's even drawn as an old lady. Where is her little dress she used to wear? She's in sweatpants and an old lady sweater. The very center of gravity changes in the drawings of the characters. They are undeniably senior citizens. They have old voices.

It's a great strip all the way through, though.

My design for the books takes some of this into account—but it's not a big part of it. The endpapers will reflect the growing minimalism of the backgrounds. The color schemes of the books reflect the changing mood of the times. Et cetera. The main thing about the design is that it is meant to be simple and to allow the strips the dignity they so richly deserve. You cross the grass lawn at the beginning of the book and enter Schulz's reality and then at the end of the book you exit out the same way.

SPURGEON: Can I ask about your general approach to designing the John Stanley books? You've written well about him in the past, so it's obviously an artist you enjoy. I wonder specifically how you avoid repeating yourself taking on yet another high-profile project like this one. What does Stanley bring out of you that maybe your other design assignments don't?

SETH: Like everything I do, I am bound to repeat myself. It's what I am all about. I like repeating myself. That's what I liked so much about my Mum and my Dad. They constantly repeated themselves.

I love John Stanley. He's way up in that personal pantheon of mine. The entire design of the series was inspired by Tom Devlin when he spoke these words to me over the phone: "John Stanley Library."

That was it. I immediately knew I wanted the books to look like a set of old-time children's encyclopedias. I love the look and feel of those books—specifically the fifties/sixties sets. What was great about them is that many of them still had thirties surface stylings to them. They were brand new sixties books but they felt instantly old. Hence, my plan.

I know that seeing the designs for Melvin [*Melvin Monster*] on-line probably doesn't transmit that feeling, but when you see the physical books—especially when they start to pile up and you have a handful of different volumes stacked up—you'll see what I am going for. I think the online pictures make it look like it's got some sort of fancy art deco design going on. I can see why you might think that (and why people might think that's a really bad design choice)—but really, with the endpapers and the texture of the cover stock and the shiny seal on the back—it will read "encyclopedia." But, of course, encyclopedia with a fun cartoon character front and center. I think kids will respond to the design. I think it has kids written all over it. But then again, what do I know? No one is less involved with children today than I am. Do kids even read books any longer?

That last part of the question—"What does Stanley bring out of you that maybe your other design assignments don't?" That brings us to a real problem with me as a designer. The truth is, when I design something it really is too much about me. I'm responding to Stanley with the love of another artist. I'm trying to create a package for him that is a tribute to him. It's not really how designers classically work. I think the best graphic designers try to remove themselves from the picture and create a package that is suited to the work being packaged. I don't really think that way—I can't keep myself out of the process. My designs end up having a bit too much of me still in the picture. It's that way with Schulz, it's that way with Stanley, and it is certainly that way with Wright. I'm probably not a very good graphic designer for that reason.

SPURGEON: I'm catching you right when you're about to head out on tour . . . you've been around long enough to know what things were like before the more sustained interest in a wider range of comics. Are you happy with the way things have developed in terms of the art and industry and opportunities that are there? Is there anything that you wish had happened that has yet to happen in terms of the arenas in which you work?

SETH: I am happy with the way things have gone.

I often repeat this story. Around 1999, Chester Brown and I were in a restaurant and I recall things looking really grim. We were worried that the whole comics "thing" was coming to an end. I cannot remember what exactly sparked these worries but I recall we were discussing what we would do if the publishers went under. This seemed a valid worry at the time. Would we go back to Xeroxing? How would we make a living? Chet and I decided we had hitched our wagons to a falling star. Who knew back in the seventies, when we were teens, that comic books (which seemed a mass medium at the time) were actually the modern equivalents of the dime novel. Doomed to extinction.

And then—everything changed.

It's a better time now. It may not last, but it really is a golden age. I feel a real enthusiasm about the medium. There are a lot of exciting young cartoonists coming up—more than have ever been. Great works are being published

Seth draws John Stanley. From *Vernacular Drawings* © Seth. Used with permission from Drawn & Quarterly.

every year, works that will be considered classics in the decades to come. The very vocabulary of the cartoonist's language is expanding as great cartoonists continue to add to it with their ambition and genius.

As a working artist, each day remains a struggle—to try and make good work. To try and get better—to learn. To try and balance the commercial work with the personal work. Frustrating. Life gets sadder as you get older . . . but it is a fulfilling struggle. Art is like a religion. You have to have faith in its transformative power.

Interview with Seth

ERIC HOFFMAN AND DOMINICK GRACE / 2013

Previously unpublished interview, conducted September 21, 2013, Guelph, Ontario.

Editor's Note: Our interview with Seth began with a discussion concerning Seth's attendance of the Small Press Expo in Bethesda, Maryland, the previous weekend. Seth remarked on the incredible talent of young comics artists he met, in addition to the casualness with which they explore certain themes, in particular superhero and other fantasy genres.

The interview was transcribed by Eric Hoffman and Dominick Grace, and edited by Hoffman, Grace, and Seth.

ERIC: I wonder if with comics we're not back where we were with fine art in the 1920s, that there is a certain playfulness and experimentation involved.

SETH: Perhaps. I think it's a little different though. For example, when you look at the aesthetic of the 1980s compared to the aesthetic of today, and I'm speaking of the pop culture in general, much of it was mocking and ironic and mostly the tone wasn't earnest. For example, when I was in my twenties, B-movies were the "cool" thing to be interested in. If you liked cheap exploitation films for example, or Ed Wood, to name the obvious, you appreciated it *because* it was poor. You didn't look into low culture in order to find the gems of it; you were actually looking for the junk and smugly kind of appreciating it. You admitted it was junk and didn't pretend it was any better than it was. I think that that ironic stance isn't so prevalent any longer; I think that young artists are really just earnestly embracing the junk. *Star Wars*, for example, I saw lots of images from *Star Wars* displayed at SPX—unashamedly displayed. These young artists aren't drawing from that imagery and apologizing for it. They're not saying, "I kind of like *Star Wars*; I know it's not the greatest thing in the world." It's more like, "no, I 100 percent like it. It's cool." *Star Wars* is actually probably on the high end of that crap spectrum. You could make a plausible case, I suppose, for why *Star Wars* might be interesting. Maybe. You couldn't make a good case for why some shitty science fiction TV is earnestly worthwhile. That's just pure junk food entertainment. Or *Twilight*. Not that I know really any of the details of *Twilight* but I'm going to assume it's junk. Junk for teenage girls, kind of Harlequin romance horror.

ERIC: There does seem to be a dearth of legitimate campiness and kitsch in culture these days.

SETH: Yeah, and I have no problem with *Twilight* existing—I don't have a problem with the junk culture. There will always be junk, and it doesn't bother me that this stuff exists. I think I have more of a problem with the people who like these unashamedly and might actually . . . honestly, I have no problem with fans having bad taste. That's perfectly fine. I think I find it strange when it enters into the culture I'm used to, the underground comics culture, and see people referencing these pop culture things with no irony whatsoever. To see a young cartoonist who's got a real out-there Fort Thunder [Art Comics movement named for the locale in which the artists originally lived; key figures included Mat Brinkman and Brian Chippendale] kind of style, doing a comic book about 1990s *X-Men*. I can tell that there's a *bit* of irony there, yet what I'm really seeing is a sense of a pride—a swelled chest about having utterly no shame in what the artist is willing to embrace, in fact a total willingness to earnestly embrace pure pop culture junk. That is a big shift from my generation which grew up with a lot of mainstream comics junk and actually tried very hard to get away from it. I think my generation of cartoonists definitely wanted to distance ourselves from all that fantasy/space opera/superheroic material. It easily took us fifteen to twenty years to return and freshly look back, without a jaundiced eye, on that pop culture material that we grew up with: to judge it clearly and possibly to see some of it in a positive light again. My point is that it appears to me that the younger generation of "art" cartoonists doesn't feel this distance between the pop culture machine and their art. It's just grist for the mill.

I think I always liked Jack Kirby and Steve Ditko during those distancing years, but it would have taken me a *long* time to come back and look judiciously at anything I had read with great pleasure as a teenager that would not have been in that exalted company. I'm not likely to become a John Byrne fan again, for example, but I might be able to look at those comics now and not feel the *necessity* to blindly react against them. I think that whole culture that my generation came out of had to be rebelled against to create a different breed of comics. If we wanted comics to be adult literature, then there clearly had to be a period where you stepped away from childish things. I suppose we succeeded well enough if the younger cartoonists don't feel that need any longer. They don't need to rebel. They don't feel the same stigma hanging over the medium.

DOMINICK: A mixed blessing perhaps.
SETH: Yeah.

ERIC: Are *Wimbledon Green* and the *GNBCC* representative of your ability to reflect on these so-called "childish" things without any sense of shame?
SETH: Yeah. It is my coming back to it. I think the funny part about that is I could not have done those comics in 1990. For a variety of reasons but mostly, I suppose, because I wouldn't have even entertained playing around with that junk-comics world. I wanted to get away from it. I mean, I was always interested in that whole wide spectrum of cartooning, but at that point in my life I was definitely thinking, "Let's get away from the superheroes entirely, and let's focus on the gag cartooning, or the old strips" or whatever. That material would have been fine to linger over or use as a subject, but the whole world of the superhero . . . I guess the point is, we had grown up when superhero comics were really the only game in town. If you said to yourself at that moment in time—"I want to make a 'serious' comic book," the answer is that the fantasy elements had to go out the door. That meant that there had to be a period where it was established that you *could* make a serious work of art out of comics, and only when that occurred do I think that people of my generation said, I don't need to carry that golem on my shoulders anymore, now I can lighten up. By the end of the nineties the idea of a comic book as a work of art seems to have pretty much succeeded. Honestly, I didn't think that was coming. I can remember very clearly throughout the early nineties being unable to explain to people what I did or have them take it seriously. Comics-as-art did kind of seem like a stupid idea to most people. It wasn't much different than saying I would like to do serious art but I want it to be on the back of a matchbook cover or something equally trivial. Why would you waste your time on that, why don't you just go do some real art? The comic book just wasn't taken seriously. Its current acceptance might actually be a sign that the culture has declined—just kidding—but today when the topic of comics-as-art comes up, regular folk aren't that perplexed, the idea that a comic can be a work of art seems to have taken root. I don't have a problem explaining what I do any longer. Maybe to some folk, but it's usually the older generations. You might run into some absolutely normal guy who's like

eighty years old and I wouldn't even bother explaining to him, because he'd really just be perplexed, but anyone my age or younger, they know what the graphic novel is; they don't think it's so strange. So I think perhaps winning that little battle has lightened up my generation to some extent. Not as much need to prove anything. It seems to have been proved.

ERIC: Is this part of the reason why you have no reservations about referring to yourself as a cartoonist and not, say a comic book artist?
SETH: No, in fact I've always been wary of that "comic book artist" title. I may occasionally refer to myself as an artist, but I've always been adamant about referring to myself simply as a cartoonist. I'm proud of the label and don't need a fancier title.

ERIC: And that's not just limited to your style of drawing?
SETH: No. No. I think of the medium itself as cartooning. That is the name of the whole broad medium. When someone says they are a comic book artist, I think that has a very specific meaning. I've never used the term "comic artist" because I think it's more closely tied to adventure comics. These are all semantics, I guess, maybe it really doesn't mean that . . . I'm a comic book artist, as well, I guess. But somehow that term has come to be more clearly tied into the adventure stuff. "Cartoonist" I think . . . I always liked it because it had the right tradition behind it. Charles Schulz was a cartoonist and Frank King was a cartoonist. Harvey Kurtzman was a cartoonist. Doug Wright was a cartoonist. John Stanley was a cartoonist. Robert Crumb is a cartoonist. There's a long tradition to the term and I think it's an unpretentious term. Even "comic book artist" has a bit of pretension to it because I think the seventies guys at Marvel and DC wanted to get away from the word "cartoonist" since they thought it was a little bit derogatory. They saw the name "cartoonist" as being connected to humor comics for kids or something like that. Or maybe it sounded too much like you were an animator. So "comic book artist" was that first step towards coming up with a new name that sounded more respectable. I think the urge for respect has been such a big thread throughout the history of twentieth-century mainstream cartooning that people keep coming up with these new names. That's also why I dislike the term "graphic novel" because it's really got a stink of pretentiousness about it. But that label's not going away. That's a battle that's over. It won.

ERIC: It's something that we have to fall back on; otherwise people don't know what you're talking about. It's shorthand.

SETH: I resisted it for years, I wouldn't even use the term, but now I definitely use it all the time. People know what it means. I even sometimes say, "I'm a graphic novelist," even though I hate that term. It's awful.

DOMINICK: On the other hand, I'm not sure I've ever actually seen it on the cover of one of your books. You've used a "picture novella," or a story.
SETH: Yeah, picture novella is a joke. It's a joke that nobody gets. I've had people ask me seriously about that description . . . It's not unheard of to come up with a silly term, in the tradition of other silly terms.

DOMINICK: You're kind of winking at your audience . . .
SETH: Yeah.

ERIC: To me, the term "picture novella" has echoes of Arnold Drake and Leslie Waller's "picture novels."
SETH: I thought it was an obvious cute joke. I keep using it for the same reason. I wanted something antiquated. In my mind it was the equivalent of coming up with another antiquated and funny term for "graphic novel." I think Dan Clowes once had some ridiculous term he used on something, you know, like a "picto-sequential graphic narrative," or some such. And Chester Brown—well, Chet always simply subtitles his books with the phrase, "a comic book," which is his way to get away from it as well. I think the thing is, I don't really like the word and I would never use the words "graphic novel" on the cover, but I really wouldn't be surprised if Drawn & Quarterly doesn't have the term "graphic novel" somewhere in the text on the back flap, and I can live with that.

DOMINICK: I haven't read all the back copy that closely, but we're basing this on how you identify the work. We don't recall having ever seen you identify your work anywhere as a graphic novel.
SETH: I'm pretty sure I haven't. I make it a point to try and not to use the term. I think nowadays it's more out of spite than anything else because I do sadly recognize that it is an important term that has gone out into the world and helped me. Librarians know what it means. You gotta live with it. That's fine. It doesn't really matter. The important thing is that these books exist and people know what they are.

DOMINICK: Maybe that takes the pretension out of it, if it's no longer identification so much as a label. . . .

SETH: Yeah, and the good thing is, when a term becomes accepted, it tends to lose its meaning. I don't think people think about what the term "graphic novel" means any longer. Like you say, it's just become a term. Like the word "comics." "Comics" is a strange term as well when you think about it—and definitely a misnomer. So little of the stuff has ever been funny! Humor never really defined the medium, and yet that's the term that we were using for a hundred years. I suspect most people never even think about what the term "comics" actually means. It's a plural, but I'm pretty sure it gets used as both a singular and a plural.

DOMINICK: You often refer to structure and rhythm when discussing how you construct a narrative; in episodic works like *George Sprott, Wimbledon Green*, and *GNBCC*, you depend on an omniscient narrator, and you often have your characters directly addressing the reader—breaking the fourth wall—something that also occurs in a largely non-episodic work like *Clyde Fans*. What is it about breaking the fourth wall that appeals to you? It seems to derive somewhat from autobiographical works—I'm thinking of Chester Brown's *The Playboy*, or Joe Matt's comics, or even Harvey Pekar and Crumb. Is this the tradition from which you find yourself drawing inspiration or is there some other reason for this somewhat self-conscious "breaking of the barrier"?

SETH: Of course, as an artist you don't often think about that sort of thing. You don't usually trace back why you're doing certain things the way you do. But if I were to think back to my most important influences when I was starting out and was trying to figure out what I wanted to do, it probably would be people like Crumb or Harvey Pekar or Lynda Barry. There's an awful lot of addressing the reader in those works. However, nowadays I'd say probably what it's most connected to is simply the fact that I talk *a lot* in real life and I'm a very gregarious person and I have a strong desire to say a lot of things in the comics. I don't mean that I have a lot to say that's important; it's just my characters, they talk a lot—I like to have them talk a lot. I like conversational writing and I like the form of a monologue and that lends itself to narration.

Years ago, when Chester and I first became friends, we talked an awful lot about what made good comics. One of the main things that we came up with was that narration was bad, that comics shouldn't be narrated, that they should show and not tell. That classic approach. I think for a long time I struggled to try and keep that true. Well, for a while. To keep narration to a minimum. But as time went on I came to realize that I was really interested in narration. Chester is still strongly a "show-not-tell" person. I like to tell. I think my comics are rapidly turning into mostly telling and a lot less showing. The pictures are often on a different level now. Of course, scenes still come up where two people are talking to each other and the pictures and words come together naturally to tell the story. However, today I think much of the time what I'm currently doing is juxtaposing text and image, where the narration is talking about something and the pictures are talking about something else. That seems to be my main mode of operation on the last couple of projects I've been working on.

The funny thing is, I don't actually think much about the breaking of the fourth wall. It seems natural to me to speak directly to the reader and to have the characters speak directly to the reader. It might have to do with the fact that I read more nonfiction than fiction. So much nonfiction is just directed at you rather than through dialogue delivered by characters. It seems to me a natural approach in comics to have the character speak directly to the reader, conversationally. It strikes me that a lot of newspaper strips are set up to have the characters basically speaking at the reader. I think we've all internalized that approach.

There are different ways to do it, though. In *Clyde Fans* for example, where I am working with a more traditional narrative, the characters don't directly speak to the reader in a normal way, as they do in *George Sprott*, where the characters are facing the reader directly while addressing them. Certainly in *Clyde Fans* the whole first chapter is a monologue. I suppose it's implied there's a listener. In my mind the listener *is* the reader. I didn't structure it that way . . . I didn't intend that you would think of him speaking directly to the reader. He's speaking to thin air. I used that approach because I was reading some old comics around that time . . . it was John Stanley's *Little Lulu* where Tubby would often talk to himself. So he would be doing something, and he would run along and he would be thinking, "I gotta get home; I've got to get there before Lulu gets there." He would basically be telling the reader plot details they needed to know but it read pretty normal. I never once thought to myself, Tubby's speaking to himself here, why is he talking aloud? But that was a device that worked very fine. So I remember I thought, wow, you know I don't want my character to have thought balloons over his head for the whole chapter and I didn't want his dialogue up in boxes at the top of the panel because that's just not direct enough. The word balloon is a very direct communication; it's very different when you're reading dialogue in a word balloon than when you're reading dialogue in a caption box. That was maybe the first time where I wanted to have the character speak to the reader but not have the character speak *directly* to the reader.

In *Clyde Fans* there are different narrative approaches to get that same point across. So, in the first chapter we have a character speaking to you in balloons, two chapters later everything is in caption boxes for Simon. That's because I wanted to distance it a bit more. In that case I was implying it was thinking and not speaking. It's funny; when you put something in a caption box it has more the texture of thoughts, but when you put it in a word balloon it has a totally different active quality to it. These are just different methods so that you *can* talk directly to a reader in a narrative, but it doesn't have to break the fourth wall in a traditional sense. *George Sprott* is definitely talking directly to the reader. But even the *GNBCC* where the tour guide is actually *speaking* through a great deal of it, somehow that's an implied listener as well. It *is* the reader, but it's not the same reader they're talking to in *George Sprott*. It's a vaguer reader. It's almost as if you're going along on a fictional guided tour whereas in *George Sprott* he's speaking only to *this* reality. Our reality. It's all kinds of shades of gray. What it boils down to is this: I really like to have characters talking and I've always had less of an interest in back-and-forth dialogue. I'm more interested in monologue.

ERIC: It's interesting that you mention Simon's character. Switching from word balloons to captions certainly helps to define his character because he's definitely an introvert. You made an interesting comment about saying one thing and then showing another thing differently. Are you trying to underline the distinctly human characteristic of fooling ourselves, of truth being relative?

SETH: Sometimes. I do like the idea of the unreliable narrator. There are times where I will undercut the pictures with the words. But a lot of what I'm writing currently just seems to be not very well illustratable. Let's put it that way. For example, in the "Nothing Lasts" story I'm now serializing in *Palookaville*, as I break it down into panels, either it's too mundane to illustrate what it says, you don't want to draw the exact thing described in the narration—so, for example, if the narration says, "I'm walking out the door" and then you draw someone walking out the door—that's dull. To be honest I will do that a fair amount even though that's really supposed to be a crime in comics. But a lot of the time I've got narration as vague as "I was feeling sad," or whatever. I don't want to draw a picture of myself looking sad. That's terribly dull. Often I realize that everything that I am writing on the page is an intangible. It's not dynamic in any way. It could be twelve panels of an interior monologue, where you're describing something you felt when you were twelve years old or something, and you realize that you have literally nothing to draw. Now that's a classic problem for a cartoonist. Some person might say well then why are you even doing this as a comic? Why aren't you writing this out as a page of text? But there's something about reading a sequential work where the text and the words are unrelated that has a power in it, too. So I might, for example, draw the neighborhood and break it into twelve panels. That creates two things at once. You establish setting and place and the mood, and the drawing doesn't have to relate directly to the text and yet it solves the problem of having to also write that boring paragraph. "We lived in a suburban neighborhood where blah-blah-blah," where you have to describe things.

DOMINICK: One of the things we found when we were looking at your work, from the perspective of how we were going to select images to illustrate this book, was that when removing a single panel from the page we discovered that we could not communicate how this work is functioning in single panels. As a result, many of the illustrations we chose consist of full pages or at the very least several panels.

SETH: That's very true. I don't think I do a lot of traditional panels anymore. I'm not that interested in drawing as much as I used to be. I've come to recognize while working that more and more now, my drawing is becoming increasingly minimalistic. I'm less interested in drawing itself and more interested in diagraming.

This is a digression here, but when I was at SPX I noticed that a lot of the young cartoonists are really quite accomplished in their drawing styles nowadays, even the twenty-year-olds have very slick, sophisticated cartooning styles. I found myself thinking back to the kind of comics that were being done when I was that age, and without a doubt my drawing ability at that age was a much less slick style than these kids have today. I found myself wondering about why this was. Why are so many of them so good at such a young age? Two things came to me: one is that they're trying to do easier stuff. This sounds like I'm insulting them but I'm not. I suspect that they're emulating artists that have simpler styles. Everyone my age was growing up trying to draw like Wally Wood or Neal Adams, stuff that, whereas I'm not crazy about the styles themselves, were very, very difficult to do a half decent version of when you're twenty years old. It is a lot easier to do a half decent version of, say, Charles Schulz's art; as much as I understand that Charles Schulz's art is more sophisticated than Neal Adams's, I'm not kidding myself about which artist would be more difficult to emulate. The other thing is I think the reason

It takes more than a panel to get the picture. From *The Great Northern Brotherhood of Canadian Cartoonists* © Seth. Used with permission from Drawn & Quarterly.

they have more sophisticated models they base their work on is that they've seen a lot more art. When I was a teenaged boy, the only art I saw was the art available in a small town in Ontario. A pretty limited spectrum. These young folks today have seen a tremendous amount of art on the internet and have already moved into areas where they can pick more sophisticated models of art to emulate at a very young age. So they might be drawing very simple drawings of figures, but well-designed simple figures—and they've mastered it at a young age.

ERIC: My twelve-year-old daughter is very enthused by manga, and she's already adept at emulating that style, seemingly by virtue of osmosis, by having been exposed to so much of it at such an early age. She has a skill at twelve years of age that I was never able to attain.

SETH: It's nice to see that kids are even still drawing. I was kind of worried that when the electronic media stepped forward . . . especially video games. I thought that there might not be another generation of little cartoonists drawing away in their bedrooms yet clearly there's no shortage of them. I figured video games would kill that impulse, that the people who would have been drawing all the time as kids would instead be playing those hateful games all the time. But no, I guess that they can somehow actually do both.

ERIC: There's also something to be said about the ease of publication now, as well, with Internet and desktop publishing, and of distribution. The relative lack of expense in producing printed or especially digital media is certainly different now than it was when you were starting out.

SETH: It's totally different. Another thing that's changed is today's kids are shameless about showing off stuff in a way that my generation isn't comfortable with. For example, people will do a drawing and post it up on their website immediately, the minute they finish it. That seems bad form to me. My approach is that you don't show anything until it's in print. There's almost something vulgar about so baldly asking for attention, but obviously they don't see it that way at all, it's all just *sharing* stuff. If you look at the cartoonists of my generation, almost none of them have any digital presence. They don't have their own websites or if they do they have someone else running it. You'll rarely see any of them *speaking* on the Internet. It's funny because for the generation somewhat older than myself, that's not so true.

ERIC: Like Stephen Bissette.

SETH: I guess. But I'm thinking more the underground cartoonists or those artists just before my time—I notice Kim Deitch, for example, commenting here and there on the internet, Ben Katchor has some kind of web presence— it's definitely some particular moment in time thing. My specific generation doesn't appear to want much of a presence on the Internet. Though who knows. Come to think of it, maybe I'm just talking about my own peer group here. Is Ben Katchor really a different generation? And Robert Crumb has zero digital presence. This might just be me talking nonsense.

ERIC: You were interviewed as part of Dave Sim's series of "Advise and Consent" interviews [see pp. 77–88] querying artists about the level of critique they are interested in obtaining before a work goes into print. Some interviewees were at ease with receiving criticism prior to publication, while others were more reticent. Do you believe that a degree of autonomy is lost when showing your work prior to publication?

SETH: Yes. I guess I do feel that some distance is needed. I ascribe to the idea that an artist should try and keep away from his audience. You don't want to get too chummy with the reader. Somehow or other that pulls you out of your ivory tower. I think it's important that you keep your ivory tower. I know it sounds elitist or something, but I think the moment you get down too close to your readers you lose some kind of "mystique." You want them to view you from a distance. If you become too familiar to them, you risk the chance of losing their respect—making it harder for them to read your work freshly. Even with some of the other cartoonists I know, it's altered my enjoyment of their work by getting to know them too well personally. You end up knowing more about them than the work and that starts to interfere with the read. I always recall a funny line Dan used on the *Eightball* letters page years ago: "maintaining an icy distance between author and reader for twenty years." Or something like that. It was a joke, but I immediately thought, yes that's absolutely true. There is some necessity in keeping away from the audience that definitely the younger cartoonists don't seem to feel. Watching someone like Kate Beaton, who's totally connected to her audience, reminds me how very different that is from my approach. She's very accessible—communicating back and forth with them in a way that, I guess, they're both benefiting. Still, I can't help but feel that it must influence the actual work she does in a way I wouldn't care for. You can see where the readers are commenting on things, suggesting things. There are instances where she's saying, "well, guys, what do you think of this" and the readers are responding, "Oh, I like that, you should publish that." That seems *very* strange to me and I'm very uncomfortable with that level of contact.

DOMINICK: Is there a balance point between a level of feedback from readers or critics that's beneficial?

SETH: Yeah.

ERIC: You mention the "icy distance" from the letters page of *Eightball*, yet in your interview with Dylan Williams—this is going back to 1994, mind you—at one point you say that when you are producing comics, you really don't have a sense of audience in mind, yet later you tell Williams that feedback from readers is important as "You've really got to feel like you're communicating with people" when you're creating comics. Now, I understand that this was twenty years ago, yet how do you account for this apparent dichotomy? I note, for example, that in that same interview you criticize Dan Clowes for "fucking around with goofy stuff, trying to please his audience."

SETH: And that's really an unfair criticism. I did a complete about face on that later, and I'll tell you . . .

ERIC: . . . is it a matter of doing what you want, maintaining your autonomy while still remaining open and receptive to criticism? Is it a matter of picking and choosing criticism you find beneficial?

SETH: For a simple answer, yes. Okay, for a more complicated answer, probably at that point what I was trying to say, but not getting across very articulately, is that when I was writing I was trying hard not to think about the reader because at that early point in my career I was trying to simply puzzle out what it I was even wanted to write. That is harder to do than it sounds. When you're young, I think that's a hard thing to figure out: what you even have to say and what's the point of even telling a story. So back then I was genuinely trying to figure out exactly what I was even attempting to write about. That took a while and mostly that's been a journey toward the idea of trying to create works that capture some quality of inner reality. I think at that point what I was trying to do, and which is very hard at any age, is to avoid perceived ideas of what a story *should* be about. That's why I would deliberately try not to think of the audience while writing. To try not to contrive things just to keep them interested—to avoid that kind of thinking. But I was also young enough at that point that I *needed* some positive feedback. Some approval from the readership. Somebody to say this worked or not.

I was talking to Chester about this not too long ago and I said to him, "Imagine that we received no positive feedback over the years, that we were doing our comics but that we'd gotten no success and had other jobs on the side but still wanted to do the comics—Question, would you have the stamina to keep doing them?" Can you keep doing the work without some kind of acclaim from somebody, someone saying it's valuable art? I think both of us kind of agreed—we probably couldn't. We *could* do it *now*—I mean, if the whole industry fell apart and we had to go back to Xeroxing minicomics and sending them out to ten people, that'd be fine, because we've already had that positive feedback. I've established in my own mind that I'm doing work of value and could do it with the future in mind, I suppose—you know, "people in the future might enjoy this work" sort of thing. But you can't do that when you're thinking, "I don't really know if I'm any good at all." That's quite difficult. You *do* need to have that positive feedback. It's a blessing to get to a point where you *can* legitimately stop thinking about the audience. Today when I write I don't think about the reader much because I don't need the feedback in the same way. Now I actually have enough confidence to say I don't care what the reader thinks. Back then I would try deliberately to not pander to the reader. I came to the conclusion that what makes for an interesting story is a story that doesn't really have much conflict in it, so I *tried* to write stories that didn't have a lot of conflict in them, even though I knew the unbreakable rule is that a story is *only* interesting if it has conflict in it. Nowadays I don't think about it at all. Bit by bit, I'm working toward telling stories of less and less conflict, but I'm proceeding without the doubts I had back then.

I always bring up Chet because he's the main person I would be talking to about these sorts of things. Anyhow, just the other day I asked him how much confidence he had about whether his artistic choices are correct or not. He answered. "100 percent," and I said, "Me, too." I no longer have the need to show work to anyone beforehand. It doesn't mean that I am doing *great* work or that it's perfect work, but I know that it's the work I want to do. I'm not so sure I could have said that when I was twenty-five.

So what am I saying here? Feedback is important when you are starting out. Maybe it's always important to some degree. I still like to read reviews or whatever. That said, too much feedback might be a problem. It affects your independence of thought. I'm certainly uncomfortable getting too chummy with the readers. I like some distance. I guess I'm comfortable with the feedback in the old traditional methods. Reviews and letters. No one writes letters any more but it was a good communication method in its day. Slow and not too close. Email is far too close. It's too much like going out for a coffee with someone. Too much back and forth. I certainly can't see myself ever chatting online with "the fans." Too close.

DOMINICK: So Chester doesn't show people his work and ask for feedback?
SETH: He does still a bit. I think Chester likes the feedback in a way I don't

care for. I almost don't want the feedback anymore. I don't want somebody to tell me when something doesn't work because I want it be MY way. That kind of feedback leads to doubts.

ERIC: Is Chester's liking of feedback what led to your contributing an essay for *Paying for It*?

SETH: He wanted the feedback. He asked Joe [Matt] as well and Joe didn't do it, and I'm not surprised because Joe doesn't do anything. Joe should definitely have written something for the back of Chester's book because he has plenty of reservations about *Paying for It*, just like I did. I was talking to Joe just yesterday about his role in the comic and he had some points to make, that he'd like to set the record straight, that sort of thing. That's why he should've written something in the back. Typical Joe.

Chester really does enjoy that whole experience of getting feedback. I think Chester was the guy who set that in motion even back then, of each of us showing the work, back and forth.

ERIC: So would you revise your comment about Dan Clowes ("fucking around with goofy stuff, trying to please his audience.")? Would you say that same level of confidence applies to his work as well?

SETH: Yes. I really didn't understand what Dan was doing back then. I recall writing a pretty insulting letter to Dan on this very matter, and Peter Bagge too. I wrote them both apologies a few years later. You see, back in the day that whole matter of trying to do "serious comics work"—it was a bit of a holy cause for me. Looking back I think I may have taken it more seriously than my peers. They were just doing their work. I kind of had some idea that we were all "fighting together" and I can remember reading *Eightball* and being very thrilled and approving of certain works like [*Like a*] *Velvet Glove* [*Cast in Iron*] or *Ghost World* but at the same time being disapproving of other things he was doing, things like "The Happy Fisherman," really goofy stories and I remember thinking, "Why is he wasting his time on this nonsense?" when he should be just working on the serious stuff. I really felt that the serious stuff was the important work, that was what important artists do, and this "Needledick the Bugfucker" [1993] et cetera was just a total waste of his time and wasn't helping "the cause." But now of course I realize it's the exact opposite: all that work was of the same level of importance to Dan. One wasn't more "real" than the other. Knowing Dan today I suspect that the "bigger" stories were where his ambition lay, but it was also part of the very essence of his personality to do the goofier stuff as well. There was no sense of . . . I'm even surprised I used the words "trying to please the readers," that seems particularly harsh . . .

ERIC: Maybe you were misquoted.

SETH: No, I'm sure I wasn't. The amusing thing here is that it makes me realize that back then I did actually think he was farting this stuff out for the readers instead of giving it his whole . . . well, I mean, today I can see that that work is just as interesting and important as the *Velvet Glove* strip. Two sides of a coin. But I obviously couldn't recognize it at the time.

ERIC: There's an overarching absurdism to all of Clowes's work.

SETH: Yeah. It's all of a piece. You know, I'm not such a huge fan of *Velvet Glove* anymore. I still like it but probably I love all those "goofy" strips more in the long run. That's great work.

DOMINICK: So you would not find much value in having an editor?

SETH: No, I'm rather opposed to editors. I've gotten into a lot of arguments with people about editing. Basically because I think editing exists . . . my harsh opinion of editing would be that it exists mostly because of the way the publishing industry developed. I find it's an unnecessary requirement for an artist to have someone to look over their shoulder and tell them whether it's good or bad or whether it could be improved. There's no arguing that an editor can improve a work. I've written a couple of introductions in the last year or so where I had to deal with an editor and there's no doubt they make your writing better, at least the prose pieces. They challenge you and . . . I mean, I was perfectly happy with the first draft and then they would be, "Well, maybe you can explain a bit here." Or maybe we should cut this section out, it doesn't really connect. Admittedly, you know, a week or two later, when we've been through it all, those were better pieces of writing. But on some level I guess that when it comes to my *real* work I don't want it to get any better because someone else is involved. It becomes a collaborative work then. I'm not much interested in collaboration. You know, there are no editors for painters, for sculptors, for composers; there's nobody standing over their shoulders saying you really should fix up the composition over here, or have you given enough thought to why this figure is in this pose. That's accepted as an artist's job. I feel that same way about cartooning, as well. I think that the only reason we talk about cartooning and editing is because of the established history of the publishing industry.

DOMINICK: Because of how it has developed as a medium?

SETH: I might be wrong but I suspect editing came into existence because the publishers had all the power and not the authors. They wished to control the final product. And I'm also betting that as an author's power and reputation grew the upper hand shifted from editor to author.

In our medium it's even worse than in prose, or in the academic world, because the editor is actually the *boss* in comics. I do understand that writers develop interesting relationships with the *good* editors and a good editor isn't the boss. A good editor says, "Well, if that's how you really want it, that's how it's gonna be." A bad editor, like at Marvel or DC, would say "Well, you're not doing that," and that's all there is to it. That really puts the artist into the position of employee. Now, if the industry would have been different, if people of my generation had come into comics *with* editors, I'd probably have a different opinion of them. But the great thing about alternative comics was there were no editors and no reason why you should submit to one. The companies were so small and ill-formed . . . Chris Oliveros never attempted to edit anybody. Basically he took the position, "I like what you're doing so I'm going to let you do what you do. I may not like *everything* you do, but my role as publisher is to publish the work of artists I like." That has given us a real luxury that we have gotten used to and I could not give that up. Even the times I've had to work with an editor, I imposed my will right from the get-go to make it so that it couldn't be otherwise.

Even working for the *New York Times* it was kind of a given that I would allow them to copy-edit but I was not going to allow them to edit the actual comic strips. I did allow them to make a few suggestions. I think the only suggestion they made was when I turned in the first few strips [of *George Sprott*] that perhaps there might be an introductory strip to help the reader since I had originally started the story right on the ground. And that was fine. I added a prologue. I didn't have any problem with that. I don't mind the occasional structural comment, where somebody asks could we have another page or something along those lines. That's fine. On the other hand a few years before that I was working on a strip for *Toro Magazine*, and I established my position right from the beginning. I proposed the strip to them. I said, "I'd like to do this strip with you and I can't have *any* editing, that's rule number one." They said that's fine. But typically in these kinds of things, later it changed. Suddenly it's "Well, that was somebody else you were talking to who promised that." They started editing, and very quickly I just had to quit because it was really turning into the kind of editing hell. They clearly didn't like the story I was telling. They were trying to get involved in the actual writing of the story. Trying to shape where it was going. For someone who's not used to having any editors, that's just unacceptable. However, things are changing for cartoonists out there, and I do tell young cartoonists not to submit to editing, but I doubt they are listening to me. There is a new world now. With big publishers coming in interested in graphic novels, they're getting used to working with editors just like regular prose authors. They like their editors, so it's hard to argue with them. They're like, "No, I have a *great* editor." What can you say to that?

DOMINICK: While we're on the subject, is George Sprott actually based on anybody in particular?
SETH: He was based on a very specific fellow from 1970s television, a Detroit TV host named George Pierrot, although very little of it is based on any of the actual details of his life. He was a travel show host and lecturer. The one real detail I took from him is that he did fall asleep on the air often, and his snoring was true, so that was kind of my initial starting point for the character, but he was also based on . . . well, a certain type of person, a type you saw more of back in those times than you see today. There's a bit of Pierre Berton in there, and the old-time columnist Greg Clark . . . and this odd guy from a book I read a few years ago, called *The Bull Cook* [*Bull Cook and Authentic Historical Recipes and Practices* (1960) by George Leonard Herter], which is a very strange book I found in a Goodwill . . . it was just this big fat book of travel stories and recipes from a really gregarious kind of charismatic character that as I read it, I was like, well, you know, these type of characters are a specific type, a kind of a stuffed shirt, very full of themselves and yet sort of endearing at the same time. There's even a bit of my dad in the character, too, so it's sort of an amalgamation, but the main guy was George Pierrot.

DOMINICK: Setting generally seems to be really important in your work. From the realistic context of a book like *Good Life*, and books on place and time rather than character (*GNBCC*) and of course the theme of landscape looms large in Canadian literature generally. Do you see yourself as part of that Canadian landscape tradition?
SETH: I certainly feel connected to the landscape tradition in that I'm very interested in it. Let's put it that way. I certainly wouldn't have given that answer when I was twenty-five. At twenty-five, I would have given little thought to the tradition of Canadian art and literature and landscape's role in it. At least I don't think I would have. I was so interested then entirely in the idea of using comic narratives as a way to tell personal stories. That was my number

one concern; anything else would have been secondary. Today, I think this has kind of changed in that I'm not as exclusively interested in the world of cartooning as I used to be. What I mean is that I'm mostly just interested in pursuing my own cartooning nowadays rather than being so enthusiastic about the medium itself and trying to change people's perceptions of it and so on and so forth. Now I just want to do my own comics. I think when I started out I would have said I was totally interested in the world of comics in every way. I was very enthusiastic about exploring comics history and digging up obscure work. Now my tastes are often more focused on less comic book–related subjects. They've broadened considerably. One of them would certainly be that tradition of landscape in Canadian art. I'm very interested in the Group of Seven and just as interested in several of the artists that followed them, especially Thoreau MacDonald. I think that my work has become progressively more about place than it is about character. I'm realizing that I'm actually inching towards stories that don't feature real characters at all. This long project I've been working on for years—the city of Dominion—that is always looming as the next possible graphic novel.

I've got two possible next graphic novels when *Clyde* is finally finished. One of them is kind of all character, and the other one is all setting. When I say the first one's all character, that's not entirely true because that one's very specific to a place. Let's just say there's five characters in a very specific place, and whereas they don't really interact much with each other, each chapter will be about one of these persons. So let's put it that way. That said, there would be a big element to that story about setting and history as well, so the place would be super important. The other story, the story about Dominion, would be all place. That's the one I'm most tempted to do first because it's completely non-plot-oriented. There are no central characters. It would just be description. It could simply be several hundred pages describing the place, and that seems really easy for me to do now. I'm ready for that. I feel like that would be an utterly natural response for me to just dive in there and go. In much the same manner that I'm doing this memoir ("Nothing Lasts") . . . it could be structured in the same way. You would just talk and talk. It would just be a long monologue, basically. There's no story conflict . . . it's just an essay essentially. Or a travelogue, I suppose. That's really quite appealing to me right now. I like the idea of getting very deeply into something that is potentially really boring but not worrying about whether it is boring.

As I've grown older, I find the works I'm most attracted to have a strong digressive quality to them. Something happens and then someone digresses and then it goes on for awhile, and then another digression, and another, and eventually maybe it catches up to where it started out. Or it gets back on thread. Or it doesn't. Or they're stories that are not heavily focused on a plot. I always use *Last Year at Marienbad* as an example of my favorite film because even though there is a genre plot in there—there's possibly a murder in there, and certainly there's a love story going on—it's really just a looping narrative of some sort, going around and around until eventually it starts to coalesce into a story that you understand. That seems to me an ideal form of storytelling. More and more as I watch traditional movies, I find myself wishing to take the plot out, or to lessen it at least. I think I was saying this to my wife just the other day about something we were watching. I said, "That was pretty boring, but I think I'd like it better if it was *more* boring." There's always some layer that I'd wish to shave off from most stories—a layer of what is considered the essential thing that the viewer/reader is supposed to be *most* interested in. I always want to cut that back a bit. I think this kind of thinking does lead you to make works that are less marketable, but ultimately I think those kinds of considerations are a mistake for an artist to worry about anyway. When you start thinking about marketing ideas and about whether people are going to like this or not, you start to change how you approach your work. I think the only consideration I keep firmly in mind for the reader anymore is clarity. Clarity is always important to me. I want the reader to understand what's going on. If they're supposed to be confused, then that's okay, but I don't want people to be confused by accident.

But getting back to landscape, I'm engaged with it simply because a lot of the time I am dealing with intangibles and therefore the place setting is very, very useful as something for the reader to enter into visually while they are dealing with less tangible elements in the writing. So landscape is very useful as a tool in my toolbox, in that sense.

ERIC: With the Dominion project, will you be drawing from the work you've already completed in the notebooks?
SETH: To some degree. I think how I'd ideally approach it is that I'd start with all the knowledge about Dominion that I've built up in my mind, of what the city's about, and elaborate out from there. I have a basic structure planned of how I would approach such a big rambling story that would keep it from just being "In 1862, the first pioneer walked into the area that would become Dominion . . ." You know, that sort of boring A to B to C kind of thing. I mean, that would come in there somewhere, but the thing is, the reason I like digression so much is that it gives a certain spontaneity to the writing. Rather than the very, very tightly controlled script method, a meandering narrative often

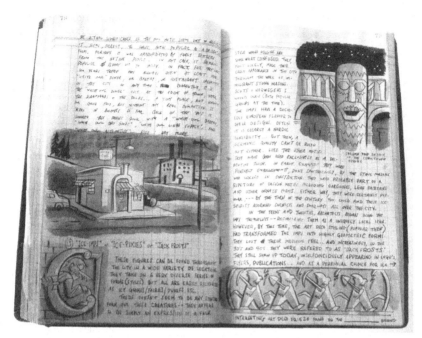

Working on Dominion: pages from one of Seth's Dominion notebooks. © Seth. Used with permission from Seth.

creates a life of its own—like a long conversation. Much like with this memoir "Nothing Lasts," the whole point of it was to not script anything out and to basically make it up page-by-page. Of course, that comic is based around places as well. So each place that I lived in becomes a starting point—a hook to hang my memories on. It's simple. I just write about the first place we lived in, and then the second and so on. In this way I don't have to worry about where the story's going. It's going to the next place we lived at. When I get there, if I realize, "Oh, I should have said something about this event that happened back then," I can just digress back and it gives it a kind of spontaneity that removes the worry and polish of a tight structure. But because of the central conceit of it all, I've built in a natural structure for it—it's all about place—that's the undercarriage for it, the motor of the story can go on top of that, which can be handled with completely spontaneous writing. If I was to write about Dominion, I would do it exactly the same way. I would just start; I have a structure in mind that I could lay that spontaneous writing on top of, and it would just roll out. At the end of five hundred pages or so, I would know where it could conclude, and even though I wouldn't get everything down on paper, it could be one helluva big digression that would have some weight . . . or texture, I guess texture is the best word for it . . . texture of a place and time that you would get from having read through all that.

ERIC: It seems to be that of all your works the *GNBCC* most closely approximates the digressive narrative style you're describing.
SETH: Mm-hm. That's very true. Because that's all just digression too. That's right. I'd forgotten about that. As I worked along on it, there were always about ten other things I wanted to talk about, and I dealt with each of them, one by one as they came up. That story works fine, I guess, but I actually think that the structure of that one might be a little *too* straightforward. A person walking through a museum is a pretty firmly directed narrative path. That's why that one sat in my notebook for a while and *Wimbledon Green* came out first. *Wimbledon* seemed more organic, more spontaneous, and more fun. I kind of only put the *GNBCC* out because *Palookaville* wasn't going to come out that year. I didn't want a complete year with nothing coming out. So, I figured, I've got this finished work, I'll put that together. It might not ever have come out as a book if I'd had another section of *Clyde* ready for that year.

DOMINICK: We're curious about the distinctions you draw between the kinds of work you do. There seem to be at least three categories: the commercial illustration work, which you have sometimes described rather dismissively (e.g. in your interview with Williams, where you suggest that if you did only illustrative work, you'd be a "hack"), your sketchbook-style work, and the more finished *Palookaville* work. What determines where something gets slotted in that spectrum? Obviously, illustration work is commissioned rather than personal, but other than that, how do you approach it in terms of your style? How do you differentiate between what should be a sketchbook-style work and what should receive the more finished approach? Is this mainly a matter of aesthetics, or the speed with which the work can be completed, or are there more fundamental questions of narrative form, or of the relationship between form and content, that guide such decisions? How do you separate commercial work from the work that you find more artistically legitimate? Does it depend on the work? Why does, say, *About Love* make the cut, but not *Classic Cocktails* or *The Wage Slave's Glossary*? Or the Aimee Mann CD but not the design for the Criterion Collection DVD release of the Leo McCarey film *Make Way for Tomorrow*?
SETH: Well, I think the one word answer to what determines things is control. That's the number one thing. That's why sometimes something that's

quite commercial actually turns out to be part of my own work. For example, right now I have a book coming out in about a month which is a designed and illustrated version of Stephen Leacock's *Sunshine Sketches of a Little Town*. I put a tremendous amount of work into it, and it's definitely a part of *my* work. There's a couple of reasons for that: one would be that it was my idea to begin with. I approached a publisher and not the other way around. Now, that's not a rule, though. If they had come to me and asked me to do it, and I still had the same amount of creative control, then I would still regard it the same way. I mean, since doing *Sunshine Sketches* we've begun talking about possibly designing a couple of other books in the same manner. The next one on the list I believe my editor might have suggested instead of it coming from me, but it doesn't matter because it's one of my favorite books, which is *The Stone Angel* by Margaret Laurence. So we're still working out the rights issues to see if we can do it, but the next book might not be my idea at all, let's put it that way, but it would still be my work. The main reason is that they gave me the absolute control I needed on *Sunshine Sketches*. They didn't make a single interfering suggestion in the whole process. Nobody said . . . well, maybe they made a few little suggestions during the process, like maybe page order or production issues or cost considerations, certain technical things like that. But nobody ever said something like, this concept isn't working or maybe you should cut out those landscapes you're using here or anything like that. It was completely understood that this was my project. If I had come to that project and encountered an immense amount of interference, at the end of the book it would be "This isn't my work anymore." I would have struck it off the list, basically. Then it would have just been work. Some work, of course, is done just for the money and so that takes it off the list right away even if I like the end results.

There's lots of illustration work like that . . . I have two boxes of original illustration art downstairs—I used to have three—the two boxes are labeled "Better Illustrations" and "Lesser Illustrations." There used to be a box that didn't have a title which was stuff that was going in the garbage. Now they don't even get into a box. Cut out the middle man. But the "Better Originals" doesn't even say "Good Illustrations" or "Favorites," or anything like that. It just says "better" because they're all kind of tainted. Every one of them is tainted by the fact that I had to illustrate *something* I wasn't that interested in, just for money, and of course, the results vary. The funny thing is it's not even a content-driven decision about which are good and which are poor, because certainly some of the better ones are often stupider in content than some of the lesser ones. With these illustrations I'm basing my opinion entirely on execution. It's like, "Oh, this one came out okay." Or "This one came out terrible." Something might make it into the bottom box if it's particularly heinous, like if the actual subject matter is beyond embarrassing. I think the worst illustration I ever did, content wise, was a few years ago and I always think of it because it was so stupid. It was a drawing of the Sistine Chapel—that famous pose of Adam and God with their hands meeting—and God's passing Adam a frozen yogurt. Now that may be the most stupid thing I ever drew. That one likely went in the bad box no matter how well I executed it. I'm sure I kept it as a brutal reminder. I should probably frame it and put it over my desk as some kind of object lesson!

That's why being exclusively an illustrator can be a bit of a grim career: at the end of your career you'll have a big box or two boxes like that and ultimately the content will be nothing of any importance or personal meaning. I think editorial illustration used to be a better career long ago because when you look back on those great years of the twentieth-century magazines you see illustrators being offered subject matter of a better sort. You see that illustrators were actually working on better articles. It wasn't just business and fluff pieces. There were serialized novels being illustrated, there were investigative pieces. You'll see some pretty remarkable stuff. There still are a few illustrators who work in that manner. Somebody like Sue Coe probably has a pretty impressive portfolio. I can't list a lot of names here because I'm out of touch. I don't follow illustration at all. Most illustrators, I suspect, when it comes down to it, will have portfolios filled with a variety of stylistically nice drawings. "Here's some coffee packaging I designed, here are some illustrations I did for the op-ed of the *New York Times*." That sort of thing. Much of that stuff is very pretty—very eye-catching—but ultimately that body of work, if collected and published, will only make a book of wallpapers at best. Even if you look at 1940s illustration; a book of that will be more interesting because its subject matter is more varied in what they were doing. That said, even the collections of older commercial illustrators don't interest me much beyond appreciating their talent and style.

As an illustrator, I *am* somewhat of a hack simply because of the commercial nature of the work. It's done for the money. I'll always do my best for them. No matter how stupid the job is, I'll try to make it look good. I give it serious effort and kind consideration. But that work is always just somewhat meaningless to me in the final analysis.

ERIC: Well, I think that shows, personally.
SETH: Right, I think you can always tell. Even Jaime [Hernandez] was

recently saying somewhere that you can always tell his commercial work is lesser because he just doesn't put his heart into it. It's hard for that not to happen.

Carrying on. After "control," I'd have to say the next deciding criterion . . . there's basically two other reasons—the first is time. Some things are done for expediency. The sketchbook work recognizes that I will never do these stories if I have to do them in the "full style," for lack of a better term. To really put the finish on the art, like on *Clyde*, is just too laborious. It means that those other works simply won't get done if they have to be done "full style." If I had waited around to begin *Wimbledon Green* after I finished *Clyde Fans*, well, it wouldn't have been done. I'm still working on *Clyde Fans* and by the time the damn thing actually gets done I'd probably have entirely lost interest in *Wimbledon Green* long ago. There are many such stories I've planned that died on the vine because I thought, "Oh, I'll never get to them . . ." Everything has a window of opportunity. When you start planning a novel, you can't wait ten years to start the thing. You'll have a better idea after ten years. Ideas have a shelf life. Doing them in the sketchbook style saves a few ideas from the graveyard.

After expediency, the other criterion is private versus public. Some stuff is just done more for me. That doesn't mean it *can't* be published, but it's not a prerequisite. I have a handful of sketchbooks that nobody has seen anything from and it's not because it's secret; there's nothing big in there that I couldn't publish. I could probably publish the whole of my diaries and it wouldn't bother me in the least. There's nothing really secret in there. I don't write about that kind of stuff. But it's not done *for* publication. It's also not done *not* to be published. It all depends on how I feel when the time comes. I don't think there's anything I do that *couldn't* be published. But there's lots of small stuff that's not really done as part of the process toward final publication.

ERIC: Beyond those factors are there certain hired jobs that you would include because they provide you with a sense of accomplishment, like, say, the covers you did for the *New Yorker*?

SETH: Well, the *New Yorker* covers are interesting in that I wouldn't include them . . .

ERIC: I mean, it's presumptuous of me to assume . . .

SETH: No, that's a good point. The *New Yorker* covers would get on a list of accomplishments because it's a career accomplishment and not because of anything I feel about those particular covers. Of the few covers I've done, I liked one or two of them, I think. But I probably don't like them terrifically more than some other illustration work I can think of. That doesn't seem important to me though. They are on a list of "real" work just because the *New Yorker* was so important to me when I was coming up and getting those covers was a tremendous career goal.

ERIC: To be part of the pantheon of *New Yorker* illustrators.

SETH: Exactly. Also, sometimes another person's project will take on personal meaning, like the Aimee Mann project. That was the result of someone calling me up, wanting me to work for them, and it wasn't because it was prestigious that it ended up on the list but because it became a more personal work for me. She gave me surprisingly sweeping control, she let me do what I wanted to do and therefore the final results felt very much like my own project.

I don't think I included anything I did for Criterion, did I?

ERIC: No.

SETH: Okay. Whereas I'm proud of those, and they do feel *kind* of like personal work . . . I mean, Eric Skillman gave me tons of control on those designs . . . they do seem to fall more into the category of commissions. As much as I was excited to be even very vaguely connected to Charlie Chaplin—I've just completed the designs for *City Lights* coming out later this year, and that's a definite thrill, when you're allowed to illustrate the DVD packaging of a Chaplin film—that still doesn't make it personal work in the same way as the Aimee Mann project. Still, I have no doubt if I were ever to do an *Art of Seth* book those Criterion designs would be in there for sure and most of that commissioned illustration work would not. So that says something.

Even the *Peanuts* books—I'm not all that sure they really fall into the personal work category, although I'm certainly proud of them and they're an important career point for me. Maybe I feel less connected to them at the moment because I've done so many of them. I'm just not sure what to say about that. I'm very happy with them and I still enjoy working on them, but I don't think about them all that much any longer. If somebody asked me what I do, it would be a while before I would think to list the *Peanuts* books. I mean, I think I've done about twenty of them now. But, you know what? When the set is finished and they are all sitting there in their slipcases I will surely feel that they are a tremendous personal accomplishment. All this seeming ambivalence I'm displaying here will vanish.

ERIC: Dominick and I were having some difficulty deciphering whether the images on the covers of the *Peanuts* books were original Schulz blown up or if it was you doing a Schulz pastiche.

SETH: Okay, that's good to hear. I'm glad you cannot tell. When I first started doing those books, I didn't intend to redraw any of Schulz's work.

ERIC: But there were instances where you had to—where panels were missing.

SETH: Well. Not really. Those re-created panels from the early books were cobbled together from Xeroxes of other panels.

And those spreads inside, where you'll see like, you know, a big landscape scene, those are about 80 percent Schulz and then maybe 20 percent me. Actually even less. Probably 5 percent. I'm cutting Schulz images apart and putting them back together in different arrangements and then I've got to fill the little spaces in between the cut images. If I have, say, the ball diamond, I blow up a bench and I put that in. Then I have a wall behind it and then I'll put in the pitcher's mound up front, et cetera. So then there'll be a few Schulz texture lines on the ground that he's put in, but I'll need a few more, okay—so I will draw those in. Then maybe there's a tree, but there's not a full trunk for it so I'll fake a bit of a Schulz trunk or something. And that's very minimal. But the covers, the problem is I don't work digitally. In the first volumes I used to simply blow up a face for the cover on the Xerox machine, a Sparky drawn face, but it would be so bit-mapped that I'd have to go in and clean it up with white out. By the end the faces were so cleaned up that I was literally reshaping every line in them. In fact, even in the first couple of books I remember somebody complaining that I was putting his drawings through a vector system. I remember thinking, "I don't even know what a vector is." I guess they suspected I'd taken Schulz's drawings and digitally made them more mechanical. Slicked them up. That was just because I was removing so much of the clutter that happens when you blow up a small image on a Xerox machine. After about ten books of that I realized, you know, there is so much manipulation going on in this Schulz-face that I might as well just re-ink it. Now I just take the bitmapped image, light box it and re-ink it. So basically it is like 50/50 now on the cover. The inside stuff is still almost 100 percent Schulz. But I'm happy you're at least *wondering* about it because I don't want it to look like I redrew it. I want it to be slick but I want it to be totally Sparky's image.

ERIC: I think my suspicion is a result of our familiarity with your work, whereas most people look at it and it would probably never even occur to them.

SETH: I haven't gotten as much blame for the *Peanuts* books as I've gotten for the other designs. People have been pretty pissy about those [John] Stanley books because they're so clearly my drawings on the covers. I have a better argument for those. Stanley worked the majority of his career with other people drawing his comics for him. In fact, the majority of his work was drawn by other hands. So it's not really that insulting to put my drawings on those covers. Stanley drew so little of it that it's not quite the same in my opinion. But even so, I sympathize with the complaints. I would have the same complaints if somebody was designing those same books and I didn't care for their particular stamp. I probably cut myself a little too much slack.

DOMINICK: There are lots of reprint projects happening right now and you've been involved with a few of them. I'm assuming that at least some of these were people who came to you and asked you to be involved. But are there others that you've spearheaded other than the Doug Wright?

SETH: Let me think about that. I guess you could say that I was involved from the beginning with each of these reprint projects. There haven't been any of them yet that began with someone just calling me up. *Peanuts*, as well. I can't remember which issue of *The Comics Journal* it was but there was an issue where they interviewed Schulz and Gary Groth asked me, since he knew I was a big *Peanuts* fan, if I would do the cover for it. At that point I recall saying to Gary, if you ever . . . and this was before any of the current crop of reprint books really got going—though Fantagraphics *had* been reprinting classic strips for years—but the modern era hadn't really hit yet. Actually, not to be immodest but I think those *Peanuts* books might be the very start of that new era. Something changed right about then.

Anyhow, I remember saying to Gary that if he ever gets a chance to publish the complete *Peanuts* that that would be a dream project and I would love to be involved. I suspect it is just because I said that to Gary at that moment in time that it led to my later involvement as the designer. I doubt Gary's first thought would have been "OK, we're gonna do this *Complete Peanuts*; call Seth." There's probably lots of artists who loved Schulz as much as I did and probably a few that loved him even more. So that was probably just a very good piece of luck for me that I was involved with it from the very beginning and had talked to Gary about it. I mean it was just pie-in-the-sky thinking when I said that. At that point he hadn't even been talking to Jeannie Schulz, but I recall him saying something like, "It's an idea we've been considering."

Even the Stanley books, I'll take some modest credit. I'd suggest that those books were somewhat prodded into existence because of my years of enthusiastically talking up John Stanley to Chris Oliveros. I can remember sending Chris Xeroxes of John Stanley's *Little Lulu* way back when he didn't even know who John Stanley was. However, that was really just the two of us being young and me wanting to share a great cartoonist with a friend. Not a book pitch or anything. At that point I think we were generally more enthusiastic comics fans and there was a lot more give-and-take, talking back and forth. I think my relationship with Chris Oliveros has settled somewhat into a publisher/artist friendship now simply because we don't see each other as much or talk on the phone as much as we used to. I don't talk on the phone to anybody nowadays.

Also, the fact that Tom Devlin came to work at Drawn & Quarterly and he had previously edited that issue of *The Comics Journal* where I wrote an essay about Stanley. Tom and I often spoke about John Stanley after that, and I think it was just kind of a given between us that if they ever did any books about John Stanley I'd be involved. Currently we've passed into yet another phase with reprints, I think. A variety of publishers have reprinted a lot more material since we started on that project. I suspect that if Drawn & Quarterly put out those Stanley books now instead of back then they might have just designed them in-house. Thinking back, right around the time of the *Peanuts* books it was somewhat standard to draft a modern cartoonist in as the designer to give some special "flavor" to the books—which I don't think anyone cares about so much anymore. I can't remember—was Chris Ware designing *Krazy Kat* before the *Peanuts* books? I'd have to look that up. [The Ware-designed *Krazy & Ignatz* series in fact predates Seth's work on *The Complete Peanuts*.]

DOMINICK: Do you think, obviously I think that there is historical value to these sorts of projects, bringing all this stuff back, but do you think that contemporary artists are now looking as this material, now that there is more to see, in terms of influence?

SETH: Yeah, it's a different world. I do think young artists *are* looking at the work, because I can see the influence. I just got in the mail a book the other day that Koyama Press put out that clearly the format is meant to imitate an early Cupples and Leon [American publishing company founded in 1902 by Victor I. Cupples (1864–1941) and Arthur T. Leon (1867–1943)] collection from the early 1920s. The work inside is very much in the style of *Little Orphan*

Annie. This cartoonist is probably in his twenties, so clearly these books are getting in the hands of young artists. I bet you though that these young cartoonists are still having the same problem that I had at that age—these books are expensive.

ERIC: Unless one has access to a good library—

SETH: Yeah, exactly, and I think a lot of them *do* go to the library to look at this stuff. And there is the *big* difference—and I hate to argue for less cultural access but that was a time where the cartoonists of my generation were forced to find their own ancestors. That was a long and meaningful process. I mean *Good Life* talks a little bit about that process of searching about in the dusty past. That process of digging up the older artists was so integral to my experience as a cartoonist in my twenties. That made me who I am. I mean, you discovered them bit by bit over time simply because you just didn't have greater access to information. What books were out there were scattered and few and usually full of inaccuracies. That big *World Encyclopedia of Comics*, by Maurice Horn, I read that book cover to cover. It's filled with mistakes but just as a source of information that was a godsend back then. There was almost no information on cartoonists available.

ERIC: Or the *Smithsonian Collection of Newspaper Comics.*

SETH: The *Smithsonian* book is a great vault of art that you might otherwise have never seen. Even today you're only just starting to see that vault opened up for real. But back then, literally, you'd just go into a bookstore and find some old book with no context about who this cartoonist was or how their work fit in to the grander scheme of things. Maybe it might mention in the back of the book where they'd published, maybe it wouldn't, but you'd slowly build up these progenitors. You'd pick which person is of interest, you'd say, "Now I'm a fan of Charles Addams," whatever, and then you'd try and figure out who Charles Addams was. Information that seems so easily acquired now; I can remember encountering Edward Gorey when I was very young and not really knowing who he was and not having an easy answer to that question. I couldn't just walk into the library and find out who Edward Gorey was at that point, and my friends didn't know any more about him than I did. I can remember someone saying about Edward Gorey, "Oh yes, he published in the *New Yorker.*" So I thought, "Oh, he's a *New Yorker* guy!" Well, of course, Edward Gorey never really published in the *New Yorker.* They were thinking of Charles Addams. They just got it mixed up because of the macabre subject matter. There were lots of incidents like that where you'd just have to muddle your way through.

I do think that was a really important process for me, a kind of artistic archaeology that you were required to go through. Ultimately, maybe that's not important in the long run. It's hard to say. It was important to my generation. It was certainly very important in shaping who I am as an artist. The whole process of collecting shaped me, too. Essentially I became a collector *because* of that lack of information. I didn't start out that way. I don't really think I was a "comic book collector" in the true sense as a kid because I didn't have any access to collecting. I lived in a very small town so, if you call buying the new comics on the newsstand as they came out each week collecting, well, yes, then I was a comic book collector. But I'd never seen a comic shop or a comic bag or a price-guide and I'd never been to a comic book convention or anything like that. My real collecting started later in bookstores. That process of collecting has shaped all my work and it's pretty much shaped the very narratives that I'm interested in writing about. They're all narratives about discovery and loss, in effect. That's all kind of linked to collecting and learning about the past. They're often concerned with mundane ephemera in some manner too. I'm interested in mundane things for some reason. I like things that are more on the boring end of the scale than the exciting end, and, as a collector, the world of old books and dusty magazines and stuff like that, that all sits comfortably in that stuffy category. If cartooning is my vocation then collecting is surely my avocation.

But the young cartoonists, they don't have to go through that process anymore—maybe a bit of it, but not so much. You can find the context of just about anything with the computer in a moment. And it does make a tremendous difference on how you view the work. The mystery vanishes from a lot of that material when it is instantly catalogued.

ERIC: You don't have that same kind of joy of discovery, of unearthing . . .

SETH: I do think that there's some unique quality in obscurity that people find enticing. When you discover something off the beaten path, you can kind of make it *your own*. It's one of the main reasons why people stop liking things when they become quite popular. "I used to like this band but now they're too popular, they're terrible." So you disown them. You can no longer pull them out of a bag and say, "Check this out! You've never heard of these guys." That process of building identity through pop culture I think is super-important to our time period. It might be the defining element of our times. Maybe people didn't do that so much in the seventeenth century. I doubt peasants identified themselves by trends or possessions or musical forms. I mean, maybe some people did, but I have a suspicion that that's an essential element of modernity. I know that my identity is largely based on the cultural forms that I've latched onto. They're *mine*.

ERIC: The world was a much larger place way back then. There wasn't so much of the printed word, there was no mass media, no radio, no television, any of these cultural artifacts and venues we have now and are constantly bombarded with.

SETH: Exactly. Culture was much more proscribed then. You would likely identify yourself by fitting into the folk culture around you. That makes sense, right? I mean, you might identify yourself as, I'm a Cooper, or I'm a Wheelwright, and that was plenty of identity for you. I'm a father . . .

ERIC: . . . a Christian . . .

SETH: Yeah, definitely important. Probably where you lived was very important, too, because you probably didn't move around that much. The actual spaces you inhabited, without even thinking about it, probably formed a huge part of your identity. But today, I think it's pretty obvious that we largely identify ourselves by wearing a shirt that has something written on it. Folks choose pop culture symbols which broadcast their taste . . . or their sense of humor, or whatever it is, and I think that artists always do that as well by picking their influences . . .

ERIC: Don't you think that experience of discovering something obscure sort of ties into that feeling of authenticity, that it hasn't been, for lack of a better word, tainted yet?

SETH: I do think that's true. I think that might be a bit of a rationalization, though. Looking for authenticity gives you the nobility of a truth seeker. I try to be hard on myself—to be rigorous—because I like to pretend I'm doing things for better reasons than others, but I'm pretty sure I'm not any different from the average Joe. I have a strong suspicion that I wrote *Forty Cartoon Books of Interest* as a way to show off that I've got forty things that aren't the same as your forty things. To make it clear, I guess, that I'm "doing my own thing." There's something about that process of defining yourself through culture, I think, that's so primary to becoming an artist, it's why you naturally narrow your vision as time goes on.

Digressing—I do think that all style in drawing is about choices; the choices an artist makes determines what their style will be. So right away you make some basic choices and for me my initial choice was to work in a clear line, so immediately you've eliminated texture from the work. I was not going to make a choice like Chester Brown's choice and use a great deal of hatching. That was out for me immediately. Every decision is a boiling down process. I will draw noses in this manner; I will draw feet in this way. My backgrounds will be sparse or my backgrounds will be detailed. The end result is a style of some kind. It might take a decade to get there or even longer. That's why young artists aren't sure what style they're going to work in. I always tell them, "Don't worry about it because you won't pick the style, the style will pick you . . . over time through a series of small choices."

You can often see where their choices begin though, and that's because people define themselves right away by whom they stylistically wish to be connected to or which artist gives them a certain feeling they like. When starting out, I recall doing pages that were all in different drawing styles, and one of them was a *very* Edward Gorey style, because I really liked Edward Gorey then. Another one was a sort of Jaime Hernandez kind of approach. Ultimately it was the Hernandez influence that won in that battle because Jaime was primarily working in a clear line, not a lot of hatching, and that was an easy decision for me, because I wasn't an artist who liked to work with all that hay. Again, that process of early selection is about trying to connect yourself to defining elements in the culture that you wish to be defined by. No matter what I thought of the look of any of the mainstream comic artists at that time, I would never have selected any of them to study because the very nature of the work they were doing would've been something I'd be horrified to identify my young self with. If somebody like, say, Mike Mignola had been around at that time, he works in a pretty clean style and I might even have liked it then. I would definitely not have added him to my list of interests because his work had the wrong context. Its pulpy aura said something unclean to me. I simply had to pick someone that was doing a clean line art style as an influence that was part and parcel of my own kind of "persona building." It had to be artists like Hergé or Schulz or Peter Arno—someone that I felt was . . . well, you carry on doing this through your whole life, you continue to do it, I think. It's interesting that people . . . they talk about their tastes changing, a lot of it is rejecting things that aren't defining you as well as they used to. A refining process of identity. So, maybe being interested in B movies in the 1980s for some might have been a real way to define one's self against the mainstream, but as the culture caught up and assimilated that B-movie irony stance perhaps that same person might move on to more extreme material: "I only like movies that have a lot of depictions of gore in them." They know that the majority of people don't want to come along for that. Of course, this seeking of obscurity to define oneself can be pretty shallow. That said, I think it is an essential element of identity. Roping off interests to possess them entirely.

You know, people are always searching for something that others can't own, too. It seems to me that most people don't want to be labeled as bland. Even people who *have* perfectly bland tastes tend to think that they're "out there." "Oh, I love that Dexter" or whatever some soccer-mom will tell you. And you think, well, that's probably because she thinks *Dexter* will define her in some way and make her more interesting than some sitcom with, I don't know, Jennifer Aniston in it. We all do it. It's stupid but it's effective too. Results vary.

ERIC: I find your comparison of comics to "poetry and design"—in particular its concern over "brevity . . . rhythm [and] breaks for silence"—fascinating [see Bryan Miller interview pp. 74]. When making this comparison, did you think this is to be the case with comics as a medium, or were you referring more specifically to your own work?

SETH: I'm not sure any more. I have to think about it. That was said some time ago. Probably when I was talking about that I was thinking of comics like my own. I might not have been thinking about adventure type comics. But I'm not sure that it makes any difference. I think that comics have always been compared most easily to film or to prose: or as a combination of the two. I think that as more people have thought about this comparison they've realized that might not be so true. The film connection, if anything, is probably in the other direction, in that comics are *trying* to be like film, rather than having anything inherently in common with the movies. Actually, I don't think comics have much in common with film except that they've taken on a lot of cinematic techniques that generally do work quite well in comics. And if film hadn't come along, I suspect comics would look *a lot* different. Though, that said, they would likely have invented many of those filmic techniques anyway. A close-up is a pretty obvious invention.

The essential element of film is that it moves. Comics don't move. For a drawn medium I'd say that animation is the one connected to film, not comics. Comics really are a still form. That is what is interesting about them, and that's why I think instead of film, graphic design is actually their more natural partner. I do think that the grammar and syntax of comics is very connected to the formal qualities of graphic designing more than simply being about drawing because it's how you arrange things on the page that matters in the storytelling. It's how you choose the panels and the shapes within the panels. That's the essential element to cartoon language. Not the finish you put on it after. Graphic design is about manipulating shapes, understanding negative space and controlling where the eye is looking. It's basically the art of composition writ large. What is a comic page but a complex graphic design with a storytelling goal? A good cartoonist is a good graphic designer because he cannot leave the important decisions on how the page operates to random chance. That sounds obvious, but think of how many comic strips or comic book pages are put together by people paying attention to only what is inside the panel they are working on.

When you talk about the writing, which always gets compared to a how a novel reads . . . well, no, I think the writing is actually closer to poetry, it's much more about compression and brevity and cadence. Comic storytelling is so much about brevity and pacing. Even big, long graphic novels, everything is about compression. Obviously the one thing that doesn't read well in comics is when there's too much text. Anybody can tell you that. "Oh, I can't read this; there's too many words in the balloons." It's an immediate turnoff. You could have three pages that have a certain amount of information that is far too dense and then take those same three pages and spread that out over twenty-five pages and suddenly that material is totally readable. It's not about the amount of information, it's about the presentation and the fact that it needs to be rolled out in a certain manner where the pacing is the most important element. Pacing and brevity are essential to any kind of good comic storytelling.

For me, I really think it boils down to no more than a sentence/balloon per panel. You might be able to have two balloons when people are speaking to each other, but the moment you get beyond a singular thought being expressed per panel it gets bogged down. You lose the essential reading rhythm. Rhythm is all important in comics. You don't have to break the rhythm up a lot, but you do have to think about the rhythm all the time. Much of the time I'm following a very simple rhythm, which is a staccato kind of rhythm, beat after beat after beat. Occasionally, I'll throw in a large panel or a double-page spread, essentially a whole note or a long pause. These pauses are essential too. You don't want three hundred pages of a staccato rhythm in a row, but you also don't need to keep changing it up on every page—where things are really slow and then really fast. I think the reader is fine with almost any

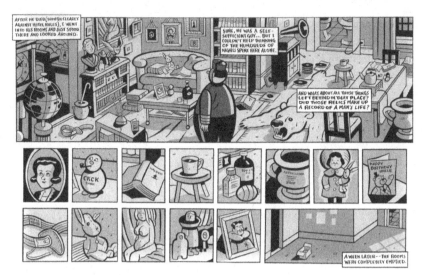

Panel size and pacing. From *George Sprott (1894-1975)* © Seth. Used with permission from Drawn & Quarterly.

rhythm but the rhythm has to be measured with the same considered thought that a poet might use. I do think that may be one of the failings of commercial comics over the century is that the cartoonists stopped thinking about the rhythm. Or they weren't *allowed* to think about the rhythm, let's put it that way. If you look back at the Atlas monster comics of the late 1950s, or any of the horror comics coming out at that time, the big problem is that they had a rather constrictive page count, maybe eight pages to tell a complicated story, and the writer clearly wasn't thinking about the rhythm at all, he was just thinking about the body count. The artists, because of the constraints of storytelling, were left with little to really think about beyond style. They weren't really allowed to tell stories properly at that time. Cartooning stagnated as cartoonists thought less about storytelling and more about showing off their drawing style. That's turning around today. Lots of interesting storytelling going on.

Let me digress: I do think I could make an argument, if I had to, about why simplified drawing styles work best in cartooning. Now, when you say "cartooning," people have an idea of what a "cartoon" drawing is. I do too, but that simplified cartoon "style" isn't *essential* to the medium. You *could* have a comic in a highly realized, steel engraving style, for example, that could be terrific if the storytelling is terrific. It's the storytelling that counts, not the drawing style. The storytelling—that's the framework, the grammar of the comics language. However, I *would* argue that simplified drawing *is* the best form of cartooning because I don't think it interferes with the storytelling language. It doesn't *fight* the language. Those steel engravings might be so busy that they interfere with the simplicity of the comics medium. Making it awkward. I don't think painted comics, for example, work so well because they inevitably slow everything down. The images tend to become deadly still and frozen. I suppose that can depend on the style of who's painting it, too. I've seen painted comics that worked alright, I guess, and I've seen ones that *really* don't work. I think the problem is when the artist aims for a really high finish in the painted artwork, they stop thinking about the storytelling as much. They start thinking of, you know, how am I going to paint this panel so that it will be particularly beautiful. They tend to think in panels—not full pages. The whole thing is a series of dead images with no movement between them. Whereas when you are working with simple line drawings, this generally leads you to think, "I'm not so concerned with just the visual impact; I'm mostly concerned with how the story's told." The drawings become more like graphic shapes you are moving around to maximize the storytelling language. I suppose it's something like comparing drawing style to lettering fonts. A nice simple sans-serif font is easier for reading clarity than a baroque Old English font.

ERIC: *Clyde Fans* has a far different pacing than most of your other work. It's your longest work, both in length of story and in the length of time it has taken you to complete it. Is this slower, more meticulous pacing a deliberate choice? Did you know from the outset that it was going to take you this long to complete? What place does it have in relationship to your other works? Do you view *Fans* as your magnum opus?

SETH: First off, the slow pacing in the story is very deliberate—actually, *whatever* pacing I'm using in there is very deliberate. The very point of *Clyde Fans* was probably more about narrative storytelling than it is about story. The story is a very thin story, if you boil it down to a couple of sentences of what it is about . . . well, I won't boil it down because then I'd have to say what's in the last chapter. The final chapter is kind of . . . if you think of an interlocking object then the final chapter is the thing that keeps it from falling apart. Right now you're just slowly getting these four pieces basically, but the heart of it comes together in the final chapter, when you'll finally put the last piece into the puzzle.

I knew from the beginning exactly what each of the chapters would be about and how they would be told. That was planned from the beginning and I've been following that plan along pretty faithfully as I slowly work my way towards completion. A few things have changed because it's taken so long; certain sequences that I was planning to get to have evolved. When I finally reached some certain scene or other, I might have changed the way I approached it or its importance had grown or diminished, but the overall structure of how it fit into the story was set in place right at the outset. A brief explanation of what I mean by that: for example, the first chapter is Abraham entirely in monologue. So I knew I wanted the first chapter to be set up so that one of the brothers would be speaking directly to the reader and everything is said from the outside; in other words, there's never a moment where he has an interior thought. We're getting a monologue from a narrator whom we believe or don't believe, but we don't have access to his inner thoughts.

I knew I needed to keep the brothers apart until the fourth chapter. They may have a minor scene or two they share together, but no real interaction exists between them. The second chapter would be composed in what I considered to be a "naturalistic" approach in which we are following the character around like a ghost watching him do things. But again, no interior access to the character. So Simon is seen entirely from the outside, naturalistically, and there's very little dialogue as he doesn't talk much. In the third chapter, that's when I get to switch to interior dialogue with Simon, that's where we now get to see him from the inside. In the fourth chapter, which I'm completing now, we see Abraham from the inside. This is the chapter where I finally get to bring them together, as well. Each chapter has some narrative purpose that had to be accomplished and this chapter's is that they have to meet and talk. After a long stretch I finally get to allow them to speak to each other.

To answer your other question—no, I didn't plan for it to take this long to accomplish. Definitely not. I mean, when I started on it, after *Good Life*, I intended to take probably about as long as *Good Life* took; I thought it would take a couple of years to do, but as I worked with this kind of storytelling, it required more pages than I anticipated. *Good Life* is five or six issues long, and each issue is a chapter in the final book, and I kind of thought *Clyde Fans* would be like that as well: five chapters, so basically five issues. Of course each chapter turned out to be three issues, or in some cases four issues. As I got older, the pace at which I was producing the issues got slower too. At some point, a lot of time had passed. So basically, I think I stopped caring about how long it was taking because around that time I was also beginning to spread myself out on a lot of different projects. When I did *Good Life*, it was very straightforward; that was all I was doing. By the time I was halfway through *Clyde* I was already producing longer stories in my sketchbooks, working on the cardboard buildings and my city, and all these little side projects. *Clyde* remained a strong interest; I worked on it when I had the time, but it no longer had that central importance in my life, that, "I've got to get this done because it's my next work." There was a lot of other work coming out too.

That said, it does remain in the category of magnum opus to me, but I have my doubts it's going to end up having that effect when it's finished. I think to current readers it will just be another book I finished, although to me it will still have that original larger vision. A primary work. I feel that when it's done and people actually read the whole thing, because I don't imagine that anyone has kept up with it—I mean, people probably don't even *remember* what's happened in it anymore, or more likely, there are probably people who have read a couple of chapters or a couple of *segments* of chapters and don't even have a clue about what's going on. I certainly never kid myself that when the latest issue appears that anybody out there is like, "Oh boy, now let's see what's going on with *Clyde Fans*." Often I encounter people that've read the first book collection, *Book One*, and then have read a couple of the more recent segments and have asked, "So, have I got all the Clyde stuff so far?" My unsatisfying response is, "No, there are a bunch of issues that are long out of print now—you haven't even read chapter three." Sigh. But anyhow, I expect when it's finally done, and I re-edit it all and put it into its final form in a nice fat book—that that book will be really for the new readers who've never read any of it, or who maybe read a little bit of it and will now sit down, read it, and say, "Oh, *that's* what that thing was all about." Sadly, I worry that the long-term readers will be the ones who've given up and may be tired of the whole thing by the time the final book appears.

At this point, I think most people just see it as some long, meandering drag that has something to do with salesmanship. My personal interaction with it is long and deep because I've been involved with it for such a long time, but in a weird way it doesn't define my work to most people. Because it is unfinished, it doesn't come up much in discussions of my work. People talk about other books. People talk to me more about *George Sprott* than *Clyde Fans* because *Sprott* is a finished work—a tangible work with a beginning, middle, and end.

I'm still excited to do it, though. And that's the thing. I look at it with a different time frame than most serialized books would be looked at. To me it's just a long project that will eventually be done. I'm not working on a schedule here. Unless you consider getting it done before I die, a schedule.

ERIC: Two follow-up questions. The first one may be a bit easier to answer, I think, than the second one, but, will there be a *Book Two*, or will you eventually just publish everything in one volume?

SETH: That's a good question. If you'd asked me this last year, the answer would definitely be, "yes, there will be a *Book Two*." And I would have said that for sure. In fact, I remember I really wanted a *Book Two*, and I remember I talked to Chris Oliveros about it, and he seemed completely in agreement with me. Now, I'm not so sure. I've actually started to think maybe I don't want a *Book Two*. I was emailing with Carol Tyler a while ago, who put out *You'll Never Know* in three books instead of one, and the first book sold reasonably well, and (from what I gather) the second book sold less, or it did worse, and the third book, worse too (I think). A lot of people who really loved the first book simply didn't follow up on it, I guess, or forgot to look for the subsequent volumes or whatever, but because it didn't come out in one chunk, it kind of fell off their radar. Carol said to me, "Should I put those together into a new complete book? I kind of feel like I'm ripping off the people who got the three books." And I was like, "Put them into a big book. It should be out there, and people should read them." You know, I've bought lots of stuff that came out in a variety of formats and then by the end, in yet another final form, and that's just life—I didn't feel ripped off. The funny thing is, I had been feeling the exact same thing about *Clyde*, that I don't want to screw all those people who bought *Book One*, but it was so long ago, part of me couldn't help wondering, "is anyone genuinely expecting a *Book Two* to come out after all this time to complete their set?" I think *I* wanted a *Book Two* mostly because I wanted to put them side by side in a slipcase and have this project done. I had a design planned out that the second book mirrored the first book—it has the same faces on it, except they're old men now, and the two books match up perfectly in the design together. But the greater part of me can't help but think that the logical answer is to simply put it out as one complete book, because that's the form that would be correct for the new reader. It gets complicated. If we put out a *Book Two*, I've got to make sure *Book One* is available at the same time, which means maybe *Book One* has to be reprinted at that same point. Maybe then I should have a slipcased edition, as well, so a new reader can buy both books at the same time. But then, do we sell a slipcase separately for the original purchasers of *Book One*? It all seems like it's getting over complicated, and maybe it's not the best business plan for Drawn & Quarterly, either.

DOMINICK: Would *Book Two* be longer than *Book One*? My impression is that it seems to be bigger.

SETH: Yeah, it is.

DOMINICK: Was that part of the plan, or has it expanded?

SETH: No, it's expanded. I'd say the storytelling has slowed down more—meaning more pages to tell the same story. I think after I did the first chapter and it was three issues, I thought each chapter would be three issues except the last one, which would be shorter, but then chapter three turned into four issues, and it looks like chapter four is about the same length, too. Chapter five, the last one, will probably stay about the length I always thought it was, which I think will be somewhere between sixty and eighty pages, which is a much shorter segment. We'll see. I still have to do some final correcting on that, so. . . . But the second section is fatter, so that does have a bit of an effect. More and more, I'm pretty sure I'm going to put it in one big complete book when it's over. It just seems to make the most sense.

DOMINICK: Is that a similar sort of growth process to the way Dominion went from a single building to building an entire town? Has *Clyde Fans* undergone a similar kind of narrative growth?

SETH: Not really. What's happened there more is that the storytelling has slowed down. I do like to digress and go further and further into things, but actually with *Clyde*, it's just a simple matter of the fact that I'm more likely now to break actions down into smaller pieces. I think when I started the book, if for example, I had two people talking, I might have the two faces in the same panel and have two balloons, one saying, "How are you doing?" and the other saying, "I'm doing fine." Now I'd be more likely to have a shot of them approaching each other, and then one saying, "How are you doing?" and then I'd put another panel in between where there's an interior thought, and then maybe one of them would take a puff of his cigarette and then the panel where he answers, "I'm doing fine." So one panel turns into five panels or some such. I think that really slows down the action, but I also think it makes the storytelling much more evocative.

ERIC: This is the second follow-up question. You talked about how you are more interested in doing a more digressive style, but *Clyde Fans* seems to be rather more straightforward, narratively speaking. With this in mind, do you consider *Clyde Fans* to be representative of your work all together? I mean, would you consider it to be *the* representative work? If someone were to ask you, what is Seth all about, is that the book that you would hand them, eventually?

SETH: Probably at this point I would hand them *George Sprott*; that's the book I feel most represents my thinking and my approach. Maybe that's just the overall tenor of my work that I've done. But maybe, I don't know, it's hard to say with *Clyde*. I feel very connected to it, and I *do* feel like it's representative, but in some odd way, you're right, it isn't. I'm using a very different storytelling style in there than I probably am in most of other stuff, and the *Clyde* approach is probably not where my work is going, either. I think that *Clyde* will represent a certain approach that I planned long ago, but clearly I am moving more into a kind of chatty digression, a digressive narrative style, that is all about telling. And *Clyde* is a much more "show, don't tell" style. It's much slowed down. I mean, sure, there is a lot of telling going on in *Clyde* too—there's a lot of narrated dialogue et cetera, but it's handled so differently.

ERIC: So it's more representative of a certain point in your career?
SETH: Yeah, I do think so. It's transitional—although it might have been a choice, like a direction—the road not taken that maybe I feel like I should have taken. There's something I really like in the *Clyde* approach, and perhaps my newest work feels more perfunctory or expedient to me. I mean it is expedient. That's why I'm doing this current work in this form. It's a good form to get ideas out to the audience with a minimum of fuss; it's not quite so artful, though. The narrative style in *Clyde* is more considered.

ERIC: But maybe it's—you can forgive the clichéd comparison—it's like an old shoe. It's comfortable, you know how to do it; the discovery may not be there, but it's something that you're confident with.
SETH: That's true. There's something about directness that's, you know— over the door on the way down to the studio I have a little engraved plaque with quotations from the Shakers on it, and I usually look at on the way down, little reminders to myself, and one of the things that they encourage, of course, is that beauty comes from orderliness, and also that orderliness and beauty are connected to utility, and I believe that so much of where my storytelling has gone, and even my current drawing style, is based on utility. It's about the form; the storytelling-need has initiated the form. So, basically I need to talk to the reader and show them certain things, but it's all boiled down to what is the most direct way to do it, instead of the most artful way to do it, or the most elaborate or exquisite way. The language I'm using is very simple and direct. I suppose it's trying to be somewhat in the spirit of the writing of E. B. White; he's using very straightforward, simple sentences that are clipped and efficient and trying to avoid ostentation. They're evocative sentences, but they're not—it's not like reading the work of, say, H. P. Lovecraft, which is overly flowing and purple and deliberately trying to drag

in grandiose word arrangements. I think my style is now rendering itself down to a very simple kind of grammar and syntax, and *Clyde* is still from an earlier time from when I was trying to figure out what my grammar was going to be.

DOMINICK: You suggested in some comments in the past that serialization might not have been the best format for *Clyde Fans*, but could it have been completed in any other way?

SETH: It would have died long ago without serialization. Or I would have had to develop a different way of thinking about it. I don't know. Serialization is still important, in my opinion, for the modern cartoonist in that you literally cannot build a career doing a ten-year book, releasing it, and then doing another ten-year book. You have to have some visibility to the readers. It really is a "what have you done for me lately?" culture, and I do think that putting out shorter books like *Wimbledon Green* and works like that has been very important in moving my "career" along, because otherwise if it was just another *Palookaville* every two years with another chapter of *Clyde Fans* in it, I think I would have been pretty much forgotten. I think Jason Lutes has suffered somewhat in that way with *Berlin*. You don't hear his name that much but if Jason had released several smaller self-contained books of some kind during this same period I wonder if that would have changed how we perceive him as an artist.

ERIC: He has a new issue of *Berlin* out this year, and there wasn't really any attention given to it. I think there were a few people who said, "Oh yes, and Jason Lutes is still doing *Berlin*, and the latest issue is out, so buy it."

SETH: It didn't receive much fanfare. That's really not good for you as an artist, unfortunately, because you do start to lose enthusiasm if you sense that people don't care enough. *Clyde* would definitely have been in that category. If *Palookaville* depended on the interest of readers following *Clyde* then I'd likely be in big trouble. It's the readers that have come along from the other books who actually pick up *Palookaville*, and that would be a readership that wouldn't have been there if I'd just worked on *Clyde*. It's tricky. Serialization is a complicated thing, and I'm not sure it's a great form for most cartoonists, but it might be necessary just to get the work done, and it might be necessary because you have to keep your face out there somehow.

DOMINICK: The time-intensiveness of producing a huge graphic novel; how many people can bang out two hundred pages a year?

SETH: There's not many, especially if you're—unless you're one of these artists who can work really fast *and* has a real facility for drawing. There are a few, but most artists don't have those qualities. The occasional person, somebody like Craig Thompson, who has a very high-finished style but also works really fast, or Michael DeForge, who maybe isn't quite as highly polished but certainly is working at a tremendous pace, but most cartoonists, unfortunately, as they get older, too, they get slower, not quicker. I'm a slow artist and I'm getting slower.

DOMINICK: Serialization seems to be slowly dying itself. Is that a problem for cartoonists, or for the future of the medium?

SETH: It's going to change the form, that's for sure. The graphic novel seems to be the mode at the moment, but it probably means we'll mostly get shorter books for a time, a hundred and fifty pages or so. You can't do a thousand-page book in a single burst. But we've got a whole new generation of artists coming up who know that from the beginning, and they seem to be already thinking in terms of shorter page counts so they may just be able to work within those parameters. Or, I don't know, we'll see much longer graphic novels from cartoonists who've crafted more expedient rendering styles.

DOMINICK: Is there something lost, though, in not being able, realistically speaking, to produce—I mean, is Dave Sim right? Does size matter?

SETH: He is right, but I'm not so sure I believe Dave really used that size as he has claimed or bragged. I think Dave produced something like seventeen graphic novels. They had the same character in them, but he didn't really create one continuous novel, in the contemporary meaning of the word. He did what, actually, adventure cartoonists have always done in the newspaper; he produced a large, rambling narrative that could be broken into logical sections. You could even look at, say, *Wash Tubbs*, and see you've got a series of separate adventures that are part of a larger whole. I think Dave did a more complicated thing, of course, but essentially it's similar. I actually think Dave would be more highly regarded as a cartoonist if he had ended *Cerebus* at the point when he was clearly getting serious about other topics, like about Oscar Wilde or whatever, and said, "Now I'm doing this Oscar Wilde book." And that book would now exist as an individual project that someone might say, "I'm going to read that Dave Sim Oscar Wilde book," whereas that same person will never say, "I'm going to read that *Cerebus* thing," because it's a completely baffling inaccessible nightmare to the new reader.

ERIC: That was Kim Thompson's criticism of it, when Sim started serializing *Melmoth*, and Dave took umbrage at that.

SETH: What doesn't Dave take umbrage at?

I have a tremendous respect for Dave's work ethic—nothing to be argued with there. He had a tremendous work ethic, and the way he worked on a tight treadmill of a deadline worked great for him. Dave seems to forget, though, that he was working in collaboration with another cartoonist. An assistant who did all his backgrounds. Dave also very much saw the artistic process as a business with deadlines and clients et cetera. This is not how most of the cartoonists work on my side of the tracks. It's less about business and schedule than it is about art making. Chester, for example, has taken longer and longer to produce his work, and that's because he's working primarily as an artist. I think most of the cartoonists of my generation now are working as artists rather than as commercial artists, and that means it takes as long as it takes, and schedules don't really matter in the way they used to matter. I think we all started out with the idea that schedules mattered, and we tried to meet deadlines back in the early days. I think in the first year of *Palookaville* I might have had three issues out, it's possible, and then, progressively, it turns into like one issue a year. At best. I think the Hernandez Brothers are among the few people who still follow faithfully the old model of trying to get out a certain number of pages a year. Not that I don't admire that—I'm just commenting on the transformation of the form away from the old mainstream models of production.

ERIC: But doesn't that get back to the problem with, say, Jason Lutes, where you're no longer in the—

SETH: No, it doesn't, does it? I mean, I'm not sure I have a good answer for that. I think for myself it's worked out reasonably well in that I've managed to keep other projects in the eye of the public, but as an artist, that's not the way you think about things or make your plans. I've gone this path mostly by accident, and in retrospect, I see that it was the smart way for me to have done things. If I'd gone the other way, I think I'd be in a worse spot today. I'm not sure I would advise another artist to follow my path, to say you should work on your big book on the side, and produce some lesser books in between. It's a good enough method for me, I guess, but it's probably not the most direct approach for creating a coherent body of work.

DOMINICK: One of the things that struck me, and it comes back to that question about the different categories of your work, is that regardless of which category it is, there's always something definably "Seth" about it; when I look at one of your commercial illustrations, it's not just an "ad," but the Seth "brand." For want of a better word.

SETH: Yes, that's true. I think the unplanned end product of the cartooning era I started out in, because there was a strong emphasis on, um, I don't know—I guess, "branding" is probably the best word for it. I don't think I set out to build my own "brand," but all cartoonists from that period, in some way, seem to have staked out their own identifiable territory, and I suspect it's because Crumb was such a powerful influence on us all. Crumb had such an identifiable "Crumb brand," if you want to call it that, and you can look at the cartoonists of my generation—look at Chester Brown, or Dan Clowes, Peter Bagge, and all these people—and they have a very, very identifiable approach. You can't help but identify them. From the second you see any of their work, you know it's them. No school of cartooning ever developed. The emphasis was on "doing your own thing." I never use the word "branding" myself; the actual term I use when I'm talking about this sort of thing to my wife or someone is "persona building." Now, of course, I've always been interested in the idea of staking personal territory—building your own identity in life. It's an essential element of my thinking.

Let me try to explain. I do think that there is some essential personality you're probably born with, and then you simply build on that for the rest of your life, adding or subtracting, as best you can, but mostly it's adding. It's a lot harder to subtract. I think you pick things (consciously or unconsciously) to identify with because the very act of choosing defines the self. You narrow the field of possibilities to carve out an identity for yourself. In this process you come to understand who you are, or at the very least, who you wish you could be. Often the things you pick end up being choices you are later ashamed of . . . or if you can be honest—you end up laughing at yourself about these choices, but they weren't picked arbitrarily. Often the reasons are obvious and pathetic in retrospect. Everything has been picked to build some kind of image or personality for yourself, and even people who probably won't admit that they're building any kind of persona are doing it just as obviously. I just know personally that I've always done this kind of thing in a really clear, direct obvious way. I've very consciously created an artificial image for myself. I've renamed myself, I dress in a very affected, specific manner, I have very carefully defined aesthetic tastes; these are all really essentially important things to me. I'm always somewhat amazed that everyone's not doing it in this more straightforwardly obvious manner like I am. Strangely to me, most people try to define themselves in less attention-getting ways. I mean, you can basically pick any affectations you want in life. Our culture is pretty tolerant. Why don't people make more outlandish choices? If you want to walk around dressed like a seventeenth-century Cavalier, you can do it, but very few people *are* doing it. My personal choices are actually all pretty conservative—backward looking. Reactionary, even. I understand that it's mostly because of conformity that people are less outlandish; we are all conformists by nature and it's very hard to step outside of it. People don't want to look foolish in life. I think—digressing again—I think that if there's one thing that most upsets me it's being embarrassed. Most people really dislike being embarrassed. There's something . . . I'd rather be injured than embarrassed; I'd rather fall down and break my ankle than be humiliated. But the funny thing is that you can overcome that fear of embarrassment fairly easily, because honestly, nobody really *does* care the slightest bit what you do in life! Most people are worried about standing out, but listen—nobody cares! A lot of people think public speaking is the most horrifying thing, but there's really nothing to be afraid of in public speaking, because for the most part people don't even remember you five minutes after you're done speaking. The same is true of every other aspect of the conformity culture. You are not important enough for others to care even if you are totally outrageous. You can be the biggest sissy, the craziest punk rocker, the most outlandish fop . . . and people can't be bothered to even remember your name the next time they see you.

I think where I got really lucky in life was being young in the 1980s, I got very involved in the punk/new wave culture, which was very much based on garnering personal attention, trying to look weird, trying to get attention in the street, and it taught me a few good lessons. It kind of freed me from all the worries that I carried around from before I got involved in that subculture, and it provided me with a licence to openly build my own persona in any way I wanted, and after that I didn't really care that much about being laughed at, or being pointed at in the street. It still happens all the time, you know; people make fun of me because I look like an oddball, but that doesn't really bother me in the least because I was lucky enough to come out the other side of that long ago. The embarrassment worries that I still carry deep inside are no longer connected to any of that trivial affected persona building. Those worries would be about things that are more meaningful to me—deeper embarrassments like someone I respect finding my work stupid or shallow—would be something more crushing than someone laughing at what I look like or being uninterested in a talk I gave. I think that process of persona building, admitted or not, is one of the essential elements of human interaction. It's funny, though, that most people don't like to talk about it in a clear manner; it's avoided because it implies inauthenticity and obvious begging for attention. I mean, on some level everything we do is simply asking for attention. We don't like to admit that and most of us spend our lives trying to conceal this fact. When you meet people who are clearly begging for attention in the most obvious way, it can either be really interesting or really embarrassing, usually the latter, so it's clear why people keep this process a secret. That's the end of that digression.

ERIC: If you had the opportunity to merchandise your brand, would you consider it?

SETH: That's hard to even imagine. I don't think I know my brand as well as people looking at my work. I'd probably be fine selling a brand if it could bring in some money!

ERIC: A Wimbledon Green action figure?

SETH: Yeah, I would do certain things immediately if the opportunity came up. That sort of thing is an easy answer.

  If there was one area of refining to my personal brand that I'd effect, it's that I probably wouldn't call myself "Seth," any longer. That's the one thing that I probably would change, if I could go back in time. I'd have kept my own name. But that was part of an earlier period of persona building, and I'm stuck with it now. It would be more embarrassing now to get rid of it than to keep it. It is my brand name. And thank God, it is an actual name, and not some fantastical made up word or something stupid. So the good part about "Seth" is that when I meet regular folk and they ask my name, and I tell them it's Seth, they just accept it as a real name. I could have picked something much stupider. I think there was somebody around at that time called "Monster X" or something. . . .

DOMINICK: Regarding persona building, there's an association attached to you that you're one of the autobiographical cartoonists. I just read an article by Bart Beaty identifying you with Joe Matt and Chester as one of the "Toronto School" of autobiographical cartoonists. I'm not sure it's true that your autobiographical work is any less fictionalized than anyone else's, but it's far more overtly "autobiography" that challenges or questions the notion of autobiography as a transparent view into the life of the artist. I assume that that's at least to some extent part of the conscious sense of what you're doing as an artist and telling people "this is a persona," as opposed to, "I am revealing myself"?

SETH: Yeah. I think the interesting thing doing anything that's autobiographical is that you can tell people very transparently, straightforwardly what you're doing, and they still do not recognize the authorial intention. Take Joe Matt for example. I recall someone saying after reading Joe Matt's comics that Matt had zero self-awareness, and I said, well, clearly you're basing this on how he chose to tell the story, and he's given you the impression that he has no self-awareness deliberately. I mean, come on people, it's not a documentary; everything you do, you *tell* the audience, and they still somehow think it's an accident, that they're just getting a peek into your life, in a way that they wouldn't do with fiction. That's why I originally decided to move towards *Clyde Fans*—though *Good Life* is basically fiction, too—to get away from that idea that you're telling people the bare truth. I think even in this memoir I'm doing, "Nothing Lasts," it's all true, in the sense that these are actually events from my life, but it's constructed on a very controlled plan, even though it's somewhat spontaneous. The way I'm telling the story, I'm deliberately placing it within a certain specific tone. I'm picking certain incidents that I want to talk about that fit this tone. There's a million memories that are not going into that story, that don't fit it. For one thing, the whole point of this is that I want it to have, for lack of a better phrase, I want it to have a slightly poetic quality, which means that it's going to be lower-key, it's not going to deal much with—there's no humor in it, really, very little humor, and there's definitely almost no specific references to pop culture. I've deliberately made it so that it's almost entirely about place and feeling, and not experience in the true sense. I don't even describe almost anything that happens in high school, I think, in the second section. It didn't fit into the narrative to be talking about, like, you know, the friends I had, and how things went with the girls I tried to date, or whatever. That seemed too plot-oriented, or "coming of age." I wanted it, from the get-go, to be about less tangible things, and in many ways, readers won't pick up on those omissions. They'll just think you're telling stories directly from your life; autobiography always kind of fakes people out in the sense that they forget how much you're shaping every element of what you're using—mostly because of the fact that you're the main character.

DOMINICK: Would that be why you incorporate overtly fictional elements, like Kalo? If I recall, there's no explicit acknowledgement anywhere in *Good Life* that Kalo isn't real.

SETH: No there isn't, and the reason I did that wasn't because I wanted a hoax, first of all; I couldn't have cared less about faking people out. I did lie to people during the initial run of the story in *Palookaville*, it's true. I remember, whenever questions came up I would lie and say Kalo was real, but nowadays, I wouldn't bother to lie to anyone about it. If someone asked me, I'd say, no, it's made up. But I still think—well, the reason I chose to do it in that way was because I thought it was a better story if you thought it was true. The belief that this guy was a real person makes the story better, and I still think that's true, and I assume that most new readers would still believe it's true while reading it. There is no real reason to doubt it. Probably most people don't bother to Google it before they read it; they might, and if they did, they might find it out right away, but you know, on the internet, what I have noticed about current *Good Life* reviews, is that, surprisingly, it's not the first point brought up about the book, so that is probably still to my advantage.

As time has passed, the lie about Kalo has become less important for the reviewers. Like I said, I think that the story is more evocative if you assume that it's true while reading it and that's why I used myself as the main character in it. Of course, a lot of the stuff in there about me in the book is basically true. Based on real events. I did go to Strathroy back then, but I actually went there just to research the town for the book, and I used that information in those chapters. I did meet that one strange woman at the motel, for example, that was a perfect little bit of something unexpected that happened on the trip and worked its way into the book.

But, you know, the conversations between Chester and me are just based on the *kind* of conversations we had, stuff like that. The whole reason for the Kalo story, really, was that when I first realized that I was no longer interested in telling anecdotes as stories, and I was more interested in the less tangible elements of what make up a story, well, at that point it seemed to me that if I wanted to tell a story that was just about rambling, disconnected, or somewhat-connected thoughts, you needed something to hang that on, and for me, what I had to hang it on was a red-herring search for an old cartoonist. That seemed to me that that could be a motor that could pull you through the narrative, and at the same time allow you to ramble on about other stuff, but I was not prepared at that point to do a story that had no plot at all. I needed that plot, somehow, and I knew that plot would read better with the audience if they thought it was real. I figured it was somehow less immediate, less vital, if it was an obviously fictional story about an imaginary cartoonist. Somehow I sensed, and I think I was right, that it would have a lot more weight if readers would believe it was true.

DOMINICK: Do you think that serialization was a factor there? I mean, this is a story that for the original readers unfolded over a long time.

SETH: Yeah, I do think that that really did figure in, and I also think it figured in that there was no Internet culture where no one could research it. I did get a letter or two during that initial run from a fellow who said, "I went to the public library, and I looked up that issue of the *New Yorker* that you mentioned, and Kalo is not in it." So, I thought, "Well, there is the one in a million person," you know, but almost nobody's going to do that; it's way too much effort, so you could count on people's lack-of-effort, but nowadays, actually, it's super easy for people to research these sort of things. There's a complete *New Yorker* that you can purchase that has every issue on a disc, and probably now, of course, you don't even need to do that, because you just do a little bit of Googling and you find out that it's not true within about ten minutes.

DOMINICK: Did you get any backlash about it after it came out, and the fact that Kalo wasn't real came out?

SETH: A little bit of disappointment in a few letters from a couple of folks, and I was a little bit worried about the idea of people thinking, "Oh, it's not so good, now I know it's not true," but the thing I most recall, that pleased me tremendously, was that Art Spiegelman said to me at the time, "I kinda liked the story when I read it, but when I found out it wasn't true, I liked it a lot better," and I thought, well, that's interesting, because it added another layer to it for him that added some complexity. I appreciated that.

DOMINICK: It's interesting because it seems to me that that kind of device is really playing with expectations of what the compact is between the reader and the author.

SETH: Yeah, that's true, and especially back then when autobiography was a bit more . . . I wouldn't exactly call it cutting edge, or anything, but there was a lot more of it going on, and it seemed like a central tenet of alternative cartooning at the time, so making it not true was a bit, I guess, mildly daring. Certainly an attempt to be clever. That wouldn't be the case today. I doubt a new reader would even consider the book's artifice as much of a surprise; they would just think that was an authorial choice of some kind. Writers today use all sorts of gimmicks that play with the reader's suspension of belief. But at the time I was very aware that by using myself as the main character, I was playing on the expectations of people who read autobiographical comics that it has to be true if you're the main character . . .

Seth's return to autobiography takes us back to his childhood. From *Palookaville* 21 ©
Seth. Used with permission from Drawn & Quarterly.

DOMINICK: And it's anchored in specific, real places. . . .
SETH: Yeah, and Chester Brown is there, and that ties it in more to a specific
truthful feeling.

ERIC: What inspired you to decide to start doing autobiographical strips
again, like "Calgary Festival" [2010], and "Nothing Lasts" [2013]? Does that
indicate that additional autobiographical work is forthcoming, and does that
revise your position, that you told Bryan Miller that you had no real plans for
finished work in that form?
SETH: Well, you know, the funny thing is, I don't think I was even thinking
about autobiography when I was working on, say, that Calgary piece; that was
just a diary entry, and I think I always considered autobiography in comics as
a more formal exercise, something you sat down and wrote an autobiographical *story*, and the story was made up of the events of your life, but you were
actually sculpting the material into a *story*. That Calgary thing was really just
like sitting down and writing in my diary, even though it's a bit less succinct,
because obviously you don't turn it out fast enough for it to be like a normal
diary entry—it's maybe twenty pages or something, and it took me a month
or something to do it—that was clearly in that impulse of, "I'm just recording
some stuff that happened to me," because it's an interesting exercise to do
this in your sketchbook.

I don't even think that when I started "Nothing Lasts" that I was thinking
of it as autobiographical work; I think, again, I was thinking of it merely as an
extension of the diaries I've been keeping now for quite a few years, the *Rubber Stamp Diaries*, but it's just that now I'm using autobiographical comics in
a less formal manner—essentially just getting events down on paper. I think
if I was to sit down—and "finish" might be the key word here—if I was to sit
down and do a finished story that was autobiographical, it probably would
be more structured, more written out beforehand, more suffered over, and

so on. There's something about the sketchbook form that actually does kind of encourage autobiography, I think. It's so direct and spontaneous, I mean, when you are trying to quickly write in a certain spontaneous manner, it is valuable for me to not have to think up a bunch of fiction on the fly. You've got the material right in your hand, your only worry is, "How do I put it down on the page?" Writing about your childhood is like, well, you've got all the material already—how do I shape it? *Wimbledon Green* was a bit more of an imaginative kind of sketchbook project, where you're entering into an imaginary world and so, that's obviously a little different, I needed to shape that a different way as I was working it through in the sketchbook. I was thinking about it more. Spending more time imagining. I think when I was working on *Wimbledon Green* I was thinking about it a tremendous amount during my day to day life, and then when I'd sit down to do a page or a segment, that's when I would take whatever I'd been thinking about, lay out a structure for it and roll. Whereas, with this autobiographical material, the structure's predetermined after the first few segments, and now I'm just moving on to the next memory that's coming up in association with this page I just finished; it's a lot more organic.

ERIC: You mentioned the *Rubber Stamp Diaries*, and you print some pages from it in the most recent *Palookaville* [21]. What inspired you to undertake that project? There are six books pictured; how many pages have you completed so far? Do you have any plans to publish more? It seems that's what you were indicating.

SETH: It might be. I don't have any immediate plans. I imagine there will be more published at some point in the future. I think I've got maybe twelve or fifteen books of them now. The books fill up very quickly, actually; it's a very expedient method for strip making. And the entries tend to be getting longer, too; I did one the other day that's like twelve pages long. I think there's a real value in keeping a diary, but I've never been very successful at keeping a diary. Even just a simple written diary is difficult for me, and I've tried it several times over the years and it usually didn't work out. The usual problems— you'd miss a day, and I'd think, "OK, well, I'll catch up on that later" so then you have to write two entries. Or you leave, go on a trip or something, fall way behind, and then eventually lose your momentum, and the whole thing dies. It was disappointing. I was caught up in this traditional diary method. Eventually as I started to see more people doing little sketchbook diaries, like James Kochalka, it occurred to me that a cartoonist probably should keep his diary in a cartoon form. But of course that just ups the ante on the amount

"Rubber Stamp Diaries" image with added art
and text. From *Palookaville* 21 © Seth. Used
with permission from Drawn & Quarterly.

of work involved—almost guaranteeing that you'll fall behind. So, I solved
both problems with the new method: one, doing it with rubber stamps, that's
pure expediency—I mean, there has to be *some* drawing occasionally because
there's not going to be a rubber stamp for everything; and two, just not writing a daily laundry list of your life, you know, writing down everything that
happened. Now, I don't feel any impulse that I've got to keep up with that
diary every day. I write in it when I feel like it—so, if I do an entry twice a
week, that's great. Or I might only do one in a week, but I feel that then I'm
writing down something I actually want to write down. It tends to be pretty
light, pretty minor stuff. I probably skip over every major event of my life, but
that's because that's not the stuff I wish to record.

I just went to the Baltimore SPX last weekend, and lots of stuff happened
there, and I talked to a lot of people—interesting conversations. Nothing
whatsoever of that weekend will end up written in the diary. That sort of
event usually won't come up in the diary, but what will come up is, I don't
know, that it rained the other day—that'll be the thing I end up writing
about. So for a biographer, this diary would be the worst case kind of diary;
it's of no use as a tool for learning what happened in my actual day to day life.
It works for me though. I think it may also turn out to be a useful exercise
that might supply future subject matter, as well.

One of the good things about keeping a diary is you can look back on it,
and it's good grist for the mill, good strip material. It's also important in a

disciplinary way; it keeps you working in a methodical manner, and if you keep at it, that's very good for your sense of discipline; that makes you feel good about yourself. I do think as an artist you have to have some kind of strong discipline and you have to win these discipline battles with yourself, so that it builds you up rather than knocks you down. Projects that you keep failing to follow through with—that's really bad for you. Also, I think it's a really good discipline because it's a way to keep in touch with yourself; keeping a diary is an exceptional way to see how your mind works, and you quickly learn that you're thinking the same things over and over again. It helps clarify your thinking. And I also think these diaries might just turn out to be of interest when I've got enough pages; I think when I have several thousand pages of them, it might be an interesting read. We'll see. I think in about ten years, if I keep going at the rate I'm going, I'll have about three to five thousand pages, so, that's a substantial amount of comics. That might turn out to be something after all.

ERIC: How many stamps are in your arsenal, and are you adding?

SETH: I think I've got about forty right now, and I just drew up another five, or something, and so I add a few every once in a while. I'm doing a lot more strips with my wife in them now. Initially she was almost never in them and now she's in quite a few. I don't have any stamps with her on them, so I'm always drawing her next to me in the panel—that's tiresome—and so now I finally designed two new stamps of her which are being made. One is just her looking, just her profile, and another is two of us in the car—that seems to be a really essential panel; we're always driving somewhere. That seems to be how it goes—if I find I have to draw something enough times, I decide I should get a stamp made for that—it's a waste of time to keep drawing it over and over.

ERIC: You told Tom Spurgeon that every project fails. Do you still feel that way? Why is it that every project fails and, assuming you still feel that way, would you say there's a project of yours that fails less than others?

SETH: Yeah, well, it's true; they all fail to different degrees, but they do all fail on some level because you're never good enough to achieve whatever you want. The big problem is that you can never really enjoy your own work. This is a big problem for artists. I always feel really sad for the artists whose work I most admire because I know they're the one person who least enjoys that artwork. You *know* that Sparky Schulz never loved *Peanuts* the way any of the fans do; he couldn't. Even if he was really proud of it, which he was, and even if he was willing to say it's great, which he might've done, he just never enjoyed the characters in the same way as the people who just read the work. You never enjoy your own work in that sense; it's always going to be somewhat dead to you—you look at it and you see how it was constructed, or you see only the flaws. Especially the drawings—where you see nothing but mistakes. All that said, I do think as you get older, it does get easier, you do start to like your own work a little bit better, and sometimes you quite like certain things much better. I think as you get older, one of the things that happens is you start to say, "Oh, I did that better than I thought I could," or, you reach a point where you're like, "I couldn't have done this ten years ago." Your skills just get better. So I will look at something like *George Sprott* now and feel pretty happy with it. I don't love it, but I'm happy with it. Whereas earlier work, it would be much clearer I am disappointed. I mean, maybe you don't get to the point where you feel every element in a work has succeeded, but you do get closer, in the ballpark at least. I don't think there's ever going to be any project where I feel like I did exactly the book I wanted to do, or really "nailed it." I think even if you worked your very, very hardest, it's not going to happen. Even the amount of effort Chris Ware puts into his books, he doesn't seem to me like he's happy with his books in the end. That's disheartening if anything is!

ERIC: I heard an interview with Ware on *Panel Borders* recently, and he said that very same thing. I think they were discussing *Building Stories* [2012] and the interviewer was talking about how perfect it was, and Ware had to say, "No. I look at it and I see the flaws." There's no way to stand outside it and see it the way the audience does.
SETH: Exactly, and the more ambitious you get, the less likely you're going to succeed at anything. *Building Stories* is so highly ambitious, and it's hard to imagine that Chris, who's very, very tough on himself, could possibly feel like he succeeded at reaching that high point he was aiming for. But even Chris probably feels better about what he's doing now than ten years ago, I bet you.

ERIC: He and I grew up in the same neighborhood in Omaha . . .
SETH: Oh, really? That's funny.

ERIC: . . . so when I look at his backgrounds—talk about being subjective— all I see are these familiar landscapes and architecture from Omaha, obviously through his filter.
SETH: I believe it too: he's very specific. I really admire Chris. He's always

making very complicated decisions in his work. It's always interesting—everything Chris does. He's so thoroughly invested himself into every piece he does. I'd be literally amazed if there's anything in Chris's work that he doesn't plan out in advance. It's kind of remarkable if you talk to him about it—*he's* thought about it, every detail, much more than most artists would, maybe to the point of . . . it sounds a bit weird, almost insane detail. I've been surprised to see how deeply he's considered every decision . . . he's a person with very specific ideas.

Actually, Chris is an interesting case because at some point you realize that an artist like Chris Ware is not really a person for emulation because he's doing something that's really very specifically his own thing. I think that many a cartoonist has been very influenced by him, including myself, and very inspired by him to try to do certain things that are probably his things alone . . . or to work harder in certain patterns that are not your own. Eventually you realize that what Chris is doing is uniquely for him; it is his own approach, and certainly he can inspire you to try harder, he can make you "up your game," as they say, but the kind of thinking he's doing on his work is not the kind of thinking most cartoonists do, and often they don't necessarily require it. For whatever reasons, Chris needs to go into those extra layers of depth, into every detail behind what's on the page; it's essential to him. It works for him. It makes great art for Chris Ware. It wouldn't be my method, and I don't think many other cartoonists of my generation *could* follow Chris's methods, but they would certainly be impressed by the depth of his thinking, the complexity of the work, and especially how hard he works. He's one of a kind. He's changed comics, totally, and I think that he's changed how everyone thinks about comics, and I believe there's a before Chris and an after Chris period. I think it's quite clear. I think in some ways, he's changed comics more than somebody like Crumb or Spiegelman even, powerful influences as they were. In some profound way, Chris has reconstructed the grammar of comics. Looked at it freshly in a way no one did before. I think it has much to do with the way his brain naturally operates; he thinks in a manner that's constantly seeking to find the underlying structure of everything. To listen to him talk about any topic, it's almost funny how much he's looking underneath the surface for what it means. Recently on line I heard him talking in some interview, and he started going on about cuckoo clocks, and he was talking about how aggressive cuckoo clocks were, and how the cuckoo is coming out, kind of mocking us with its movement and sound. I'm probably butchering his point but I recall thinking that it was a very interesting insight. But at the same time I was also thinking, that's really funny, I can totally see that insight coming from Chris alone because that seemed like an insight specific to his personality and his brain. Maybe he's right but of course, for myself, I was thinking, "cuckoo clocks aren't about aggression, cuckoo clocks are just sweet charming mechanical toys that say coo-coo because people in Switzerland love the charming sound of the cuckoo." Chris couldn't help but wring out this deeper and harsher viewpoint, because I think that's essentially how his mind works. He was looking for the underlying meaning of the cuckoo clock and coming up with a totally Chris Ware insight.

ERIC: Segueing, about composition, and to get back to your work, you mentioned in that same Spurgeon interview that you prefer a more naturalistic approach to storytelling, which is moment to moment transitions rather than big jumps in time, and that seems interesting given that your three most recent works—*George Sprott, Wimbledon Green,* and *GNBCC*—all involve big jumps in time.

SETH: Yeah, it might be an evolution that I'm undergoing. I think that on a certain level my natural impulse would be a slow progression storyline. I think *Clyde Fans* is really based around that kind of, you know, the character gets up, walks to the bathroom, walks to the next room, you follow the character doing everything—very small progressions. Show, don't tell. I do like that style a lot, but I think as time has gone on, I've ended up developing this more direct grammar I was talking about earlier; there's a realization that that is a very laborious form and to do that you have to be willing to engage in a long process that I'm not as willing to engage in when I'm telling a story now. Certainly not with the kind of stories I'm trying to tell. Right now, I am more interested in that direct grammar of straightforwardly giving the information out in a manner that is simple and emotionally effective. I think if it comes down to a real preference of how I like a story told, I probably do still like that slow form best because it ties into my basic belief of why comics have become more interesting in the last few decades, which is that they have the space to tell the story in any way they want, and you *can* tell a very long, slow, moment to moment progression story nowadays and you didn't have that luxury before the medium became artist-centric. The trick is, though, do I have the stamina to be able to produce those kinds of works, and I'm not sure that I have the stamina at this point to say, "I'm going to do one more book before I die." It's a grim point but it has to be faced. It's a very laborious approach to storytelling. I mean, if I can get a fair number of books done before the grave, but it will mean probably doing them with a slightly different comics grammar or a more perfunctory drawing style—then so be it. I *will* probably still do another book in that slower "naturalistic" manner—if I do get the books done that I'm thinking in my head about right now, then there's definitely one more book that is all told in that very slow, moment to moment progression, but there certainly are a bunch of books that are all jumps in time; that Dominion project I was talking about will likely have very little real sequential action in it. It will probably resemble "Nothing Lasts" quite a bit. There's almost no real sequential action going on in those pages. It's mostly, again, what I was talking about with graphic design, mostly just how to keep the eye engaged and moving from panel to panel. It's not really about following characters around, or interestingly visual storytelling devices. Just meat and potatoes grammar.

DOMINICK: On that privileging of a more natural approach, what is interesting for me about much of your work in that it's, in a way, fantasy. Dominion is *like* a real place, but it's an *alternate* real place. GNBCC is like alternate history—and with a high degree of fidelity to our expectations about reality. Does that emerge out of the fact that in your more formative years you were interested in the more fantastical worlds of the superhero comics, does it emerge from other literary traditions, or is it just that it's convenient for the kind of stories that you want to tell?

SETH: I wouldn't have known this when I was working on *Good Life*, for example, but I think I just have an inclination to create—I like world-building, and even *Good Life* is about building a world—creating a fictional cartoonist and his life. I guess that's what all fiction is about, but as I've gone on, a lot of the works I'm attracted to are works where someone has built a kind of realized world for their characters to operate in. I really enjoyed Dan's *Ice Haven* [2011], probably more because of the creation of the place Ice Haven than the story itself. I loved that he created a little town and brought it to life so fully. It often gets compared to *Winesburg Ohio* [by Sherwood Anderson, published in 1919], which is also a work I really like, mostly I think because of the interconnected nature of creating stories that all take place in the same little place. I think that the places I create are mundane places, and the histories are elaborate but not fantastical—pretty perfunctory in some ways. It's not so much the fantasy element of an imaginary place that attracts me—it's not so much the mirror to real life quality either; rather it's the *inner world* element of the whole thing. I really am fascinated by the idea of inner life, that you have an imaginative world inside yourself that you can elaborate endlessly on. I like building a world inside yourself and then trying to let some of it out on paper.

Seth's personal childhood superhero pantheon, revisited. © Seth. Used with permission from Seth.

When I was a kid, that inner world was a superhero world. I had my own little superhero world that I endlessly elaborated upon, and looking back it turns out that was essentially what I was interested in more than the superhero characters that I was making up. Most of the characters were just rip-off characters anyway. It was the idea of building up a world for them to live in together that kept me dreaming about it. I mean, let's not overstate anything. That superhero world of mine was just a cheap emulation of what I was reading in comics back then . . . but the process of elaborating that place in my fantasy life was more engaging to me than drawing the little comics I was making back then. I mean, drawing my own comics was really a way to actively enter into that fantasy world, and I think to some degree that's still what I'm doing today. My adult stories are an access point for me into an inner reality. I have a Dominion inside me that I'm always elaborating on, and I find that I go to it when I'm daydreaming. I think about this place, and I think about the streets, and about what's going on—not what's going on like, "the Mayor is going downtown today" but more like, "how does this historical element intersect with that one?" So, basically, the interface between inner reality and outer reality is pretty much what most of my work is about, even if it's not obvious. Even something like *Wimbledon Green*, the world-building in it is another part of that same inner reality, and I think a process has begun where everything is slowly being boiled down into becoming a part of this Dominion project. More and more, I'm finding that world-building is the core of what I'm most interested in and maybe I don't need to put a story over top of that any more, maybe the world-building is enough of a story right there. *GNBCC* is a good example, I suppose, because it's *just* a history. The pleasure was in making up the history. I didn't bother to make up a plot to squeeze it into. There's something about that imaginative kind of play that is probably the key reason I'm even an artist at all. It seems to be essential for me, and I think, as you get older as an artist, you do try to nail down what it is you're most interested in and try to follow that thread. I can't imagine it's going to stray much from this direction from now on. That seems to be where the work is going. It might elaborate itself in ways that I don't expect, but I think that will always be at the core of my work.

DOMINICK: Are comics especially receptive to that sort of world-building, and intermingling of internal and external, and revealing the internal life more than, say, film or prose?
SETH: I think they are. I think the fact that you're both drawing and writing allows you to build a world in a much different way than prose. I'm talking here about things that are *very* self-indulgent, very airy-fairy—building little inner worlds—but at the same time I'm also planning things out in a real meat and potatoes way. In comics you get to world-build with pictures and that makes it pretty concrete. Film can do that as well of course, but I think film is limited by the fact that it is a moment to moment kind of medium, and you're required to constantly move things along. There's something wonderful about the still nature of comics, the frozen quality of it, that allows you to present that world-building in a way that would be much more boring in any other medium. There's something essential in the very nature of reading comics that if they're structured correctly, everything is interesting. No matter how slow or non-narrative or catalogue-like. To be fair, I guess that could be true in prose or film, too, but as a cartoonist, I guess I'm prejudiced towards cartoons, and it does seem to me that there is something in there that really works well for the kind of approach that I am leaning toward. I think I could just describe the city of Dominion in comics form, and if I did it well, it would be engaging in a way that it might not be in another form.

DOMINICK: Might it be that with the visuals in comics you get something concrete, in contrast to prose, but in film, it's almost impossible to escape from realism as that predominant visual mode?

SETH: Yes, that it. That's true, and a cartoonist's style has a lot to do with the building of their world, as well. The very style infuses that world, which isn't quite the same in film; as you say, you're kind of held in the sway of absolute reality. Although I suppose that's probably not so true anymore, what with the allegedly fabulous special effects they can do now.

DOMINICK: Less true, but even there the impetus with special effects is to create the most maximally realistic special effect possible.

SETH: You're absolutely right about that. I hadn't considered that. With film, the fact that it's moving, it doesn't feel the same, somehow. There's some deep quality inherent in the still nature of comics that produces more a catalogue than a travelogue. I mean, when you're watching a film, the fact is that you don't stop to look at things, you can't pause and study the world in the same way you would when you're reading a comic. The fact that much of the background is merely something the actors stand in front of, rather than a carefully calculated tableau composed by the artist . . . there's something richer to me in the comics medium for what I like and what I want to do. Yes, comics have the illusion that something is moving, yet because it is a still form, it is just a series of drawings, a series of graphic designs, I think that it allows the reader to take in information very differently. To take it in at their own pace, and that's fundamentally different than in film. Of course, you can take a novel at your own pace, but without the visuals, it is almost an entirely different form. The medium that comics are supposedly closest to, film—well, I think they're so essentially different. Comics have different strengths than film, and one of them just might be world-building. Certainly all the strips that I love have a strong sense of place to them, and when they don't—even if they're not specific enough about it—I can't help but to kind of try and add it in there myself.

To explain—I thought it was real interesting that when the Another Rainbow collections of *Little Lulu* came out in the 1980s, that they felt the necessity to try and map out the world that the characters lived in, and to try to find just exactly where that place was in the real world, and especially interesting that they did nail it down to a specific town, in maybe Connecticut or something, but what interests me about this is that Little Lulu's world isn't really that highly defined in the comics, and yet, as a reader, I had a really clear sense—well, clear might not be the right word for it—but you *felt* everywhere that the characters went. That's true for *Peanuts*, as well; it's not well-defined, yet you know that neighborhood very deeply—there's the curb, there's the psychiatry booth, the ball diamond, the doghouse, the school, et cetera. Schulz wasn't even that specific about drawing these backgrounds the same from strip to strip, yet that world was built, somehow.

ERIC: It's iconic, in a way.

SETH: Yeah. These icons are islands of place in a very foggy world and yet somehow that adds up to a deeply clear reality he's built for the characters to reside in.

DOMINICK: His somewhat more abstracted form makes it less objectively realistic but in some ways more real—more experientially real.

SETH: Yeah, you take it inside the body in some way and build it up inside. Elaborate it with your own feelings. I think this is kind of what we were talking about earlier, now that I think about it, something that is very hard to put into words; the cartoonist's *style* builds the world itself. For example, *Spider-Man* by Steve Ditko is in New York. I don't know if any of those backgrounds are based on any specific buildings, I literally have no idea, but Spider-Man didn't live in New York, he lived in a Steve Ditko world. I don't really know what New York was like at that point, and it didn't matter, but I knew what Steve Ditko's world looked like. That world was fully realized in some way by Steve Ditko, even though I don't know if Spider-Man ever even visited the same location twice in those stories, except maybe the *Daily Bugle*, and even there, I'm not really sure what the *Daily Bugle* looked like, but I can sure *feel* the *Daily Bugle* in my brain.

ERIC: Or Greenwich Village in *Doctor Strange.*

SETH: Yeah. They exist because the cartoonist's style itself built that world; they laid something unique in their style overtop of our world and brought somewhere else to life, a kind of world-building that exists for itself, even when it wasn't that important to the story. I mean, let's face it, *Doctor Strange*'s "reality" is that strange Ditko world of the supernatural, and there's no consistency to that except style itself, and yet that world was a really developed otherworldly place. The cartoonist's style, the kinds of shapes or symbols he uses, sets in motion a sort of program in the reader's brain that elaborates a world beyond the panels—beyond what is drawn. If that makes any sense.

ERIC: Focusing again on some of the things that perhaps weren't discussed in other interviews, I wanted to talk to you about your work being displayed in galleries. Specifically, I guess, what led to your first art show? Had you intended to show your art in galleries? Was there a certain point where you said, "I'm going to start making work for that particular milieu"?

SETH: I've never been particularly interested in gallery art. As a cartoonist, you're generally more interested in print. I wasn't opposed to it, and I probably did have some work hanging in the usual comic art shows in the nineties, and I'm sure that I had stuff in a few European shows here and there, a few things like that, although I don't think I gave it much thought whatsoever. To me, the real changing point was that show at the AGO [Art Gallery of Ontario], and that basically came about in the most prosaic of manners, the curator just calling me up and talking and later working out a show and putting that show together, and that is where my cardboard city of Dominion was first displayed, and I think showing the city made all the difference in my thinking. I've been in quite a few shows since then that display primarily original comic art and I'm never quite fully engaged in that approach, and I think it's because I don't really think of that art as being for display; these are just artefacts of the printed works.

The city always makes more sense to me as a display item because it is something that is physical and it was meant to be looked at in person, not meant to exist in any other form. Each time I've shown it, Andrew Hunter and I have displayed it separate from my comic art and created a couple of new elements for each of the shows. We made a big archway for one show where you pass through and go into the little city, and another time we built a life-size movie theatre. I find that very fun, very engaging. We've got another show coming up in about a year, and I've some plans for new things I'd like to build.

If I were presented the opportunity by a big gallery and I had some real money to work with, I would truly love to do an original installation of some kind. I would really enjoy that, I think; that would be a great pleasure. But I wouldn't be all that creatively excited if I got a call from an important gallery and they said, "We want to hang some of your comic work." I'd be "career" excited, I'd be, like, "That's great"—looks great on a résumé. That'll make me feel important and maybe even bring me some more exciting opportunities later as an artist. But that's just hanging more comic art on the wall, and I don't really think comic art is meant to be hung on the wall, except as artefacts, in the same way that maybe hand-hewn tools weren't meant to hang on a wall, but they could be interesting if you went into a pioneer museum or something.

But I do like the idea of gallery art in itself, and somebody like Shary Boyle, I don't know if you know her work. She's a contemporary Canadian artist who's done some cartoon work, not unlike the Royal Art Lodge folks, I suppose. What I mean is, these artists are more about the world of fine art galleries, but they do have some connection to the world of comics. They do drawings, and they sometimes do sequential narratives and stuff, but they also do sculptures and installations and videos and music. A wide range of stuff. Shary Boyle does a lot of porcelain figures and a lot of installation work. When I see that, that looks very exciting, and I like how some elements of cartooning end up as part of that installation work. Cartoon drawing style, or the gag cartoons form . . . sometimes they use narrative or sequential approaches. All over the place. But this work is meant to hang on walls—not be printed in books and that's where cartooning seems to work in the gallery because it's meant for the gallery. They're not printed books that they're hanging on the wall; it's actual art that belongs there. And that could be a project of tremendous interest to me if I was ever granted the time and the opportunity. Or if someone ever came to me and said, "We'd like you to design a building,"—oh boy, I would totally want to do that. Probably a nightmare of logistics to work on such a project . . . but what a dream job.

In a sense, these are all aspects of enjoying the role of an artist, but not really that connected to being a cartoonist. As an artist or designer, so many visual projects sound like fun. But when it comes to cartooning, it's a different urge—with cartooning, my interest lies purely in telling stories that will be printed as books, and anything that happens after that like hanging them in galleries is just by-product.

Art Spiegelman and I curated a big show out in a Vancouver art gallery about comics, and that was satisfying. Mostly, though, I just thought of it as a pro-comics thing: "This will be good for regular people to come into a gallery and see some good cartoons." But whether I thought, "Is this an exciting show?" I don't really think I thought of it in those terms, I just thought, "Well, let's get eight (or whatever number it was) really good cartoonists and get some of their best art and put it before the public." They would see it in a way that they wouldn't if you just put out some books on a table. Chances are they wouldn't buy those books. So, perhaps in a sense, I wasn't really doing a good job as a curator, I was being more of a propagandist or something; pushing the cause.

DOMINICK: But there is value in that.
SETH: Oh yeah, I thought it was valuable. It was valuable just to spend time

with Art Spiegelman and hash out who each of us wanted to be in that show. Art's a natural curator and it's interesting to see his mind at work.

ERIC: The paintings from *Vernacular Drawings* seem to indicate that you continue to draw in single images that would be well-suited for gallery presentation, I would think.
SETH: They're too boring. They're just pure image. Nothing much interesting going on there. Y'know, if I was to present my sketchbook for someone to look through, I might be kind of embarrassed if they thought of it as a work of art, but if they saw it in the gentler light of "I'm just drawing things for pleasure and practice, or to learn," that's okay. I don't produce sketchbooks like Crumb produces them, or Chris Ware, where you feel like they are visual diaries as well. My sketchbooks literally are just images I'm interested in, and in a certain way, I guess that seems empty. At best, I feel that what people might get out of it is an understanding of my aesthetics. Everyone's got their own kind of iconography, and I just draw the same things over again, little landscapes, buildings, things like that. It's not meant to have a great deal of meaning, and so in a sense, they are kind of empty.

DOMINICK: It sounds like the narrative is the central element for you, then, for you to see it as a successful overall work of art.
SETH: I think it's true. I think even most of the visual art I like is narrative art, even when they're not sequential artists; I have about seven or eight artists that are my favorite artists in the world, and most of them aren't cartoonists.

ERIC: Who are they?
SETH: Okay, let's see if I can list them out. Edward Gorey would be one; Glenn Gould [Canadian pianist best-known for his interpretations of Bach]; Henry Darger [the definitive outsider artist, whose voluminous writings were unknown and unpublished until after his death]; L. S. Lowry, a painter from England; Stanley Spencer, another painter from England; Norman McClaren, animator; Max Beerbohm, the caricaturist; Thoreau MacDonald; and probably Robert Crumb, and I'm not sure, I might add Schulz in there too. There might be somebody important I've forgotten since this is off the top of my head. It's a pretty consistent list I've had for years. It changes occasionally—people have come and gone. There are lots of great artists who aren't on this list—people I love too, like someone like [film director] Mike Leigh, for example—he's not on that list. It's not that kind of list.

0 3 AUG 2009

Nothing much interesting going on here? From *Vernacular Drawings* © Seth. Used with permission from Drawn & Quarterly.

As this list developed, I realized, in some ways, it wasn't really so much about the art as it was about the artists, and I think they became important to me because their personal narratives, their lives, are so interesting and inspiring to me in a way that made them rise up above other people whose work I like as much or much more. The reason I am not 100 percent sure that Schulz is on that list but that Crumb definitely *is* on that list is because Crumb's life is more interesting to me than Schulz's life. Darger's life is more interesting to me than Darger's art, and that's true of almost everyone on this list—I not sure I'm even that big a fan of Edward Gorey's art, but I'm a tremendous fan of Edward Gorey himself. I think it's because they're all kind of strangely solitary figures who had a very rich interior life, and that doesn't mean that they were all necessarily isolated people. Crumb obviously has a longstanding very successful marriage, but there's something about Crumb that seems essentially solitary, and all these artists have that very deep, rich inner life that's coming out through the work in some way or other. There's no one on that list that's a primary influence on me. No Kirby. No one that's much of a stylistic influence for me. Peter Arno's not on that list, Hergé is not on that list. There's an enormous number of important-to-me artists not on that list. No Alice Munro, no Lynda Barry, no Edward Bawden [landscape painter] or [Alain] Resnais [film-maker]. No Tolstoy or Chekhov or Salinger or Katchor or Hernandez or even Chester Brown. I could go on and on. It's not a list about art and it's not about the surface or about aesthetics, but it's about some essential element that these artists have in their lives and in their work that has been deeply inspirational to me in some way, and that has been an object lesson for me.

Obviously, you don't want to pattern your life on Henry Darger—he's not an inspirational figure in that sense—but there's something in Darger, for example, in that his art was not about producing art; it was about finding something to save his life. To keep him from dying of loneliness. He had to make that art; he had to have that world to escape into just to exist. He would have just died if he hadn't had a fantasy world. That to me is the essential thing I take away from him. With somebody like Gorey, what I've taken away is that incredibly expansive curiosity he had in life; he was engaged with everything. Whenever you read interviews with Gorey, you get this sense of a man who read every book, saw every movie, went to every performance of the ballet; it's remarkable. He was a total omnivore; he took in everything. So admirable. But then you look at somebody like Glenn Gould, it's not only about him being a great pianist or a great thinker, and I'm not 100 percent convinced of the "great thinker" part anyway, but he was someone who really appreciated and understood the depth and value of being by yourself. The power of singularity. Each of them has some essential element that singled them out for me as object lessons. McClaren for his example as pure artist; even though he was working for the [National] Film Board [of Canada], he followed an absolutely pure line of interest. Never wavering. Spencer is about following pure eccentric belief and personal imagery. A deep understanding of the mystical power of love. Lowry has a miraculous understanding of pace. Beerbohm for his foppishness and his floating life of play and guile and sophistication. Crumb, of course, for his uncompromising example of how to be an artist. Resisting all compromise. Steadfast honesty. A truth teller. Thoreau Macdonald for his humbleness, his love of nature over art and his ability to stay put. Schulz for his sweet melancholy. I could go on and on. Elaborating on each of them. There are artists who might be hovering on the edge, someone like Edward Hopper [American painter and printmaker], but the ones that I listed definitely fall into that category of—that's the kind of artist I wish to be. Each taught me an essential element about being alive and about making art.

ERIC: This rich interior life that you're referring to, is that what inspires you to produce the handmade books, the fake trophies, all the private ephemera?

SETH: Yup. It's about trying to have a fully realized artistic world that isn't just about career-building. Being a cartoonist, you come out of the world of commercial art. Maybe cartoonists now are emerging as pure artists, but that was certainly not the case when I came up. My thinking was shaped by the middle brow nature of comics—and that's the model I was presented with at a formative age and that is what I embraced. It took me a long time, I think, to come to see myself as an artist, and so I think a lot of what I do is to try to keep firmly in mind that making artwork is not just part of a plan for career-building. It has to be about exploring the world as an artist. "Real" artists know this from the start, but I think coming out of the world of cartooning, the commercial element is something that you must work your way away from, and even among cartoonists themselves, there's an awful lot of "professionalism" that taints the idea of being an artist.

We were talking about Dave Sim earlier. Dave's a classic for basically judging other comic book artists on whether or not they can make their deadlines. A deadline. Other artists don't deal with deadlines. I mean, not in the true sense; I'm sure Edward Hopper might have had a show coming up and needed to have twelve paintings done or something, but he wasn't judging his other artist friends on whether they were good at meeting their deadlines. There's

Invented awards, granted to members of *The Great Northern Brotherhood of Canadian Cartoonists* © Seth. Used with permission from Drawn & Quarterly.

still a lot of that weird commercial artist stuff lingering around on the edge of the comics community. You're not a real cartoonist if you can't turn out twelve issues in a year; that sort of thing. That's the kind of nonsense that still hangs over the medium, and I think that it'll take a long time to get away from it. You really have to push yourself to see that this isn't about that; I may have to meet some deadlines to make a living or to keep Drawn & Quarterly from kissing me goodbye, but ideally what you must try to do is to try and understand what being an artist is, and for me, an artist is someone who's trying to interpret the essence of their inner life and somehow share it with other people. It's as simple as that. And that is not the goal of traditional cartooning; traditional cartooning is concerned with coming up with a successful property, publishing on a regular schedule and marketing it to the public—these kinds of things. As I get older, and I find that there are ways to make money that don't involve doing those specific things, I try to focus more and more on digging deeper into that interior life.

ERIC: This forthcoming documentary, which includes a never-before-seen puppet show, "The Apology of Albert Batch," and significant animation, I assume this all falls into this category of the complete artistic life. Now you've done comics, you've done installations, you've done the sketchbook work, a variety of different things, even briefly mainstreamish work . . .
SETH: Yeah, it's all just my work. In some ways I have to admit I don't feel as interested in the *world of cartooning* any more, but I do still love doing my own cartooning. What I mean by that is it doesn't mean I'm not paying attention to what's going on in the medium. I am probably as up on current cartooning as much, if not more, than most cartoonists of my generation. It doesn't mean that I'm not interested in old cartooning anymore; I am still pursuing and collecting old cartoonists and stuff like that. But I don't feel 100 percent defined by comics any more. I do feel I've come around to just following my muse as any artist would, and wherever that takes me will be fine, but I do still identify primarily as a cartoonist, and I think I always will. I think even if I didn't do any more comics for ten years and just did installations, or something, and if someone asked me what I did, I would still say I was a cartoonist.

ERIC: It's the core aesthetic from which all these other things branch out.
SETH: Yes, and these other ventures only enrich my cartooning in some manner. They enrich what I'm doing in a way that probably couldn't be done by *just* making more comic books. They add something else that's connected to the cartooning but isn't cartooning. I guess I do like the idea of that wider career. I admire a diverse body of work in other artists—say, if I were to look at Crumb's career, for example, I love all the other stuff he's done, I like the things he's made, the records he's designed, his devil girl statue, et cetera. I like all those different projects he's worked on over the years, I love his sketchbooks. It wouldn't be a fair trade to give up all the sketchbooks he made to have a bigger pile of comics from him.

ERIC: How did this film come about?

SETH: Well, the film came about because I did a talk some years ago—several years ago, about seven or eight years ago maybe—and a nice fellow, Luc Chamberland, who had come to see it said, "I'd love to make a documentary about you," and I think we talked a little bit about it, and I said okay, and later when I found the process awkward, I wondered why I had agreed to this so easily! I don't think I'm going to enjoy any of the documentary elements of it when I finally see it; I don't like to see myself on screen, I don't feel like I said anything of great interest on film—I suspect that there was a lot of stilted dialogue that went on in those interviews. Not to say anything unpleasant or unkind about Luc—he's been great—but I'm not sure that we clicked when we were talking on screen, and I bet that there were definitely points where it'll look just like pulling teeth; I was awkward and bland. We'll see what he does with all that material, how he pulls it together. If he can manage to pull it together, I will be very grateful. I've already told him I will only watch that film once, and I wouldn't even watch it once if I could get out of it. But, of course, it would be completely disrespectful of someone who has put so many years and so much work into a film and then for me to say, I won't even look at it. Still, he knows why I will only watch it once. [Jestfully:] Just watching it once will likely scar me for the rest of my life.

ERIC: Was the puppet show something that was in gestation before the film came about that somehow got incorporated in?

SETH: Yes, I kind of made the mistake of mentioning it to Luc, and then he was like, "That's great, we're going to film that," and so at one point I said, well, I never should have mentioned that, because I've got to finish the damn thing. Of course the good part of this is that it forced me to get it done. It had been lingering for years in a half-finished state. I'm grateful he pushed me to finish it.

ERIC: So you constructed a setting, puppets?

SETH: Yeah, a little theatre, puppets, et cetera. I created them more out of a desire to construct those things, not out of a longing to perform. In fact actually making the film, performing the "play" on film, made me realize that this is the only way it could ever have been performed, because when we performed it, I realized I could not actually act it out it as an actual puppet play. I'm not a performer and it turned out to be more complicated than I was capable of doing. I couldn't actually act the characters and talk and move things around at the same time, and thank God for the mechanics of film that allowed us to fake much of it, so that we could pull it all together.

ERIC: You actually act out the puppets on film?
SETH: Yeah.

ERIC: You didn't hire actors?
SETH: No. I wasn't playing "parts," but I still found it very difficult to perform it. I realized that I'm no puppeteer, that's for sure. But they're not really puppets in the traditional sense anyway, they're more like toys, but you'll see that in the film. Basically, the problem was that it was really difficult for me to speak the dialogue. I didn't have the dialogue memorized—I was just reading from a script but I couldn't read and move the figures at the same time. So what really worked well was, we had someone else reading it while I did all that was required visually, and then we would do another version where I was reading it. So in the end we had three or four different shots we could cut back and forth from, and it will probably look like I am speaking and moving the characters and all the lighting is changing, and the scenes are changing et cetera. What that means is that this is the only way it could have ever existed in the world, in this filmed version that Luc's done. So it kind of worked out great, because otherwise I would have just built it and then put it in the attic, and it would have never existed in any more realized form. The story would never have been performed live. So now there will be a little film of exactly the only way it could exist. I'm very grateful. I couldn't have done it without Luc. They also did such a fabulous job of filming this puppet show. It was unbelievable. We went into a studio in Toronto and we had this truly unbelievable million-dollar camera set-up that could do these incredible tracking shots. I was amazed. That thing alone was worth agreeing to the documentary for. They did a terrific job with that. The animation they've done looks really exciting as well, from what I've seen so far. I think for those two elements, it was totally worth it. The other part, me interviewed on film—I may live to regret; we'll see.

ERIC: How involved were you in the animation?
SETH: Not much involved. Actually, this was more Luc's cup of tea. He's an animator.

ERIC: Are they taking stuff from the books and animating it?
SETH: Exactly, yeah, and he's made pretty smart decisions, I think, about how he's managed to take the work and make them into little films rather than little segments. He's made about ten tiny little animated films.

DOMINICK: Is this going to have a theatrical release or go on TV?
SETH: As much as any other NFB film; it'll be out there, but we'll see what

that means. It will probably show in a couple of art film places, maybe a couple of festivals. I imagine it will be on TVO [the Province of Ontario's public broadcasting network] or something, but it's not going to be *Crumb*, let's put it that way; I would be highly surprised if this had any wider audience. That's no knock against Luc Chamberland. It's simply recognizing how interesting Crumb and his family are and how small and dull my life is in comparison.

ERIC: Is there a guiding thesis to the film?

SETH: I don't really know, he filmed a great deal of stuff, but we'll see what he shapes it into. I personally can't imagine how it's going to be coherent, the actual documentary, but that could be because I haven't seen it. In my mind, I'm too concerned only with my appearances in it to have been able to see anything overarching that he's doing. It's probably not the film I would have made about myself, if I was a documentary maker. I think that I'd probably be more interested in trying to capture something less structured. More of my day-to-day life. I felt like it was a lot of interviewing, rather than just stuff happening. But to tell you the truth, I'm grateful for that, because then he'd have been following me around with a camera for years and I couldn't have borne that.

ERIC: So you're worried it's going to be more, kind of talking heads?

SETH: Yeah, I'm a little worried that I'll just be boring. I mean, I'm not too worried about it, but I think there's a good chance of it. We'll see.

ERIC: You would have preferred a more verité approach?

SETH: Maybe, but I have a feeling that would have been just as boring. Maybe more so. That's the problem. He did try to film Chester, Joe, and me together, but it really died; it didn't work very well in my opinion.

ERIC: How long has the filming been going on?

SETH: A long time, six years or something.

DOMINICK: Do you think part of your discomfort with what might happen is that this is in effect a construction of Seth that's not under your control?

SETH: Yes, and I'm a little worried that maybe it's not who I think I am, and that maybe it's some of the worst elements on display of that persona I built. I'm a little worried that it's, you know, the Mister Nostalgia, Mister Old-timey, and that image will override the "real." I understand he can't help but bring that out—it's a key thing to focus on, but it's not what I really want my work to be seen as entirely about.

DOMINICK: That's interesting; we went back and forth on this, because you've been asked that nostalgia question too many times, so we were going to skip it. But when we've read your work, we can see where that comes from, but I wouldn't say that either of us sees you as a nostalgia artist.

ERIC: Yeah, you sort of eloquently addressed this point, I thought, authoritatively; I mean, there doesn't seem to be much to add to that—what was it, the television interview?

DOMINICK: The Jian Gomeshi interview. [Q TV interview, October 15, 2009: http://www.youtube.com/watch?v=_m5D9kGmxlk]

SETH: I don't think I remember what I talked about.

DOMINICK: What I think I came away with from that interview and from things you've said before is that it's probably a logical and valid response to *now* to feel that there are viable alternatives to now, not necessarily that the past is better but that there are elements of the past that are better. But what's interesting for me about this goes back to what we were talking about before with alternate history and the fantastical elements, that there seems to be a real interest in your work in exploring alternatives that I wouldn't say are nostalgic, in the sense that they're simply directed towards trying to reclaim an idealized past, but that are interested in creating—or transmuting—elements of the past into an artistic alternative to a now.

SETH: Exactly.

DOMINICK: And that might even be a future, as opposed to a past; it doesn't have to be a backward-looking thing.

SETH: Yes. I think that all artists on some level are utopians, and that if I were to create a utopia, it would not be the past. It would be something incorporating favorite elements from the past—aesthetics from the past, ideas from the past—but I think that that's not so different from other utopias that others might envision. The differences would be only in the specifics. I think Tom Spurgeon actually said, when he interviewed me on stage recently at SPX, that, looking over my stuff now, he didn't really think my work was so much about looking back to the past, so much as a narrative about decline. And that hits the nail right on the head: I think that every story I'm working on is about somebody or something that's going into a long decline, or coming to the end of melancholy, on the vanishing itself.

DOMINICK: What is it that's passing in *Wimbledon Green*? Is it the world of a cohesive comics enthusiast?

SETH: You know, what's passing in *Wimbledon Green* is in the final chapter, when he talks about his life—all the other stuff in the book is just window dressing to get to that final chapter where he talks about his life moving on. I think that the core narrative underneath any of my stories is the recognition that there is an underlying melancholy to life. An inherent sadness because everything is always moving into the past. So in *Wimbledon Green* at the end there's the nostalgia, that's probably the most nostalgic thing I've ever written, that final chapter of him reflecting on his childhood and his mother and his travels across the country, and that's all meant to show how we are burdened by all this stuff from the past, and that's why the only time Wimbledon Green is truly happy in the story is when he loses his memory, when he becomes a hobo for a while, because he's freed from the narrative of his life. In my daily life, I'm always thinking about this process of things moving beyond your reach into the past. I mean, you might have the longing, say, to hang out with your friends from twenty years ago, but you don't want to go find them *now* and hang out, you want to go find them *then*. They're still alive, but they're not the people you're looking for. I think *that's* the essential element of the decline in all of the stories; it is always about something moving beyond reach.

ERIC: But that feeling of decline is exacerbated by the overall crumminess of the modern world.

SETH: Oh yeah, it goes without saying that I hate the modern world. That's a given. I mean, that's the main thread in the whole city of Dominion, too. If you were to look at that in my notebooks about each of the buildings, every one has got the same history, practically. There was once a good period and they go into a decline, and they either survive the decline in a diminished form, into the modern era, or they disappear entirely. I think that's because, again, what I was just talking about, about things moving into the past. That's the narrative of everyone's life; it doesn't matter what kind of life you have, it's not that you have one particular golden era, but there is always this feeling of things moving further and further into the past. It doesn't necessarily mean that my life is worse than it was ten years ago; in fact I'm much happier now than I was then, but there's something in the very quality of just being alive and getting old that is about constant decline. I'm fifty-one years old, now, and I'm not thirty-one years old anymore, so you're always working down toward the end. And it's not even about the specifics so much; I think that's just the underlying feeling I can't help but have in every story. George Sprott's a perfect example. I mean, George's golden age isn't much of a golden age. Even though he was very popular at one point, where he has his moment in the sun, I never wanted to give the impression that his golden age was a truly great event, that he'd really done something terrific, or that his TV show was actually important, or that he was a good person, only that there was a high point, and now there is a low point, or a lower point.

ERIC: That also sort of underlines the reality that we tend to look at the past with rose-tinted glasses. There were miseries, and there horrible times in the past . . .
SETH: Yeah. Oh yeah. I'm always aware that I couldn't have lived in the actual past . . .

ERIC: . . . not only the past, but your own past, as well. I mean, all of us hearken back to this "golden age" that in reality was never quite as good as we remember it being.
SETH: It's interesting that even in our own lives we romanticize the past, even though you know the real details! I often think back to times that I've romanticized and remember that I was very unhappy then, but it doesn't stop the romanticizing process. I think it's easier to actually look at your own life with rose-colored glasses than to look at times before you were born. I think that you *can* envision golden ages before you were born, lots of people do it, you know, the "I-should-have-been-born-in-the-Edwardian-Era sort of thing," but that's actually pretty easy to do if you don't bother with any facts—you don't need to know that much for that nonsense, but it's odd when the romanticization is about your own life, when you know *all* of the facts, and you can still indulge that same process, and say, like, "Oh, I was so happy when I was twenty," even though you *know* you were miserable most of the time. . . . I find I'm even looking back and somewhat romanticizing the times that I was unhappy because I was unhappy. It's like there's something appealing about being sad that you can look back on it fondly, because you're not actually feeling those feelings any more. I'll think to myself, "Oh yeah, I was really depressed and lonely in those years," but I'll still think of it in nice terms, like it was a pleasant feeling.

DOMINICK: That's why someone else's sadness can be entertaining.
SETH: It's only when you're *actually* unhappy that it *is* unhappiness. "Good Grief," as Schulz called it. As long as you're not into crippling, crushing depression, melancholy is a perfectly enjoyable experience. But yes, deep depression is not so enjoyable. Sadness isn't all bad, in a way. There is a sweet sadness, and I think of that as a very distinct emotion that hasn't been as

fully classified as it should be. Perhaps because even though most everyone has felt the emotion of sweet sadness or good grief, little effort has been made to distinguish it from basic unhappiness. They are very different things. When you're unhappy, or really lonely or depressed, there's nothing pleasant about that whatsoever.

DOMINICK: But good grief, it's ephemeral, that's part of why it can be good grief.

SETH: Yes. You can wallow in that kind of good grief; you can't wallow in unhappiness. You want to put that away from you.

INDEX

Page numbers in **bold** refer to illustrations.

About Love (Seth), 166
Acme Press, 57
Adam, 168
Adams, Neal, 153
Addams, Charles, 174, 175
Alice In Wonderland (Carroll), 118
Allen, Woody, 41, 106, 140
All the Wrong Questions series, xx
Alternative Comics: An Emerging Literature
　(Hatfield), viii, xvi
American Flagg! (Chaykin), viii
American Splendor (film), 119
American Splendor (Pekar), 12, 24, 119
Anderson, Sherwood, 203
Andy Capp, 7
Andy Capp (character), 115
Aniston, Jennifer, 178
Another Rainbow, 206
Anthology of Graphic Fiction, Cartoons,
　and True Stories, xix
"Apology of Albert Batch, The" (Seth), xx,
　215, 216, 217
Arcade, viii
Archie, 7, 40, 91
Arno, Peter, 134, 177, 212
Art Gallery of Ontario (AGO), xviii, 90, 98,
　138, 208
Art of Seth (Seth), 127, 170
Atlantic, The, xvii
Atlas, 180

Bach, 138, 210
Bagge, Peter, x, 46, 47, 50, 61, 73, 159, 190
Baker, Chet, 55
Bannock, Beans and Black Tea (Gallant),
　xviii, 90, 92, 97
Barks, Carl, 24
Barnaby (Johnson), 39
Barrier, Michael, 27
Barry, Lynda, xix, 24, 64, 150, 212
Bateman, H. M., 134
Batman, 48
Bauhaus, ix, xiv, 4
Bawden, Edward, 212
Bear, The (Briggs), 40
Beaton, Kate, 156
Beaty, Bart, 192
Beck, C. C., 51
Beerbohm, Max, 210
Beguiling, The (comic book store), 12, 51, 91
Berlin (Lutes), 187
Berton, Pierre, 162
Best American Comics 2007, The, xix
Best American Comics 2008, The, xix
Betty Boop, 98
Birkemoe, Peter, 83, 91, 95, 98
Bissette, Stephen R., 155
Black Eye Press, 58
"Blue Italian Shit" (Clowes), 46
Bobcat, The (character), 94
Bordeaux, Ariel, 56
Bosco the Clown, 98
Boyle, Sharry, 209

Bradley, Buddy, 46, 47

Briggs, Raymond, 40

Brinkman, Mat, 146

Brown, Chester, x, xv, xvii, 12, 15, **18**, 22, 23, 24, 26, 27, 30, 32, 38, 50, 51, 54, 61, 63, 64, 73, 77, 78, 79, 81, 82, 83, 97, 98, 119, 143, 149, 150, 157, 158, 159, 177, 189, 190, 192, 194, 196, 212, 218

Brubaker, Ed, 50

Brunetti, Ivan, xix

Buenaventura, Alvin, 139

Building Stories (Ware), 140

Bull Cook and Authentic Historical Recipes and Practices (Herter), 162

Busiek, Kurt, 60

Byrne, John, 146

Cabinet of Doctor Caligari, The, 6

Cage, John, 123

"Calgary Festival" (Seth), 196

CA Magazine, 97

Canadian Notes and Queries (CNQ), xvii, xix

Caniff, Milton, 114

Capra, Frank, 41

Captain America, 43

Captain Victory and the Galaxy Rangers (Kirby), 43

Carver, Raymond, 41

Catcher in the Rye, The (Salinger), 46, 116

Cathy (Guisewhite), 36

Cerebus (Sim and Gerhard), 188, 189

Cervantes, Miguel de, 132

Chamberland, Luc, xx, 216, 217, 218

Chandler, Raymond, 58

Chaplin, Charles, 170

Charlton Comics, vii

Chaykin, Howard, viii

Chekhov, Anton, 212

Cherry, Don, 132

Chester Brown: Conversations, vii

Chippendale, Brian, 146

Christenberry, William, 140

Christmas Days (McCormack), 90

City Lights (Chaplin), 170

Clark, Greg, 162

Classic Cocktails: A Modern Shake (Kingwell), 90, 166

Clooney, George, 130

Clowes, Dan, x, 45, 46, 47, 50, 62, 73, 82, 91, 97, 98, 123, 149, 156, 157, 159, 160, 190, 203

Clyde Fans (Seth), xi, xii, xv, xvii, xviii, 68, **69**, 71, 75, 79, **80**, 90, 91, **104**, 110, **117**, 122, 130, 133, 150, 151, 152, 163, 166, 169, 181, 182, 183, 184, 185, 186, 187, 193, 202

Clyde Fans, Book One (Seth), xviii, **69**, **80**, 90, **104**, **117**, 183, 184

Clyde Fans, Book Two (Seth), 91, 184

Clyde Fans, Part One, xviii

Coe, Roland, 28

Coe, Sue, 168

Cole, Jack, 39, 45

Collected Doug Wright, The, xix, 121, 135, 172

Collecting, xii, xv, 37, 68, 69, 70, 101, 110, 135, 175, 215

Collier, David, 26, 65

Comic Art, xvi, xviii, xix, 110

Comics Journal, viii, xviii, 13, 141, 172, 173

Complete Peanuts, The (Schulz), ix, xviii, 75, 76, 91, 105, 121, 140, 141, 170, 171, 172, 173

Craig, Johnny, 27

Crane, Roy, 29, 35

Crime Clinic, 38

Criterion, 170

Crumb (Zwigoff), 218

Crumb, Robert, x, xi, 12, 21, 41, 63, 97, 106, 136, 137, 138, 148, 150, 156, 190, 201, 210, 212, 213, 215, 218

Cupples, Victor I., 173

Cupples and Leon, 173

Daily Bugle, 207

Darger, Henry, 210, 212

Dark Knight, The, 118

DC, vii, 4, 13, 27, 43, 50, 56, 57, 66, 67, 148, 161

Deadpan (Heatley), 123

DeCarlo, Dan, 39, 40, 52

DeForge, Michael, 188

Deitch, Kim, 155

Dell Comics, vii, 28

Dennis the Menace (Ketcham), 137

Destroy All Comics, 21, 27, 32

Devil's Advocate, The, xix, xx, 138

Devlin, Tom, 127, 142, 173

Dexter, 178

Dexter (character), 178

Diamond Distributing, 66

Dirty Plotte (Doucet), 31

Disney Studios, 52

Ditko, Steve, 23, 42, 43, 51, 146, 207

Doctor Strange, 42, 43, 207

Dominion City Project (Seth), xii, xiii, xiv, xix, 90, 122, 130, **131**, 163, 164, **165**, 165, 185, 203, 204, 205, 208, 220

Dominion exhibit, xii, xix, 208

Don Quixote (Cervantes), 132

Dorkin, Evan, 17

Doucet, Julie, 31

Doug Wright Award, xviii, xix, 135

Doug Wright's Family (Wright), xix, xx

Dragon Lady, The (comic book shop), 12

Drake, Arnold, 149

Drawn & Quarterly (comics anthology), 15, 19, 30

Drawn & Quarterly Publishing, viii, x, xiv, xvi, xvii, xix, 8, 15, 18, 26, 48, 53, 57, 69, 72, 74, 80, 93, 96, 97, 104, 117, 121, 124, 126, 127, 131, 136, 144, 149, 154, 173, 180, 184, 196, 198, 211, 214

Duchamp, Marcel, 140

EC Comics, 27, 43, 85

Eclipse Comics, viii

Ed the Happy Clown (Brown), 119

Eichhorn, Dennis, 17

Eightball (Clowes), x, 45, 46, 47, 56, 82, 156, 157, 159

Eisner, Ann, 85

Eisner, Will, 39, 51, 56, 85

Eisner Award, xviii

Elder, Will, 52

Epic Illustrated, 85

Fantagraphics, viii, ix, 44, 57, 58, 74, 75, 105, 172

Feldstein, Al, 27

Fires (Mattotti), 60, 61

First Comics, viii

First Kingdom, The (Katz), viii

Fleischer Studios, 52, 98

Forbes, xvii

Fort Thunder movement, 146

Forty Cartoon Books of Interest (Seth), xix, 110, 176

Fountainhead, The (Rand), 119, 120

Franny and Zooey (Salinger), 41

Frise, Jimmie, 135

Gallant, John Henry (father), xvii, xviii, 90, 92, 103

Gallant, Violet Daisy (mother), xvii, 7, 92, 113

Garfield (Davis), 105

George Sprott (1874–1975) (Seth), xii, xv, xix, 110, 121, 122, 123, 125, **126**, 127, 128, 129, 130, **131**, 131, 132, 133, 150, 151, 152, 161, **180**, 183, 185, 200, 202, 220, 221

George Sprott (character), 128, 129, 130, 131, 132, **133**, 133, 162, 220, 221

Ghost World (Clowes), 45, 46, 47, 91, 159

Ghost World (Zwigoff), 115

Gillespie, Dizzy, 55

Globe and Mail, The, xvii

"Glue Destiny" (Clowes), 45

GNBCC. See *Great Northern Brotherhood of Canadian Cartoonists, The*
God, 168
Gold Key Comics, vii
Gomeshi, Jian, 219
Goodwill, 162
Goodwin, Archie, 85
Google, 194, 195
Gorey, Edward, 101, 174, 177, 210, 212
Gould, Glenn, 138, 210, 212
Gray, Harold, 22
Greatest Golden Age Comics Ever Told, 27
Great Northern Brotherhood of Canadian Cartoonists, The (Seth), xiii, **xiv**, xx, 147, 150, 152, **154**, 162, **165**, 166, 202, 203, 205, **214**
"Great Return, The" (Machen), 140
Green, Wimbledon, xii, 102, **124**, 192, 219, 220
Grey Owl (Archibald Belaney), 65
Groth, Gary, 172
Group of Seven, The, 139, 140, 163

Hansen, Thor, 140
"Happy Fisherman, The" (Clowes), 45, 159
Hardy, Thomas, xii
Harper, Lynn, 92
Harris, Lawren, 140
Harvey (Kurtzman) Award, xviii, 60, 61
Hate (Bagge), 46, 47, 73
Hatfield, Charles, viii, xvi
Heatley, David, 123
Heckle and Jeckle, 7
Hergé, 22, 100, 101, 107, 109, 134, 177, 212
Hernandez, Gilbert, 189
Hernandez, Jaime, 3, 4, 168, 169, 177, 189, 212
Hernandez Brothers, ix, x, 3, 13, 51, 97, 189, 212
Heroes World, 66
Herriman, George, 39
Herter, George Leonard, 162

Hignite, M. Todd, ix, xvi
Holden Caulfield, 46
Hopper, Edward, 213
Horn, Maurice, 174
Horrocks, Dylan, 58, 65
Howard Roark (character), 120

Ice Haven (Clowes), 127, 203
Ignatz Award, xvii
Image comics, 50
Incredible Hulk, The, 42
Indeterminancy (Cage), 123, 129
I Never Liked You (Brown), 54
Influences, ix, x, xi, 3, 4, 7, 8, 21, 26, 39, 41, 101, 105, 106, 107, 110, 134, 150, 177, 190, 201, 210, 212, 213
Inkpot Award, xix
Irving, John, 97
Itchy & Scratchy Show, The, 118
It's a Good Life, If You Don't Weaken (exhibit), xx
It's a Good Life, If You Don't Weaken (Seth), x, xi, xii, xiii, xiv, xvi, xvii, xviii, **8**, **18**, 18, 21, 48, **53**, 68, **72**, 90, 97, 113, 115, 116, 133, 134, 162, 174, 182, 193, 194, 203

Jaka's Story (Sim), 86
Johnson, Crockett, 39
John Stanley Library, The, x, xix, 121, 142, 143, 172, 173

Kalo (character), xi, **18**, 18, 19, 22, 48, 193, 194, 195
Katchor, Ben, 155, 156, 212
Katz, Jack, viii
Kawabata, Yasunari, 107
Ketcham, Frank, 137
King, Frank, 148
King-Cat Comics and Stories (Porcellino), 56
Kingwell, Mark, 90

Kirby, Jack, viii, 4, 9, 43, 51, 146, 212

Kitchen Sink Publishing, 25, 28

Kochalka, James, 81, 82, 197

Koyama Press, 173

Kramers Ergot, 121, 138, 139

Krazy & Ignatz (Herriman), 173

Krazy Kat (Herriman), 39, 173

Krigstein, Bernie, 27

Kurtzman, Harvey, 27, 44, 52, 137, 138, 148

Last Year at Marienbad (Resnais), 140, 164

Laurence, Margaret, 167

Leacock, Stephen, xii, xx, 167

Lee, Stan, 61

Leigh, Mike, 41, 210

Leon, Arthur T., 173

LeVine, Jeff, 21, 48

Liberace, 138

Lichtenstein, 107

Liefeld, Rob, 14

Like a Velvet Glove Cast in Iron (Clowes), 47, 159, 160

Lil' Folks (Schulz), 20

Little Lulu, 27, 28, 60, 90, 151, 173, 206

Little Nipper. See *Nipper*

Little Orphan Annie, 22, 173, 174

London Free Press, The, 7

Lost In the Stars (Mann), xviii, 166

Love and Rockets (Hernandez Brothers), ix, x, 4, 12, 13, 54

Lovecraft, H. P., 186

Lowry, L. S., 210, 213

Lucy (character), 142

Lulu (character), 151, 206

Lutes, Jason, 187, 189

MacDonald, J. E. H., 139

MacDonald, Thoreau, xix, 121, 138, 139, 163, 210, 213

MacKay, Brad, xviii, 135

Machen, Arthur, 140

Mad Magazine, 44, 52

Make Way for Tomorrow (McCarey), 166

Man, The (Briggs), 40

Mann, Aimee, xviii, 166, 170

Marge's Tubby, 28

Marks, Bill, 3, 6, 13, 77, 78

Marvel, vii, ix, 4, 9, 12, 13, 14, 40, 43, 46, 50, 51, 52, 54, 56, 57, 60, 66, 67, 148, 161

Marvel Masterworks, 42

Marvels (Busiek and Ross), 60

Matchcard, Abraham (Abe), xi, 71, 91, 182

Matchcard, Simon, xi, 68, **69**, 71, 79, **80**, 91, 92, **93**, 152, 182

Matt, Joe, x, xv, xvii, 20, 21, 23, 24, 25, 26, 27, 28, 30, 46, 50, 51, 52, 77, 78, 81, 98, 150, 159, 192, 193, 218

Mattotti, Lorenzo, 17, 60

Maus (Spiegelman), xi, 40, 54, 91, 108

Mayer, Sheldon, 24, 27, 51

Mazzucchelli, David, 13, 14, 16

McArthur, Glenn, 140

McCarey, Leo, 166

McClaren, Malcolm, 140

McClaren, Norman, 210, 212

McCloud, Scott, 100

McCormack, Derek, 90

McFarlane, Todd, 49

McLuhan, Marshall, 105

McSweeney's Quarterly Concern, xviii

Medium Is the Massage (McLuhan), 105

Mellencamp, John, 111

Melmoth (Sim and Gerhard), 188, 189

Melvin Monster (Stanley), 142

Mickey Mouse (cartoons), 52

Mignola, Mike, 177

Miller, Bryan, 178, 196

Miller, Frank, 39, 85

Mishima, Yukio, 107

Mister X, ix, xiii, xv, xvii, 3, 4, **5**, 6, 12, 13, 14, 15, 77, 78, 97

Mister X (character), ix, 3

Mother Jones, xvii

Motter, Dean, ix, xiii, xv, xvii, 4, 6, 14, 78
Mouly, Françoise, viii
Mr. A, 42
Mr. Deeds Goes to Town, 42
Mullins, Katie, xi, xvi
Munro, Alice, 41, 92, 105, 107, 212
Muth, Jon J., 60

Nancy (comic strip), 7
National Film Board of Canada (NFB), 90,
    118, 213, 217
National Post, The, xvii, 140
Neat Stuff, x, 47
"Needledick the Bugfucker" (Clowes), 159
New Gods, The (Kirby), 43
New Yorker Magazine x, xvii, xviii, xix, 8,
    16, 41, 90, 108, 109, 110, 121, 122, 127,
    128, 134, 169, 170, 174, 195
New York Magazine, xvii, 16
New York Post, 28
New York Times, xii, xv, xvii, xviii, xix, 8,
    108, 110, 121, 122, 123, 128, 134, 161, 168
Nipper, xx, 7, 135, **136**, 137
Nostalgia, xi, xv, 9, 70, 71, 218, 219, 220
"Nothing Lasts" (Seth), 152, 163, 165, 193,
    196

objectivism, 120
Oliveros, Chris, viii, 57, 58, 59, 74, 97, 135,
    136, 137, 161, 173, 184
OMAC: One Man Army Corps (Kirby), 43
Ontario College of Art (OCA), xvii, 3, 9, 10,
    11, 12, 31, 77, 94, 97

Pacific Comics, viii, ix, 43
Palestine (Sacco), 47
Palookaville (Seth), x, xi, xii, xiv, xvii, xviii,
    xix, xx, 7, 15, 17, 19, 20, 23, 28, **34**, 49,
    52, 64, 77, 78, 81, 89, 90, 91, 92, **93**,
    94, 95, **96**, 97, 98, 99, 152, 166, 187,
    189, 194, **196**, 197, **198**
Panel Borders, 200
Parker, Charlie, 55

Parker, Dorothy, xix
*Paying For It: a comic strip memoir about
    being a john* (Brown), 159
Peanuts (Schulz), 7, 20, 42, 75, 76, 91,
    105, 106, 120, 121, 137, 140, 141, 172,
    199, 200, 207
Peepshow, 24, 25, 28
Pekar, Harvey, xi, 24, 119, 150
Peppermint Patty (character), 141
Peters, H. G., 52
Pettibo, Raymond, 107
Picasso, Pablo, 140
Pickle (Horrocks), 58
Pierrot, George, 162
Plastic Man, 90
Playboy, The (Brown), 150
Popeye, 28
Porcellino, John, 56
Portable Dorothy Parker, The, xix
Portis, Ben, 98
Prince (musician), 111
*Progressive Traditionalist: John M. Lyle,
    Architect, A* (McArthur), 140
Psychotecture, ix, 6
Punch, 62

QTV, 219
Quimby's (comic book store), 12

Radiant City, ix, xiii, 3, **5**
Rand, Ayn, 42, 120
Raw (magazine), 4, 12
Raw (publishing), viii
Resnais, Alain, 212
Reynolds, Chris, xviii
Richie Rich, 7
Rockwell, Norman, 63
Rolling Stone (magazine), 54
Ross, Alex, 60
Royal Art Lodge, 209
Rubber Stamp Diaries (Seth), 196, 197,
    198, 198, 199
Russian Constructivism, ix, xiv, 4
Ruthie (character), 63

Sacco, Joe, x, 47

Salinger, J. D., 21, 28, 41, 106, 212

Saturday Night Magazine, xvii

Schulz, Charles, 20, 42, 75, 76, 101, 106, 120, 134, 136, 137, 138, 140, 141, 142, 143, 148, 153, 171, 172, 177, 199, 207, 210, 212, 213, 221

Scribbly (Mayer), 27

Seth: and animation, 116, 117, 118, 215; and autobiography, x, xi, xv, 17, 20, 23, 24, 63, 64, 65, 73, 91, 150, 152, 163, 165, 192, 193, 195, 196, 197, 198; and cartooning, 100, 109, 114, 115, 116, 148, 180, 181, 209, 213, 214, 215; and clean line, 100, 101, 177; and collecting, xii, xv, 37, 68, 69, 70, 101, 110, 175; and commercial art, ix, x, xii, xiii, xv, xvii, 3, 10, 15, 16, 17, 23, 30, 33, 35, 36, 37, 38, 63, 90, 97, 102, 121, 144, 166, 167, 168, 169; and design, ix, x, xiii, xv, xvi, 4, 11, 14, 74, 75, 76, 90, 91, 102, 103, 105, 115, 121, 127, 128, 134, 138, 140, 141, 142, 143, 166, 167, 168, 170, 172, 173, 178, 179, 184, 203, 206, 209; and film, 108, 112, 113, 114, 115, 116, 117, 118, 145, 146, 178, 205, 206; and gallery shows, xviii, xix, xx, 31, 90, 98, 208, 209; and identity, ix, xii, xvi, 44, 95, 111, 112, 131, 133, 134, 175, 176, 177, 178, 190, 191, 192, 203, 204, 205, 218; influences of, 105, 106, 107, 108, 138, 139, 140, 174, 175, 176; and nostalgia, xi, xv, 9, 70, 71, 218, 219, 220, 221; and poetry, 103, 104, 106, 115, 178, 179; and pseudonym, ix, 95, 111, 112; and serialization, xi, xii, xv, xvi, 46, 47, 48, 49, 50, 121, 122, 123, 125, 126, 127, 128, 134, 152, 183, 187, 188, 195; and sketchbook, 166, 169, 197, 210; and style, 4, 6, 13, 32, 36, 44, 61, 71, 74, 75, 76, 87, 95, 100, 101, 102, 103, 104, 105, 115, 116, 123, 127, 128, 129, 130, 133, 134, 139, 140, 141, 142, 143, 150, 151, 152, 153, 163, 164, 166, 169, 171, 177, 178, 179, 180, 181, 182, 184, 185, 186, 187, 190, 191, 192, 193, 194, 202, 203, 204, 205, 206, 207; working process of, 102, 103, 152, 153, 182, 183

"Seth in the Studio" (Hignite), ix, xvi

"Seth on Thoreau MacDonald" (Seth), xix, 121, 138, 139

"Shamrock Squid" (Clowes), 45

Shore, Stephen, 140

Silly Symphonies, 52

Silver Snail, The (comic book shop), 12

Sim, Dave, xv, 84, 87, 156, 188, 189, 213, 214

Simon (character), 152

Simpsons, The, 47, 118

Sistine Chapel, 168

Skillman, Eric, 170

Slave Labor Graphics, 38

Small Press Expo, 145, 197, 219

Smithsonian Book of Comic Book Comics, The (Barrier and Williams), 27

Smithsonian Collection of Newspaper Comics (Blackbeard and Williams), 174

Smyth, Fiona, 31, 32, 33, 36

Snicket, Lemony, xx

Snoopy (character), 141

Snowman, The (Briggs) 40

Spawn, 49

Spencer, Stanley, 210, 212

Spider-Man, 9, 42, 91, 207

Spider-Man (character), 120

Spiegelman, Art, viii, xi, 16, 54, 91, 107, 195, 201, 209, 210

Sprang, Dick, 40, 52

Spurgeon, Tom, 199, 202, 219

Stanley, John, x, xviii, xix, 51, 142, 143, **144**, 144, 148, 151, 172, 173

Star Wars (Lucas), 145

Steacy, Ken, 12

Stone Angel, The (Laurence), 167

Stukavsky, ix, xvi

Sturges, Preston, 41

Sturm, James, 98
Sugar and Spike (Mayer), 24, 26
Sunshine Sketches of a Little Town (Leacock), xii, xx, 167
Superman (character), 115
Superman (comic book), 49, 107
Swain, Carol, 56

Tanizaki, Jun'ichirō, 107
"That's Life" (Crumb), 21
Thompson, Craig, 87, 188
Thompson, Kim, 189
Tingley, Merle (Ting), 7
Tintin, 52, **53**, 100, 101, 105, 107, 109
Tintin in Tibet (Hergé), 109
Tomine, Adrian, 56, 64
Toro Magazine, 122, 161
Toronto Life Fashion, xvii
Toronto Life magazine, xv, xix
Truscott, Steven, 65, 92
Tubby (character), 151
TVO, 218
Twain, Mark, xii
Twilight, 146
Tyler, Carol, 184

Uncle Scrooge, 24
Underground comix, vii, viii, ix, x, xv, 12, 14, 53, 55, 73, 109, 146, 155
Understanding Comics (McCloud), 100
Underwater (Brown), 26

Van Spyk, Tania, xviii, 76, 85, 89, 98, 112, 164, 190, 199
Varley, Lynn, 85
Vellekoop, Maurice, 15, 31, 94, 95, 98
Vernacular Drawings (Seth), xi, xviii, 90, **136**, **144**, 210, **211**
Vertigo (DC imprint), 50
Vidor, King, 119
Village Voice, 139
Vortex Comics, viii, ix, xvii, 3, 5, 12, 13, 19, 97
Vortex Magazine, 13, 19

Wage Slave's Glossary, The (Glenn), 166
Waller, Leslie, 149
Washington Post, The, xvii, 16
Wash Tubbs (Crane), 29, 46, 188
Watchmen (film), 118
Watchmen (Moore and Gibbons), 118
Walrus, xvii
Ware, Chris, xviii, xix, 15, 32, 33, 40, 57, 62, 82, 83, 98, 108, 123, 173, 200, 201, 202, 210
Warhol, Andy, 107, 140
Warren Publishing, vii, 85
Weirdo, 4, 12
Welles, Orson, 41, 49
When the Wind Blows (Briggs), 40
White, E. B., 186
Wilde, Oscar, 98, 188
Williams, Dylan, 157
Williams, Martin, 27
Willis, Steve, 58
Wimbledon Green, xi, xii, xviii, xix, 90, 102, 122, 123, **124**, 134, 147, 150, 166, 169, 187, 197, 202, 203, 205, 219, 220
Winesburg, Ohio (Anderson), 203
Wolverton, Basil, 43, 44, 52
Wolverton Bible, The, 44
Wonder Woman, 52
Wood, Ed, 145
Wood, Wally, 153
Woodring, Jim, 54
Woozy Winks (character), 90
World Encyclopedia of Comics, The (Horn), 174
Wright, Doug, x, xiii, **xiv**, xvi, 7, 135, **136**, 136, 137, 138, 139, 143, 148, 172

Xeric grant, 123
X-Men, 9, 146

You'll Never Know (Tyler), 184
Yummy Fur (Brown), x, 12, 26, 54, 77

Zingarelli, Mark, 17

Printed in the United States
By Bookmasters